Things and Places

The Jean Nicod Lectures
François Recanati, editor

Things and Places

How the Mind Connects with the World

Zenon W. Pylyshyn

A Bradford Book

The MIT Press

Cambridge, Massachusetts

London, England

MIT Press books may be purchased at special quantity discounts for business or sales promotional use. For information, please e-mail special_sales@mitpress.mit.edu or write to Special Sales Department, The MIT Press, 55 Hayward Street, Cambridge, MA 02142.

This book was set in Stone Serif and Stone Sans on 3B2 by Asco Typesetters, Hong Kong, and was printed and bound in the United States of America.

Library of Congress Cataloging-in-Publication Data

Pylyshyn, Zenon W.
Things and places : how the mind connects with the world / by Zenon W. Pylyshyn.
    p. cm.—(The Jean Nicod lectures)
"A Bradford book."
Includes bibliographical references and indexes.
ISBN 978-0-262-16245-6 (hardcover : alk. paper)
1. Visual perception. 2. Cognition. 3. Mental representation. I. Title.
BF241.P953   2007
152.14—dc22   2006035507

10 9 8 7 6 5 4 3 2 1

Contents

Series Foreword

The Jean Nicod Lectures are delivered annually in Paris by a leading philosopher of mind or philosophically oriented cognitive scientist. The 1993 inaugural lectures marked the centenary of the birth of the French philosopher and logician Jean Nicod (1893–1931). The lectures are sponsored by the Centre National de la Recherche Scientifique (CNRS), in cooperation with the Ecole des Hautes Etudes en Sciences Sociales (EHESS) and the Ecole Normale Superieure (ENS). The series hosts the texts of the lectures or the monographs they inspire.

Jean Nicod Committee

Jacques Bouveresse, President
Jérôme Dokic and Elisabeth Pacherie, Secretary
François Recanati, Editor of the Series
Daniel Andler   Jean-Pierre Changeux
Stanislas Dehaene   Emmanuel Dupoux
Jean-Gabriel Ganascia Pierre Jacob
Philippe de Rouilhan   Dan Sperber

Preface and Acknowledgments

This book is based in part on the Jean Nicod Lectures that I delivered in Paris in May–June 2004. The temporal gap between the lectures and the publication is not entirely due to my slow typing, but arose from the need to assimilate the rather wide range of publications that are relevant to the thesis I am presenting. The thesis, it turns out, is one that I have been gestating over many years, and hints of it occur in fragmentary form in a number of my publications. Many of these are reports of experimental work carried out with graduate students over the years, whose contribution is much appreciated.

The thesis rests on a growing appreciation of an idea I first learned from David Marr, who refers to it as the *principle of natural constraints*. The mind has been tuned over its evolutionary history so that it carries out certain functions in a modular fashion, without regard for what an organism knows or believes or desires, but because it is in its nature, or as I more often put it, because of its architecture. So far this is an innocent enough idea that fits many different schools of psychology (and in fact is a familiar part of J. J. Gibson's direct realism theory, though used there to very different ends). The particular constraint I am interested in here takes the form of a mechanism that allows the modular perceptual system to do things that many philosophers have said (correctly) can only be done by using the sophisticated machinery of concepts and the logical machinery of induction, deduction, and what Charles Sanders Peirce called abduction. The mechanism includes the capacity to select individual things in one's field of view, to reidentify each of them under certain conditions as the same individual thing that was seen before, and to keep track of their enduring individuality despite radical changes in their properties. I claim that so long as we are in the kind of world we live in there are mechanisms that allow the visual system to do these things without using the heavy equipment of concepts, identity, and tenses (which are needed for other tasks).

For example, this is a world in which most surfaces that we see are surfaces of physical objects, so that most of the texture elements we see move coherently as the object moves; almost all elements nearby on the proximal image are at the same distance from the viewer; and, when objects disappear, they frequently reappear nearby, and often with a particular pattern of occlusion and disocclusion at the edges of the occluding opaque surfaces, and so on. Identifying things as ones we have seen before and keeping track of them as being the same individual objects over time is at the heart of my research, which has shown that we are very good at doing this in a way that does not use encoded properties (or the conceptual category) of the things that are tracked and reidentified. This mechanism is important to us because if it were not for the existence of such nonconceptual processes, our concepts would not be grounded in experience and thus would not have the meaning that they do.

I have proposed that the capacity to individuate and track several independently moving things is accomplished by a mechanism in the early vision module that I have called *FINSTs* (I call them "Fingers of INSTantiation" because they were initially viewed as a mechanism for instantiating or binding the arguments of visual predicates to objects in the world). This primitive nonconceptual mechanism functions to identify, reidentify, and track distal objects. It is an ability that we exercise every waking minute, and it has also been understood to be fundamental to the way we see and understand the world.

I came upon these ideas in quite a different context, initially when I (along with my colleague Edward Elcock) attempted to develop a computer system for reasoning about diagrams, and later when I was carrying out experimental research on vision, visual attention, and mental imagery. This may seem like a circuitous route, but it has turned out that all these endeavors involve the same puzzles, which I later discovered were also the puzzles that preoccupy many philosophers: how concepts are grounded in experience; how we manage to encode and represent properties of the world when there are so many of them; why we feel that we are conscious of seeing an enormous number of things but are unable to report most of them, while at the same time a great deal of information of which we are not conscious can affect our behavior. These puzzles appear in their most striking form in discussions of two related problems: What are the properties of mental images that allows them to function in thought, and how do certain kinds of thoughts—thoughts about spatial layouts—manage to display properties very similar to those of perceived space?

In this book I examine a number of critical functions of early vision (the part of vision that is informationally encapsulated from the rest of the mind) in the light of the FINST mechanism. Chapter 1 looks at the nature of the problems that FINST are intended to solve, from our initial encounter with the problem of incrementally building a representation over time as various aspects are noticed, to the deep problem of grounding concepts in sensory information. This chapter also introduces FINST theory in terms of a number of experiments that illustrate their nature as pointers to things in the perceived world. It also offers the suggestion that FINSTs serve to provide what philosophers have called *demonstrative reference* or *demonstrative identification*. Chapter 2 focuses on a particular function that FINSTs serve, namely, the nonconceptual *tracking* of individual things that move and change their properties. Since tracking is one of the critical aspects of our commerce with the world, these experiments serve as concrete examples of the role that FINSTs play in this process. It also provides a basis for a number of additional properties of this mind–world connection: it shows that things can be tracked as unidentified things with an enduring numerical identity (where by "unidentified" I mean they are not represented in terms of any conceptual category or in terms of distinctive properties). The notion of tracking also links this work to some findings in cognitive development where it has been shown that very young infants (under six months of age) are able to track things that briefly disappear and are able to anticipate how many hidden things there are (as long as there are three or fewer).

Chapter 3 looks more closely at another of the functions that FINSTs perform, that of selecting things through something like attention (FINSTs are not exactly the same as focal attention and I discuss the differences). This chapter raises some of the controversial aspects of attentional selection. It argues that selecting is nonconceptual and does not depend on the prior encoding of any properties of the things selected—including their location. I argue that the reason this seems unintuitive is that we fail to distinguish between the various roles that the properties of things play in this process. Properties are involved in picking out things to which FINSTs are assigned, and they are involved in determining whether things can be tracked, but they need not be encoded and used in the process of maintaining the identity of the things that are tracked. I spend time in chapter 3 distinguishing between causes and codes and suggest that we should be conservative in describing certain mind–world connections as representations. This brings us to an important function that FINST selection plays, solving what has been called the *binding problem*: the problem of encoding certain sets of properties as being conjoined, as being properties of the same thing, as opposed to being properties that merely occur simultaneously in the scene. Whereas much of the psychological and philosophical literature sees the binding problem as being solved in terms of the collocation of properties, my proposal is that properties are considered conjoined if they are properties of the same FINSTed thing. This brings us to a point where we can say roughly what FINSTs attach to—what it is that I have been calling "things" (or even FINGs, to indicate that they are interdefined with FINSTs, as those things that FINSTs select and refer to)—they attach to what, in our sort of world, typically turn out to be individual visible physical objects. I discuss the frequently cited notion of nonconceptual representation and suggest how this idea is closely related to the story I am telling about FINSTs. In chapter 3 I propose that the only nonconceptual representational content we have is that secured by FINST indexes.

The view that only properties of FINSTed things get represented puts me in conflict with those who appeal to the richness of conscious experience in defending nonconceptual representation. For this reason I devote chapter 4 to a discussion of the role of conscious contents in the process of connecting mind and world. What I claim is that the contents of conscious experience are only one source of evidence for mental contents, and not even a very reliable one. I claim that there is no level of representation that corresponds specifically to the content of conscious experience and, therefore, that equating nonconceptual representation with the content of conscious experience is a mistake. The discussion of the content of conscious experience brings the topic to the nature of the mental images that we experience when reasoning about concrete sensory appearances, about spatial layouts, or when we use spatial mental model models in reasoning. In chapter 4 I focus primarily on what we can make of the contents of conscious experience, and I use theories of mental imagery as the example of how we are misled when we view conscious content as a type of representation.

It is not until chapter 5 that I focus directly on the problem of the representation of space in active working memory (as opposed to long-term memory). Here I review some of the proposals on how some mental representations manage to exhibit certain sorts of spatial properties. Most of these proposals hypothesize some internal constraints on representations of spatial layouts. The most widely accepted and intuitive proposal is that the spatial character of representations of space arises because the representations themselves are instantiated by spatial layouts in the brain—what I call *neural layouts*. I review this proposal as well as some related ones that attempt to retain the benefits of neural layouts without assuming a spatial arrangement in the brain. Of these, the one referred to as *functional space* fails to have any explanatory value, and the other, which I call the *spatial architecture proposal*, reduces essentially to the literal space alternative. In this discussion I distinguish representations involved in long-term memory from representations I refer to as *active spatial representations* (ASPARs), which are constructed both by vision and by reasoning that relies on imagined geometrical of spatial layouts. I then list what I take to be some of the conditions that an ASPAR must meet, which include its capacity to represent magnitudes, its spatial configurational stability, its amodal nature, and its intimate connection with the motor system. The latter brings us to an overview of Poincaré's proposal.

I finish chapter 5 by presenting what might be seen as a fairly radical and speculative proposal for an externalist theory of spatial representation in ASPARs (i.e., in spatial reasoning). The hypothesis, which arises from the ideas about FINSTs that I discuss in the first part of the book, is what I call the *index projection hypothesis*. This proposal claims that in constructing a spatial representation from approximate, partial, and qualitative information stored in long-term memory, we pick out things in the concurrently perceived world using FINSTs and associate imagined objects with them (we think of the imagined objects as being located at the sensed objects). This allows us to use the perceptual system to draw inferences by pattern recognition rather than logical reasoning. I then generalize the projection hypothesis to nonvisual modalities such as proprioception, which requires that I deal with the multiple frame of reference problem (as opposed to a unitary allocentric frame of reference). In this task, coordinate transformation mechanisms, which are plentiful in the brain (especially in parietal cortex, as well as in superior colliculus and premotor cortical areas), play a central role.

Throughout this essay I try to draw morals for a number of philosophical issues such as whether there are nonconceptual representations, how concepts are grounded in perception, and how the mind deals with spatial properties. Clearly this palette is more than can be dealt with adequately in one book. Yet there are some clear themes that run through these puzzles, especially when they are considered against the background of experimental findings in psychophysics, cognitive science, cognitive development, and neuroscience. So this is my attempt to find a way through that forest by focusing on one or two sunny spots where I think progress has been made in the past two decades.

In this pursuit I must express my gratitude to the Institut Jean-Nicod, who generously invited me to give these lectures, the Centre Nationale de la Recherche Scientifique (CNRS), L'École des Hautes Études en Sciences Sociales (EHESS), and L'École Normale Supérieure (ENS), who funded the Jean Nicod Prize and provided space for me the following year as I worked on this book. In particular I wish to thank François Récanati, who chairs the Nicod Prize committee and looked after the logistics of my visit; Pierre Jacob, who directs the Institut Jean-Nicod; and the many people from the Institute who made my stay memorable, especially Roberto Casati, Jérôme Dokic, Élizabeth Pacherie, Joelle Proust, and Dan Sperber. Michel Imbert and Sylvia Duchacek-Imbert were most welcoming and helped make our stay pleasant and memorable.

I also acknowledge the help I received, intended or not, from discussions with my friend Jerry Fodor and with friends and colleagues Charles R. Gallistel (who helped to educate me on the subject of navigation), Georges Rey (who carefully read an earlier version of the manuscript and tried his best to keep me from making some embarrassing philosophical slips and misusing some philosophical terms of art), Joseph Levine and Jonathan Cohen (who provided helpful comments on an earlier draft), Alan Leslie and Lila Gleitman (with whom I have taught some of this material in joint courses), Susan Carey, Ned Block, and Luca Bonatti. I am also grateful to the participants of the conference on Spatial Frames of Reference held in Paris in November 2005, including organizers Jérôme Dokic and Élizabeth Pacherie, and participants with whom I had a chance to try out the ideas in chapter 5: Jean-René Duhamel, Yves Rossetti, Charles Spence, Barbara Tversky, Yann Coello, Paolo Bartolomeo, and Sylvie Chokron.

Finally, I wish to thank my editor, Judy Feldmann, who displayed an uncanny knack for finding words for what I meant instead of what I wrote.

1 Introduction to the Problem: Connecting Perception and the World

1.1 Background

Just as Molière's Monsieur Jourdain discovered that he had been speaking prose all his life without realizing it, so I discovered not too long ago that what I had been doing without realizing it occupies a position in the philosophical landscape. I discovered that coming from a very different perspective I had taken a position on a set of questions that philosophers have been worrying about for at least the past fifty years: questions about how concepts connect with the world, about whether there are nonconceptual representations and if so what they are like, about the grounding of mental states in causal connections with states of the world, and, most recently, about how mental representations—such as those underlying mental imagery—attain their apparently spatial character that allows them to be used in thought the way diagrams are used. I propose, in this first chapter, to illustrate the questions that led me to work on these problems and then to describe, with the aid of some laboratory experiments, why there is a special problem of connecting representations with the world.

The central topic is the relation between the mind and the world. To a vision scientist this sounds like a strange topic. Isn't all of vision science about this relation? What's wrong with a story that begins with light falling on objects in the world and being reflected to the eye, where it is refracted and focused onto the retina, from which it is transformed into nerve impulses, which encode various properties of the retinal stimulus and transmit them to the visual cortex, where they are transformed once again, in ways that neuroscience is currently making good progress studying? Apart from many missing details, it is of interest to ask what's missing from this general kind of story—which is in large part what cognitive science and neuroscience are all about. Is there something missing in principle from this *kind* of story?

The answer I will offer is that there are important aspects of vision that such a story does not address. In this monograph I will attempt to describe some of what is missing and to illustrate the claims by describing relevant empirical research. The ideas come equally from philosophy, psychophysics, and neuroscience.

1.2 What's the Problem of Connecting the Mind with the World? Doesn't Every Computational Theory of Vision Do That?

The basic problem is a familiar one in cognitive science: there are different levels of explanation, and different kinds of questions must be addressed in different vocabularies. The reason we need different vocabularies is that the world is organized in certain ways so that there are different generalizations that can only be captured in different vocabularies. Notwithstanding our belief in the unity of science, we do not address questions of economics or even of geology (which is concerned with such things as rivers and mountains) or meteorology (which is concerned with weather patterns) through theories of physics or chemistry, despite the fact that the tokens in all cases are physical. Let me illustrate the case for perception with a very simple example.

The goal of understanding what has been regarded as humans' most noble sense has a long history, starting, as usual, with the ancient Greeks and taking a great leap forward in the late eighth century Arab world under al-Kindi, when the science of optics was brought into contact with the study of visual perception. This path reached its peak with Johannes Kepler's brilliant solution, in the early seventeenth century, of the problem of the optics of the eye, and his seminal recognition of the critical role that the retinal image plays in vision. But in the century that followed, this sudden spurt of progress seems to have gone into a hiatus. Kepler himself recognized that he had gone as far as he could with the concepts available to him. He wrote (quoted in Lindberg 1976, p. 202):

I say that vision occurs when the image of the whole hemisphere of the world that is before the eye ... is fixed in the reddish white concave surface of the retina. How the image or picture is composed by the visual spirits that reside in the retina and the [optic] nerve, and whether it is made to appear before the soul or the tribunal of the visual faculty by a spirit within the hollows of the brain, or whether the visual faculty, like a magistrate sent by the soul, goes forth from the administrative chamber of the brain into the optic nerve and the retina to meet this image, as though descending to a lower court—I leave to be disputed by [others]. For the armament of the opticians does not take them beyond this first opaque wall encountered within the eye.

In this quotation, Kepler touches on a number of problems that are still concerns today, particularly the balance between top-down and bottom-up analysis of visual information (which he describes in terms of an administrative metaphor). But the quotation also provides a glimpse of Kepler's insightful acknowledgment that there remained serious problems that could not be addressed given the concepts of the day ("the armament of the optician"). What made Kepler particularly pessimistic is that, despite years of trying, he could find no way within geometrical optics to deal with the problem of the inverted and mirror-reversed image on the retina. This puzzle left a generation of brilliant mathematicians and thinkers completely stymied. Why? What did they lack? It is arguable that they lacked the abstract concept of *information*, which did not fully come along until the twentieth century. The concept of information made it natural to see *right side up* and *upside down* as mere conventions, and allowed a certain barrier to be scaled because information requires only a consistent mapping and not the preservation of appearance. As Dretske (1981) points out, so long as the visual pattern is (nonaccidentally) correlated[1] with and thereby carries information about some state of affairs, the information is then available to the right sort of processor which can, in principle, interpret it appropriately, taking into account how the information relates to subsequent uses to which it is put (e.g., object recognition and motor action). But even after we see that the information carried is the same in the right side up as in the upside down image, there is still an obstacle at least as inscrutable as the one that held back Kepler; it is the gap between the incoming causally linked information and *representational content*. If similarity of appearance is eliminated as a criterion, then what makes something a representation of a particular scene rather than of some other scene from which it could equally be mapped in a consistent (information-preserving) manner, and indeed, why are some states representations at all? This puzzle will occupy us throughout this book; its resolution (or at least clarification)

1. The sense of correlation relevant here is any consistent correspondence between values of input and output. Unlike the usual product–moment correlation or even nonparametric correlation measures, metrical or ordinal values of variables need not be preserved—only correspondences. This sense of information is one that is captured by the shared information or shared entropy measure $H(x, y)$ discussed in Attneave 1959.

is central to our understanding of how the mind connects with world in perception.

It is now widely accepted in cognitive science (as well as in computer science) that many generalizations cannot be stated without recourse to the notion of representational content: Many of the things we do can be explained only if we refer to how we represent the world, what we see it *as*, what beliefs and goals we have. There is, of course, much to argue about here (especially if you are a philosopher), but it will scarcely come as a surprise to a cognitive scientist to be told that, for example, the reason you are where you are—in this particular room, at this particular time—is because of what you believe and what your current goals are. Even if it does not require appeal to such notions as beliefs and goals, vision science still has to refer to perceptual contents. As the examples provided by Julian Hochberg (1968) nicely illustrate, how you see a certain part of a scene (what you see it *as*) depends on how you see some other part of the scene. How you see one particular line in a drawing determines (or at least constrains) how you see another line. What color you see this patch of a stimulus to be affects what color you see this other patch to be, regardless of the physical causes of the color perceptions. Many perceptual regularities have to be stated in terms of how things appear to you, in other words, in terms of how things are represented.

The need to appeal to representational content results in another explanatory puzzle, beyond the one that led to Kepler's problem of the inverted image. Not only do we need an informational view of sensory encoding, we also need a way to talk about representational content. A complete story of perception ought to have something to say about why some perceptual state is about X (has the content X) rather than Y. For Hume (and presumably for Kepler) what makes an internal state a representation of X is that it *looks like X*. But if "looks like" is replaced by "carries information about," then the problem of where the content comes from must be confronted once again, because the information-carrying relation is concerned only with correlation; and there are indefinitely many properties of the world that are correlated with the internal states of the mind (e.g., the temperature, or most other properties of the objects under consideration). Picking out the right one is hard enough; but the content is not only some thing in the world, it is also the way the thing is seen (e.g., the Necker cube pattern shown in figure 4.1 is correlated with two different percepts, so how do we specify the different percepts in terms of properties of the world?). To vision scientists, who take representations and representational content for granted, this question generally does not arise. The implicit understanding is that what representations represent is in some way traceable to what caused them, or at least what might have caused them in a typical setting (without the latter qualification, we would be hard put to explain illusions or representations of imagined things that do not originate from immediate causal links with the perceived world). This is certainly a reasonable starting assumption, but it is incomplete in crucial ways; there are generally very many ways that any particular representation could have been caused, yet the representation may nonetheless unambiguously represent just one scene.

Although it may seem at first glance that we should be able to give a purely mathematical account of what all these causal antecedents have in common (e.g., we should be able to provide a geometrical account of all the distal objects that result in a particular representation or appearance), this turns out not to be the case because the mapping between distal shape and proximal image (or, perhaps more perspicuously, between proximal information and percept) is indeterminate or not reversible. What something looks like (even if we could state that with unambiguous precision) depends on factors other than the geometry of the proximal image. In recent years significant progress has been made in making such factors explicit, and the current state of understanding the relation between the geometry of the proximal image and the perceived 3-D shape is relatively advanced (see, e.g., Koenderink 1990; Marr 1982); but we are still far from having an account of why we see things the way we do, let alone why certain of our brain states are about some things and not others. Indeed it is not clear what sort of answer might be adequate for the latter, which may account for why neuroscience celebrates findings of topographical projections of a scene as among the clearest exemplars of (at least visual) representation. But the Humean idea of representational content being defined in terms of similarity will not suffice—as anyone who has taken an introductory course in philosophy of mind knows, *similarity* is the wrong sort of relation to bridge the gap between the world and its representation (many things are similar but do not refer to one another, and many things, such as words, refer without bearing any similarity).

There are at least two distinct kinds of relations between mind and world. There are *semantic* (or *referential*) relations and there are *causal* relations. The first is the sort of relation that exists between, say, a sentence and what it expresses (its content). This is sometimes referred to as the relation of satisfaction—if the sentence is true the world satisfies the sentence (or, to put it the other way round, what the sentence expresses is a state of affairs that would satisfy the sentence). The second sort of relation is one that concerns the mathematician, physicist, and biologist—it is the one to which Kepler contributed important insights and the one that continues to be the goal of neuroscience. One of the perennial projects in philosophy of mind has been to reconcile these two, presumably by showing how the intensional is grounded in the causal. Despite some progress I think it is fair to say that the results have been limited. One elaborate theory has been concerned with the question of how the referents of proper names are grounded in a series of causal links to an initial a dubbing or "baptism" event (Kripke 1980). Another theory builds on the concepts of information and information-carrying states (developed by a number of people, but perhaps best represented by Dretske 1981). In contrast, the causal connection between the proximal pattern (e.g., the distribution of light on the retina) and the three-dimensional layout of the world is well enough understood in principle, although of course there is an enormously complex story that would have to be told to explain how it works in particular circumstances. This is an area of cognitive science where considerable progress has been made, on many fronts, in the past fifty years: on optical processes (including the study of the relation between 3-D geometry; the material composition of surfaces and the patterns of light they reflect to the eye); on biological, cellular, and biochemical processes that take place in the eye itself; on psychophysical relations that hold between optical and geometrical properties and perceived properties; and on the neural circuits leading from the eye to the cortex via several distinct pathways. Much remains to be discovered, but at least in the short term the kind of story it will be is unlikely to rest on brand new concepts, as it did in the time of Kepler and Descartes, when some of the basic concepts we now take for granted were unavailable.

The semantic or intensional[2] connection is quite a different matter. Philosophers (with a few notable Platonist exceptions) have understood that when you postulate representations—as everyone in cognitive science does—you are assuming that the contents of the representation corre-

---

2. The terms *intensional* and *intentional* are used in a somewhat special sense. *Intensional* (with an *S*) is a term that appears in discussions of semantics and is used to refer to the meaning (or sense) of an expression as opposed to the things in the world of which it is true (its *extension*)—so it is relevant to the *form* of a mental representation. On the other hand, *intentional* (with a *T*), often used informally to mean "done with some particular intent," is also a technical term introduced by Brentano (and discussed by Sartre and Husserl), which refers to the property that mental states and acts have in virtue of which they directed at or are *about* something (see next paragraph).

spond, or could correspond, in some way to entities and properties in the world, or at least in some possible world. Yet there is no straightforward way that the world *causes* the particular contents that our representations have, at least not in any transparent way; rather the world may *satisfy* the representation, or the representation may be *true of* the world. A moment's reflection should convince you that if you claim to have a theory of how the world causes your representation to be about X rather than Y the account would be missing something. For one thing, the very same pattern in the world (e.g., of a Necker cube) can be perceived as (represented as) one sort of thing at one time and another sort of thing at another. Psychology is full of examples that illustrate that what you see something as is not determined solely by how or what it is. Illusions provide convincing demonstrations of this, but the principle runs through normal veridical perception. In chapter 1 of Pylyshyn 2003, I provide many examples of this principle, including examples from color-mixing (the "laws" of color mixing apply over perceived colors, not over spectral properties) and shape perception, that show that how one perceives one part of a scene depends on how one perceives (represents) another part. This is not the place to rehearse these examples, but it should be kept in mind that the question of *how something is represented*, or what it is represented as, is at the heart of the study of cognition—one might even say that it is constitutive of cognitive functioning.

Examples are not hard to find: It was not the holy grail that caused the knights of the round table to go out on their searches, but rather the knights' beliefs about the grail, and those beliefs have no causal connection with the grail (since there is no grail to be causally connected to). The need for talk about representations is thus completely general and unavoidable in cognitive science (see, e.g., the discussion in Pylyshyn 1984). Because of this it has often been assumed (and at one time it was argued explicitly by Fodor 1980a) that an account of cognitive processes begins and ends with representations. The only exception to this, it was assumed by many (including, implicitly, Pylyshyn 1984), occurs in what are called transducers (or, in the biological literature, "sensors"), whose job is to convert patterns of physical energy into states of the brain that constitute the encodings of the incoming information. According to the computational view of mind, which these days represents the most widely accepted foundation of cognitive science, these states enter into the causal story of how the brain computes—how it makes inferences and decisions and ultimately determines behavior. Given the view that the bridge from world to mind resides in transduction, the problem then becomes to account for how transduced properties become representations, or semantically evaluable states and, in particular, how they come to have the particular representational content that they have; how, for example, when confronted with a red fire engine, the transducers of the visual system generate a state that corresponds to the percept of a red fire engine and not a green bus.[3]

The problem arises because of how representations are related to what they represent—how their contents are related to the world. Representational content is related to the world semantically, by the relation of *satisfaction*, and satisfying is very different from causing. Satisfaction is the relation that holds between a description and the situation being described. Franz Brentano (Brentano 1995/1874) understood that this sort of relation is unique to the study of mind; it does not appear in physics, chemistry, or biology. Because of this it presents special problems for the scientist—problems that are unappreciated by many people working in empirical cognitive science where it has typically been assumed that the causal story, or at least some abstraction over the causal story, will eventually render obsolete such distinctions as those between satisfying and causing. But the question of how the semantic relation can be naturalized remains as deep a mystery as we have in the field.

Needless to say, I will not be taking on what Brentano called the problem of intentionality. I will instead confine myself to a very small corner of this problem. Yet it is a corner that has ramifications throughout cognitive science. In trying to make headway in understanding the distinction between the causal and the semantic connections—between causing and

3. At one time it was seriously contemplated that this was because we had a "red-fire-engine transducer" that caused the "red-fire-engine cell" to fire, which explained why that cell corresponded to the content *red-fire-engine*. This clearly will not work for many reasons, one of which is that once you have the capacity for detecting red, green, pink, etc., and fire-engines, buses, etc., you have the capacity to detect an unbounded number of things, including green fire-engines, pink buses, etc. In other words, if you are not careful you will find yourself having to posit an unlimited number of transducer types, because without some constraints transduction becomes productive. Yet even *with* serious constraints on transduction (such as proposed in Pylyshyn 1984, chap. 9) the problem of content remains. How do we know that the fire-engine transducer is not actually responding to wheels or trucks or engines or ladders, any of which would do the job for any finite set of fire engines? This problem is tied up with the productivity and systematicity of perception and representation. Failure to recognize this is responsible for many dead-end approaches to psychological theorizing (Fodor and Pylyshyn 1981; Fodor and Pylyshyn 1988).

satisfying—I will draw heavily on empirical findings as well as on ideas from computational vision. Many of these results come from over three decades of experimental research in my laboratory as well as my earlier attempts to build computational models with computer science colleagues. Others come from recent experiments by psychophysicists and cognitive neuroscientists around the world.

What this work has highlighted for me is that at the core of the connection between mind and world lies the question of how vision is able to select or pick out or refer to individual *things* in a scene—tokens or individuals rather than types. It turns out that on this seemingly simple problem rest many deep issues, from the set of problems concerned with reidentifying individual things in the world, often referred to collectively as the correspondence problem, to the grounding of concepts in nonconceptual relations to the world, and perhaps even the problem of sentience itself. (This may be a good place to interject a note about terminology. I often use the term "things" because that makes it clear that I am not intending a technical term, but at other times, when I want to invoke the usage in philosophy or psychology, I may call them sensory individuals or visual objects or sometimes just objects. The question of what these things really are is obviously of central concern and will be addressed in due course.)

What I hope to do in this chapter is introduce this family of issues in two ways. First I will recount an early experience I had in trying to build a computer system that could reason about geometry by drawing a diagram and in the process noticing particular properties of what it was drawing that could lead to conjectures about more general necessary properties and thus to possible lemmas to prove. I confess that we did not get very far along that particular road, but thinking about this problem did serve to alert us to some of the prerequisites for making progress, and it is these prerequisites that I want to share with you. After this introductory example I will outline a number of apparently diverse phenomena in vision that raise the same problem—the need for a nonconceptual connection between thoughts and things in the world. Following this I will sketch the theoretical idea of a mechanism within the visual system that I call a visual index or FINST that arose from this experience, and I will describe some experiments involving attentional selection and multiple object tracking that illustrate the function of this mechanism fairly directly. In subsequent chapters I will expand on the points raised here and develop them in a way that makes contact with some contemporary philosophical issues. In every case, however, I will keep close to the empirical phenomena that motivated the initial exploration of these issues.

1.3   The Need for a Direct Way of Referring to Certain Individual Tokens in a Scene

1.3.1   Incremental Construction of Representations (and a Brief Sketch of FINSTs)

Many years ago I was interested in the question of how diagrams function in reasoning. So, I and my computer science colleague, Edward Elcock, set ourselves the ambitious goal of developing a computer system that would conjecture lemmas and prove theorems in plane geometry by drawing a diagram and noticing interesting adventitious properties in the diagram (this work was described in Pylyshyn et al. 1978). Since we wanted the system to be as psychologically realistic as possible we did not want all aspects of the diagram to be "in its head" but, as in real geometry problem-solving, remain on the diagram it was drawing and examining. We also did not want to assume that all properties of the entire diagram were available at once, but rather that they had to be *noticed* over time as the diagram was being drawn and examined. If the diagram were being inspected by moving the eyes, then the properties should be within the scope of the moving fovea. Even without the eye movement complication, what is noticed has to be constrained in some way so that some degree of sequential construction of a representation is necessary. Consider the following problem, which these constraints immediately raised.

Suppose the system began by drawing a line, then another line, then a line that happens to intersect a line that was already there, forming a vertex, illustrated in figure 1.1. Assume that as these three lines and the first intersection were drawn, representations of them were constructed in working memory (the memory where active representations are stored while they are being used). Working memory now contains a representation of three lines and a vertex. But do we know which line is which, and which of the represented lines form part of the vertex? Since we have drawn three lines at this point we can infer that the vertex involves two of these lines; but which ones? And of the two that form the vertex, which is which? So far it hardly seems to matter. We can easily distinguish them by their orientation. But what if we could not—what if two of them had the same orientation (as in the first and third line in this example)? Surely we know that there are two lines and that one was drawn before the other, but how do we represent this fact? We might recall where the lines were in some global (allocentric) frame of reference. But there is reason to think that we cannot localize things very well in a featureless global environment. And even if we could, knowing their location would not help if they were in motion (a common condition we will explore later). In general

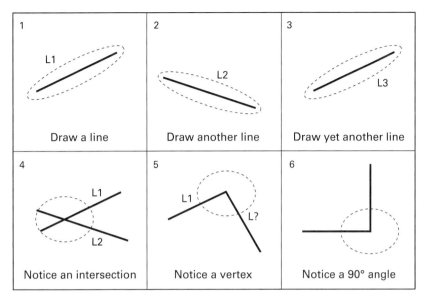

Figure 1.1
As we draw lines (which we see through a narrow foveal view shown by the ellipses) we need a way to refer to particular ones. We can do that by associating them with a description (e.g., "... is at 28° from horizontal") or by placing a label near them. What else do we need in order to re-recognize them when they recur as an intersection or a vertex, or when a second vertex is recognized, or when another property of a vertex (e.g., being 90°) is noticed?

what we need is to be able to refer uniquely to the individual lines so as to think *"this* line was drawn first." In other words we need a way to refer uniquely to a token item (line, vertex, endpoint, etc.) in the scene.

To pursue this story, suppose that the system scans the figure being drawn and notices a vertex that looks to be a right angle (as in panel 6 in fig. 1.1). Is this the same vertex as was just examined, or is it another vertex that was not seen before, or which may have been noticed before but not encoded as a right-angled vertex? As the figure grows in complexity the question of whether some newly noticed property is a property of a new or a previously noticed thing becomes more difficult, and the number and precision of properties that we would have to store in order to tell which line or vertex was which would increase greatly. In order to tell, say, that the line labeled L1 in the first panel of figure 1.1 is a different line from the line labeled L3 in the third panel, but the same as the line we have conveniently labeled L1 in the fourth panel, we would need to encode it as a line and then check that line against each line encountered so far and determine whether it is that one by referring to its defining properties (e.g., its orientation or its location in the scene). We will see later that there is very good empirical evidence that under many common circumstances we do not re-recognize a token thing as the same identical thing previously encountered by checking its properties, and that indeed we *could not* in general do it this way because of the intractability of the problem of storing unique descriptions and matching such descriptions to solve the identity problem (or the "correspondence problem," as it is known in vision science). Moreover, the properties of items often must be ignored, as when we notice only the configurational pattern that holds among tokens and not the properties of individual tokens (in determining, for example, whether there are things in a display that are collinear).

But the situation is even worse than this characterization suggests, because the same question arises in the case of things whose properties change over time. The world is dynamic, and some individual thing you now see that has a certain shape and color and is at a certain location may be the very same thing that you later see with a different shape, color, or location. It turns out that this problem is completely general since the same individual can look different at different instants in time and will clearly be in different locations on the retina and probably in the world. The problem I have just hinted at arises from the fact that standard forms of representation can refer to a *token individual* only by picking it out in terms of a description that uniquely applies to it. But how do we know which description uniquely applies to a particular individual and, what's more important, how do we know which description will be unique at some time in the future when we will need to find the representation of that particular individual token again in order to add some newly noticed information to it? Moreover, to determine whether some particular object is the same as one seen earlier, we would have to look it up by the description it had been given earlier—but how do we know what description it had been given earlier that made it unique in that previous context?

This problem of keeping track of individual token things by using a record of their properties is in general intractable when the things can move and change properties. But the problem exists even for a static scene since our eyes are continuously moving, the lighting changes with different points of view, and so on—which means that the problem of unique descriptors applies to every thing in a perceived scene. In fact it remains even if the scene and the point of view are fixed (as when a static scene is viewed through a peephole) since the representation itself is changing over time as the scene is explored with moving focal attention. There is ample evidence that percepts are built up over time. It takes time for certain perceptual phenomena to appear; for example, it takes up to half a second for hidden parts of simple figures to be filled in or for illusions to be produced from the context of the figure (Reynolds 1981; Reynolds 1978; Schulz 1991; Sekuler and Palmer 1992), as well as for visual processes, such as those involved in the perception of faces (Bachmann 1989; Calis, Sterenborg, and Maarse 1984; Hagenzieker, van der Heijden, and Hagenaar 1990), to complete. All these phenomena require that tokens of individuals—parts of figures or other token things—be tracked so that the information developed over time can be properly merged and attributed to the appropriate things in a scene.

For now my argument concerns the sort of reidentification or correspondence computed by the visual system in the course of normal perception of scenes over relatively brief times. It does not apply when you recognize objects after some absence, as when you recognize someone you have not seen for some time. There are clearly many cases where re-recognition proceeds by matching information stored in long-term memory, and cases in which re-recognition fails when properties of the individual change. The present discussion concerns the sort of tracking of identity that occurs automatically and generally unconsciously as you perceive a scene while scanning it with your gaze or your attention. It is a function of what we call *early vision* (Marr 1982) or of the *modular visual system* (Pylyshyn 1999). When we look at some empirical examples in the next chapter we will see the sort of time scales and conditions over which this operates.

When my colleagues and I first came across this problem in the context of incrementally constructing a representation of a geometrical diagram it seemed to us that what we needed is something like an elastic finger: a finger that could be placed on salient things in a scene so we could keep track of them as being *the same token individuals* while we constructed the representation, including when we moved the direction of gaze or the focus of attention. What came to mind is a comic strip I enjoyed when I was a young comic book enthusiast, called "Plastic Man" (figure 1.2). It seemed to me that the superhero in this strip had what we needed to solve the identity-tracking or reidentification problem. Plastic Man would have been able to place a finger on each of the salient objects in the figure. Then no matter where he focused his attention he would have a way to refer to the individual parts of the diagram so long as he kept one of his fingers on it. Even if we assume that he could not detect any information with his finger tips, Plastic Man would still be able to think "this finger" and "that finger" and thus be able to refer to individual things that his fingers were touching. This is where the playful notion of FINgers of INSTantiation came on the scene, and the term FINST seems to have stuck.

Figure 1.2
"Plastic Man" is able to extend his limbs flexibly. Even if his tactile sense did not permit him to recognize what he was touching, he would still be able to keep track of things in the world as the same individual things despite changes in their location or any of their perceptual properties. (From "Police Comics" #21 © DC Comics. PLASTIC MAN™ DC Comics. All rights reserved. Used with permission.)

1.3.2 Using Descriptions to Pick Out Individuals
I have been speaking of the need to keep track of things without using their properties, or more precisely, without using a conceptual description. But how can we keep track of a thing unless we know something about it? In particular, how can we keep track of it unless we know *where* it is? What I will suggest in the next chapter is that *selection*, which is the central function of what has always been called *focal attention*, is based on individuals, which in vision means that it is "object based" or sensitive to the individual token and not to its properties. But for now let us reconsider the geometry example and ask how we might attempt to keep track of individual parts of the figure by using a stored description. This requires that we be a bit more precise about what constitutes a description. The everyday sense of a description is both too strong and too weak. It is too strong for our purposes because it implies that there is a description in some natural language, whereas we do not need that restriction in the case of a mental representation. All we need is that a description be constructible from basic concepts (other restrictions, such as compositionality, are also required but will not be discussed here; see, e.g., Fodor 1998; Fodor and Pylyshyn 1988). So for our purposes a description is any encoded representation that picks out some individual token by referring to properties that it possesses. The question is: Can such a description uniquely pick out and refer to a token

individual under a wide range of circumstances—in particular, can it refer to an individual token under conditions such as those we were concerned with in the geometry example? And, even if it can, a second question is: Is this how our visual system in fact does it?

In the example sketched earlier, where we are constructing a description of a figure over time, we need to keep track of individual things so as to be able to determine which is which over time—that is, we need to be able to decide between "there it is again" and "here is a new one." We must be able to do this in order to put new information into correspondence with the right individuals already stored in memory. We also need to be able to decide when we have noticed a new individual thing or merely renoticed one we had already encoded earlier. Being able to place individual things into correspondence over time—or to keep track of individual tokens—is essential to the ability to construct a coherent representation. When we notice an individual thing with property P we must attribute P to the existing representation of that very token (if we had encoded it before), or else we must augment our stored representation to include a new individual thing. One way to place individual things into correspondence is to associate a particular token thing with what Bertrand Russell called a definite description, such as "the object x that has property P" where P uniquely picks out a particular thing. In that case, in order to add new information, such as that this particular thing also has property Q, one would add the new predicate "Q" to the representation of that very thing.[4] This way of adding information would require adding a new predicate "Q" to the representation

4. The way a mechanism based on updating descriptions would be used to solve the correspondence problem would be something like this (using the predicate calculus notation is inessential but convenient). The perceptual system notices an individual with property P and stores a description that identifies it at that time, say, $\exists(x)P(x)$. If the description is to specify that P picks out a *unique* object it would have to be augmented to $\exists x\{P(x) \wedge [\forall(y)(P(y) \supset (x = y)]\}$. When an additional predicate Q that happens to pertain to the same object is to be added, the previously stored descriptor for that object is retrieved and a new expression added that asserts that the object also has property Q, thus: $\exists x \exists y[P(x) \wedge Q(y) \wedge x = y]$. The process is repeated each time a new property of some object is encountered. This process of continually inferring the previous unique description and updating it with the currently noticed predicate is clearly not a plausible way to incrementally build a visual representation. Even if there were some rational way to determine the previous description, the matching and updating process demands increasingly complex storage and retrieval processes based on pattern matching, a process that is in general computationally intractable for tree-matching.

of an object that is *picked out by a certain descriptor*. To do that would require first recalling the description under which x was last encoded and then conjoining to it the new descriptor. Each time an object was encountered once again, we would somehow have to find the description under which that same object had been encoded earlier.

The alternative to this unwieldy method is to allow the descriptive apparatus to make use of the equivalent of singular terms or names or demonstratives. If we do that, then adding new information would amount to adding the predicate $Q(a)$ to the representation of a particular thing a, and so on for each newly noticed property of a. Empirical evidence that I will review below suggests that the visual system's Q-detector recognizes instances of the property Q *as a property of a particular visible object*, such as object a. This is the most natural way to view the introduction of new visual properties to the sensorium. This view is consonant with considerable evidence that has been marshaled in favor of what is referred to as object-based attention, and I will have more to say about this idea in the next chapter. In order to introduce new properties in that way, however, there would have to be a nondescriptive way of picking out a. This is, in effect, what the labels on objects in a diagram are for and what demonstrative terms like "this" or "that" allow one to do in natural language. So what I am in effect proposing is that the visual system needs such a mechanism of demonstratives.[5]

The object-based view of how properties of objects are detected and encoded would suggest that when we detect a new property we detect it as applying to a *particular* object, rather than as applying to any object that has a certain (recalled) property. It is also more plausible that properties are detected as applying to particular objects since it is objects, rather than empty locations, that are carriers of properties—as I will argue in the next chapter. Intuitions, however, are notoriously unreliable, so I will later examine empirical evidence that this view is indeed more likely to be the

---

5. Both *demonstrative* and *name* are misleading ways of referring to indexes. In speech what a *demonstrative* refers to depends on the intention of the speaker and the context of utterance, which is not the case with FINST indexes. On the other hand the term visible *name* is misleading because names allow us to think about things in their absence, whereas FINST indexes have a restricted existence, corresponding roughly to when their referents are visible. Levine (forthcoming) eschews the term "demonstrative" in relation to FINST like mechanisms, reserving the term for constituents of thoughts as opposed to constituents of percepts. Since none of the existing terms quite fits, I will tend to use the technical term FINSTs or visual indexes.

correct one. For example, in chapter 2 I will describe studies involving multiple-object tracking that make it very unlikely that objects are tracked by regularly updating a description that uniquely picks out the objects.

The empirical part of this story is the hypothesis that what perception initially detects is *things* or *objects*, as opposed to properties or locations. The more general claim, that *something* in the world is detected without prior specification of its properties, is more than an empirical hypothesis. In order to be able to provide an explanation of behavior and its relation to environmental conditions we must allow for a purely causal connection from world to mind. Later we will see that in principle there are two ways in which properties of the world may affect a perceptual system. It may affect it in a purely causal manner: A property *P* in the world can simply trigger a chain of events that culminates in some change in the perceptual system. Alternatively, the perceptual system may, in effect, *ask* whether property *P* is present. The first of these corresponds to what in computer systems is called an *interrupt*, and the second corresponds to a *test* for *P*. We often refer to the first as *bottom-up* and the second as *top-down*. What is important for us is that there is no such thing as a purely top-down process, or rather, a process cannot be top-down all the way out to the world. If representations are to have a content that is about the world, then the world must impose itself upon the perceptual system—which is to say it must act from the bottom up at some stage. What I am proposing here is that what is bottom up is what will be needed to produce the predicate-argument pairs that constitute a conceptual encoding of the world (encoding that something has the property *P*). To prevent circularity, the arguments of such predicates must be identified (or, as I say, "picked out") by a process that itself is not conceptual (does not use other predicates or properties to identify the referents of the arguments). This desideratum also entails that things that are bearers of properties must be selected and referred to in a bottom-up or data-driven manner. I will return to this topic in the next chapter, where I hope to show that this requirement is entirely reasonable and in a certain sense even obvious.

1.3.3   The Need for Demonstrative Reference in Perception

The sort of "link" I have been referring to is very close to what philosophers have called an *indexical*. Indexicals are terms that refer only in particular contexts of an utterance. They also occur in thoughts where mental indexicals refer in the context of particular token thoughts. In natural language indexicals are instantiated by such terms as pronouns (*me, you*), temporal and spatial locatives (*now, then, here, there*), and, of particular interest to us here, demonstratives (*this, that*), which pick out particular token individuals. Since my concern will be with the selection of things and not with other sorts of indexicals, I will follow common practice and use the term *demonstrative* rather than indexical.

The easiest way to see what this sort of link is like is to think of demonstratives in natural language—typically words like *this* or *that*. Such words allow us to refer to things without specifying what they are or what properties they have. While this gives a flavor of the type of connection we will be discussing, equating this sort of reference link with the role of certain words in a natural language would be misleading in many ways. What a word such as *this* refers to in discourse depends on the intentions and state of knowledge of the speaker (as well as the speaker's beliefs about the state of knowledge of the hearer). Such terms typically occur together with nouns, so we speak of "this chair" or "that table" and so on, and in such contexts they can pick out extremely general things that include things not in our perceptual field, as when we say "this house" while pointing at a wall or "this city" while pointing out the window. Such complex demonstratives occur frequently and there is even a lively debate about whether all uses of demonstratives involve (unstated) complex demonstratives or whether there can be "bare demonstratives" (see, e.g., Lepore and Ludwig 2000). We need not enter this particular debate since what I am proposing is clearly not identical to a demonstrative in a natural language. To the extent that it is like a demonstrative it is clearly like a "bare" demonstrative—it picks out things without doing so by their properties. It does it because the perceptual system is so constituted that things of certain kinds and not other kinds are picked out in certain contexts. Spelling this out will be left for a later chapter, but the details clearly rest on empirical findings concerning such questions as how attention is allocated and how the world is parsed and indexed.

The study of the connection between demonstrative thoughts and perception has been a central concern in philosophy of mind. Most philosophers acknowledge that demonstrative thoughts are special and essential to linking mind and world. They also recognize the important role that perception plays in establishing such connections—through what are referred to as *informational links*. Many philosophers have also argued that, in order to link perception to actions, individual things in a scene must be selected, and that such selection requires demonstrative reference. A reason given is that, finally, the motor system must act on things that are picked out directly rather than by description. We are able to reach for *that* without regard for what "that" is. We can reach for it without representing any its visual appearance properties (such as color or shape) since those are irrelevant to reaching for *it*. Of course the motor system must issue commands in some quantitative frame of reference, but as we will see in chapter 5, this need not be in a global frame of reference, or in any frame of reference available to other parts of the nervous system. How the visual system can provide the information to command an eye or limb movement when the mind does not know where the item is located is a puzzle that is more apparent than real, as we will see later.

John Perry (1979) has argued that such demonstratives are essential in thoughts that occasion action. Perry offers the following picturesque example:

The author of the book *Hiker's Guide to the Desolation Wilderness* stands in the wilderness beside Gilmore Lake, looking at the Mt. Tallac trail as it leaves the lake and climbs the mountain. He desires to leave the wilderness. He believes that the best way out from Gilmore Lake is to follow the Mt. Tallac trail up the mountain.... But he doesn't move. He is lost. He is not sure whether he is standing beside Gilmore Lake, looking at Mt. Tallac, or beside Clyde Lake, looking at the Maggie peaks. Then he begins to move along the Mt. Tallac trail. If asked, he would have to explain the crucial change in his beliefs in this way: "I came to believe that *this* is the Mt. Tallac trail and *that* is Gilmore Lake." (Perry 1979, p. 4)

This point—that demonstratives are essential to such thoughts—is important and easy to overlook. In fact it was glossed over in the earlier discussion of the need to keep track of individual visual objects, illustrated in figure 1.1. There I labeled the vertices and lines and suggested that what we need in order to encode the diagrams over time in a coherent manner is what such labels provide. Although labels do help in thought and in communication, they can do so if (and only if) we have an independent way to refer to the things to which the labels apply. As in Perry's example, we can think about the labeled items if we can think thoughts such as "*this* is the line labeled L1." If we cannot refer to the line in our thoughts independently of their printed label then we cannot use the information that the label provides. Even being able to think of a line as "the line closest to label L1" will not do because determining which line is closest to the label requires referring to the line in question directly, as in "*this* is the line closest to label L1." The alternative would be to search for something that is a line and is closer to L1 than any other line. But that too requires having in mind the thoughts "$this_1$ line is x distance from label L1 and $this_2$ line is y distance from L1 ..." We may have no awareness of such thoughts, but unless we can entertain thoughts with such contents (however expressed) we could not make use of the labels. The importance of demonstrative

"Are we in this Starbucks or the one down the street?"

Figure 1.3

identification has been recognized for some time; it has also been the source of humor in such cartoons as that of the person lost in the desert who comes up to a sign with an X on it and the words "You are here." One of my favorites (by David Sipress, which appeared in the *New Yorker* on April 22, 2002), is shown in figure 1.3. The problem illustrated in these examples is generalized in the next section to the claim that we need a way to bind representations of individual things to the token things themselves—we need a symbol-to-world binding mechanism.

The point of this discussion is that the mental representation of a visual scene must contain something more than descriptive or pictorial information in order to allow reidentification of particular individual visual elements. It must provide what natural language provides when it uses names (or labels) that uniquely pick out particular individuals, or when it embraces demonstrative terms like *this* or *that*. Such terms are used to indicate particular individuals. Being able to use such terms assumes that we have a way to *individuate*[6] *and keep track of particular individuals* in a scene *qua individuals*—even when the individuals change their properties, including their locations. Thus what we need are two functions that are central to our concern in this book: (1) we need to be able to pick out or individuate distinct individuals (following current practice, when discussing the experiments I will call these individuals *visual objects*, reserving the more general question of what they really are for later discussion), and (2) we need to be able to *refer to* these visual objects as though they had names or distinct demonstratives (such as *this*$_1$, *this*$_2$, etc.). Both these purposes are served by the proposed primitive mechanism that I have called a *visual index* (or more generally a *perceptual index*), or a FINST.

I might point out that even though the postulation of FINST indexes arose from the theoretical need for something like demonstrative references to fill the gap between symbolic representations (perhaps in the *language of thought*) and perceived physical things in the world, such indexes can now be seen as important for explaining certain human skills. Among these is the ability to play team sports, like basketball or hockey, in which a player must keep track of moving objects (e.g., players) as they weave around the field or ice. There have been reports of exceptional tracking ability among these "experts," and we now have evidence that tracking can be improved substantially with practice. Moreover, we have evidence that people are able to track moving things far into their periphery, as long as they do not get too close to one another. Some of these results will be presented when we talk about our multiple object tracking experiments in chapter 2. But for now it might help us appreciate the generality of the mechanism that I will be discussing if we think of them as connecting familiar moving things in the world with mental things, as illustrated in figure 1.4 for the case of the game of basketball.

6. As with a number of terms used in the context of perception research (such as the term "object"), the notion of *individuating* has a narrower meaning here than in the more general context where it refers not only to separating a part of the visual world from the rest of the clutter (which is roughly what it means here), but also providing identity criteria for recognitional instances of that individual. As is the case with *objecthood* and other such notions, we are here referring primarily to perceptually primitive cases, such as ones provided directly by mechanisms in early vision (in the sense of the term "early vision" used, e.g., in Pylyshyn 1999) and not constructed from perceptual/conceptual resources.

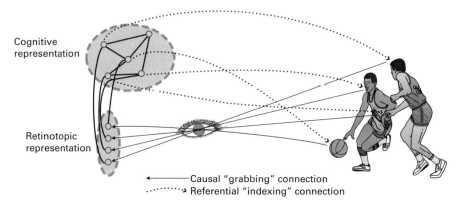

Figure 1.4
An illustration of how being able to pick out and track several individual moving things, even when there is not enough time to encode their properties, might be useful in team sports.

In the rest of this chapter I will provide some empirical illustrations of the claim that the visual system does in fact embody a primitive mechanism of this sort by showing that they provide a natural account of a number of empirical phenomena. In the next chapter I will introduce other experiments and will discuss the philosophical issues raised by this claim.

1.4   Some Empirical Phenomena Illustrating the Role of Indexes

1.4.1   Tagging/Marking Individual Objects for Attentional Priority
There are numerous other reasons why the visual system needs to be able to pick out particular individuals in roughly the way singular terms or demonstratives do (i.e., without reference to their properties). This need is quite general and arises from the fact that properties are predicated of things, and relational properties (like the property of being collinear) are predicated of several things. So there must be a way, independent of the process of judging which property obtains, of specifying which objects the property will be predicated of. Ullman (1984), as well as a large number of other investigators (e.g., Ballard, Hayhoe, Pook, and Rao 1997; Watson and Humphreys 1997; Yantis and Jones 1991), talk of the objects in question as being "tagged" (or in some cases "marked"). One of the earliest uses of the notion of tagging was associated with explaining why things that had attracted attention (e.g., by being flashed or by suddenly appearing in the field of view) had priority in such attention-demanding processes

as detecting a faint dot or making a visual discrimination. For example, Yantis and Johnson (1990) showed that in a search task, subjects told to find specified letters in a multiletter display showed superior performance when the letter had been signaled (highlighted), and he attributed this to a "priority tagging" process.

Tagging has also been used to explain why certain items have a *low* priority in search. Under certain conditions, irrelevant but potentially confusable distractor items can be inhibited in a search task by being tagged (Watson and Humphreys 1997 refer to this as "marking" rather than "tagging," but the idea is the same). The notion of a tag is an intuitive one since it suggests a way of *marking objects* for reference purposes. But the operation of tagging makes sense only if there is something *out there* on which a real tag can be placed. It does no good to tag an internal representation since the object one wishes to examine is in the world (recall that one of the reasons for tagging objects is to be able to move focal attention to them, to examine them further, and to evaluate predicates over them). But how do we tag parts of the world? What we need is a way to refer to individual things in a scene *independent of their properties or their locations*.[7] This is precisely what FINST indexes provide.

1.4.2   Argument Binding

When we recognize visual patterns we recognize them as patterns constituted by particular tokens. Consequently, prior to detecting the pattern we must select or pick out the relevant elements of the pattern and then recognize the configuration that these elements instantiate. Shimon Ullman (1984) described a number of simple patterns that he claimed require, by their very nature, a serial process (called a "visual routine") to be undertaken involving certain selected token elements. For example, in order to detect the pattern "inside," the elements to which this pattern applies must be specified. Ullman (as well as Marr 1982) uses the notion of *tagging* to refer to this selection. Some form of a selection and specifying operation is essential because there must be some way to specify the particular token items to which the pattern detection routine is applied. The pattern-detection process may simply involve judging whether the specified items

7. As we will see in the next chapter, it would not help the problem of incrementally constructing a representation even if we *could* tag the objects in the world since it would not solve the problem of representing unique individuals. For example, it would not let us think thoughts such as "*this* is the object labeled L1," without which the label would be of no help. The use of demonstratives in thought is so natural that it is easy to forget that they are indispensable.

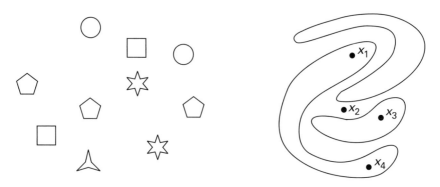

Figure 1.5
Collinearity (left panel) can be computed over objects only after they have been
identified (i.e., individuated) and bound to the argument of the "collinear" predicate. Similarly, the "inside" predicate (right panel) can be computed only if all relevant objects (dots $x_1 \ldots x_4$, and appropriate contours) are bound.

form a particular shape (as in the left panel of figure 1.5) or whether a certain more abstract relation holds among them (as in the right panel of
figure 1.5). In the case of more abstract relation, a visual routine such as
"contour tracing" or "area painting" must then be undertaken, but this
cannot be done until the things on which the process must be performed
have been identified and a reference to them established. My way of putting this is to say that certain items must be bound to the argument of a
visual predicate (or a computational function) before the predicate can be
evaluated. In these examples we need some way to bind the arguments of
predicates such as **Collinear**$(x, y, z, \ldots)$ or **Inside**(x, c), as shown in figure
1.5.

   In these examples the things over which the predicate is evaluated have
to be selected. How does such selection occur? Is it voluntary or automatic?
We will return to these questions in chapter 2. But for the moment we
might note that some form of voluntary selection must be possible. Look
at a flecked wall or any surface not totally uniform. You can pick out a particular fleck or texture element with no trouble. Now pick out a second and
third such fleck without moving your eyes. It is not easy, but it can be done
(or, rather, it can be done easily but it feels like an effort—an experience
that may have little to do with how the process itself unfolds, as I will argue
in chapter 4). Experiments (see, e.g., Intriligator and Cavanagh 2001) have
shown that so long as the items are not too close together, people can keep
their eyes fixed on a particular selection while moving their attention to a

specified second item (they can follow the instruction to "move up one" or "move right two"). We have also carried out experiments (section 1.4.4) where the selection is automatic—where the FINST index is captured or grabbed by an onset event.

1.4.3   Subitizing

I want to give two additional experimental examples of the need for such argument-object binding because they make an important point about how the selection works and why it might be generally useful. Among the processes for which binding is needed is one that evaluates the cardinality of the set of tokens. There is a lot of evidence that when the number of items is four or fewer, the process of recognizing their numerosity, called subitizing, involves a different mechanism from that used in estimating larger quantities. The evidence comes from both psychophysics and neuroscience and has been studied in adults, infants, and animals (nicely summarized in Dehaene 1997). Although counting is involved in both the subitizing range ($n \leq 4$) and the larger counting range ($n > 4$), the former has certain signature properties, among which is a faster and more accurate enumeration and an independence from item location (e.g., telling the subject in advance which quadrant of the visual field the items will appear in does not alter subitizing though it does improve counting; see below). These characteristics can be explained if we assume that subitizing does not require searching a visual display for the items to be enumerated, because what is being enumerated is the number of active FINST indexes. But the explanation that involves indexes assumes that the relevant items are individuated automatically and quickly and a reference is established at the same time. When this precondition is not fulfilled, subitizing cannot occur, we discovered (Trick and Pylyshyn 1994b).

There is independent evidence that certain conditions of element properties (and spacing) allow automatic individuation whereas others do not. For example, when items are too close together they cannot be automatically individuated but require focal attention, as evidenced by a person's inability to pick out, say, the third one from the left, even though the distances are large enough that person can easily judge when there are two items and when there is just one (the usual two-point threshold test for acuity). See figure 1.6.

Given these independently established individuation parameters we can then ask whether elements that cannot be individuated without our serially attending to them (as in the panel on the left) can be subitized. The

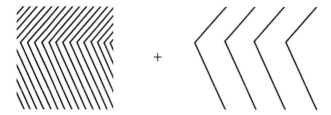

Figure 1.6
The spacing required for individuation is greater than the spacing required for two-point resolution. The first is measured by the ability to select a particular element (e.g., third from left) while the latter is measured by the ability to distinguish one from many. (Based on Intriligator and Cavanagh 2001.)

answer we obtained from experiments is that when items are arranged so that they cannot be preattentively individuated, they can't be subitized either, even when there are only a few of them (Trick and Pylyshyn 1994b). For example, items that are too close together or are distinguished only through operations that must be performed serially or that require serial focal attention in order to individuate (e.g., objects characterized as "lying on the same curve" or elements specified in terms of conjunctions of features, such as elements that are both red and slanted to the left) cannot be subitized. In other words, with such displays we don't find the discontinuity in the rate of enumeration as the number of objects exceeds around four (as shown by the fact that the graph or reaction time as a function of number of items does not have a "knee").

An example of elements that can and that cannot be individuated preattentively, along with typical reaction-time curves, is shown in figure 1.7. When the squares are arranged concentrically they cannot be subitized, whereas the same squares arranged side by side can easily be subitized regardless of their relative size. Lana Trick and I argued that the difference between counting and subitizing lies in the need to search for items in the world when counting large numbers ($n > 4$) of items, which requires attentional scanning that takes time and memory resources. By contrast, the cardinality of smaller numbers of items that have been indexed can be ascertained without having first to find them. This can be done either by counting the number of indexes deployed or by evaluating one of several cardinal predicate over them (TWO(x,y), THREE(x,y,z), etc.). Since there is a (small) increase in time taken to respond correctly as number as the number increases from two to four, the first of these appears more natural.

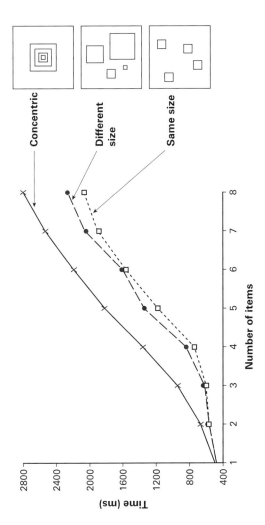

Figure 1.7

Graph of reaction time versus number of items enumerated, for several conditions examined in Trick and Pylyshyn 1993. Time to enumerate concentric squares does not show the characteristic "knee" in the curve that is the signature of subitizing.

1.4.4   Subset Selection

I have claimed that a central function of indexes is to select and refer to (or bind arguments to) several visual elements at once so that visual predicates can be evaluated over them. This is important not only for recognizing certain patterns as I suggested above; if we make certain assumptions concerning how the indexing mechanism works, it may also help us to understand how visual stability is attained in the face of rapid saccadic exploration of the visual world. Let me illustrate with two experiments.

The first study (Burkell and Pylyshyn 1997) was an experiment in which a subset of (2–5) items sprinkled randomly among an additional set of identical 11 items (Xs) was precued (by appearing after the other items, thus capturing attention), following which all items turned into distinct search items (by dropping one of the bars and changing colors, yielding left-oblique and right oblique bars in either red or green), and the subject had to search through only the precued subset for a specified target (e.g., a left-oblique red bar). The patterns were such that we could tell whether the subject was searching through only the precued subset or in fact ended up searching through the entire set of items.[8] What we found is that subjects did confine their search to a subset of cued items among a larger set of similar items. Moreover, their performance in finding the target was not slowed when the distance among members of the subset increased, as one would expect if subjects had to search through the subset items by scanning the display. These results suggest that subjects could hold the subset in mind during the search and also that they did not have to search for the subset items themselves; they had only to search for the target among those subset items. This is despite the fact that subset items were interspersed among the other (distractor) items. We concluded that the late onsets caused indexes to be assigned to the designated subset, which could then be used to direct a rapid search of that subset while ignoring the irrelevant intervening items—much as the enumeration operation could be confined to the selected items in the subitizing task, providing there were four or fewer of them.

8. The technique involved presenting all 11 Xs and then using sudden onsets of additional Xs to precue a target subset of 3 to 5 Xs. All the Xs then turned into either a "popout" single-feature search or a slow "conjunction" search. Since the elements in the entire display always constituted a set of conjunction-search items, we could tell by the different search rates whether subjects were able to confine their search to the subset alone. More details on all these experiments can be found in Pylyshyn 2003.

The second set of experiments (carried out with Christopher Currie) used the same procedure, but introduced a saccadic eye movement after the subset had been cued but before all the "*X*" items changed into search items (left- and right-leaning colored bars). We found that under certain saccade-inducing conditions (in particular when subjects moved their gaze to any one of the targets, though not when they were told to saccade to a second fixation point or to the edge of the display), observers were still able to confine their search to the subset. This finding lends support to the proposal that what makes the world appear stable in the face of several saccades each second may be that the correspondence of a small number of items between fixations is made possible by a mechanism such as a FINST. Others have also shown that only a limited amount of information is retained across an eye movement. In fact Irwin (1992; Irwin and Gordon 1998) has shown that only information for about four objects could be retained, which fits nicely with the FINST account.

The power of FINSTs to select and to hold on to objects also accounts for a number of findings reported in the literature in which recalled patterns are superimposed onto patterns that subjects viewed visually. For example, they can account for how illusions such as the Müller-Lyer illusion can apparently be induced by *imagining* arrows superimposed on perceived lines. All one has to assume to account for this is that indexed endpoints and arrows allow attention to be moved to them. Since the Müller-Lyer is known to depend on attention, this is enough to induce the illusion. Many such demonstrations are discussed in Pylyshyn 2003, chaps. 5 and 7.

1.5   What Are We to Make of Such Empirical Demonstrations?

I have devoted rather more space to these examples than perhaps is merited by the small point I wish to make. I simply want to point out that there are many reasons why the visual system needs to pick out individual token things in a perceptual scene. Moreover, the picking out entails two separate operations. First, it entails a form of individuation—a primitive separation of the thing from its background and from other things. Second, it entails being able to refer[9] to the individual directly—in an unmediated

9. John Campbell has suggested that I might avoid some philosophical arguments if I refer to FINSTs as "epistemic instruments" which serve to find out about physical objects in the world and to act on them, rather than treat them as demonstratives, since the latter raise questions such as whether they refer to real physical objects or "proto-objects," whether they play an inferential role similar to proper names, and

way that does not require using a description of the thing in question. The reason for separating these two functions may not be apparent at this stage, but I will return to it in the next chapter where I distinguish them empirically, with the first function (individuation) being carried out in parallel and without drawing on limited resources, and the second being limited to the four or five indexes postulated in FINST theory.

---

whether they are two-place relations (as implied by my term "direct reference") or three-place relations involving a reference, an object, and some encoding of the object's properties (e.g., an object file). These are all valid and helpful observations and I am grateful to Campbell for his comments. For a number of reasons having to do with my expository goals (which I hope will become apparent later) I will persist in my claim that indexes directly refer to proto-objects or *things*. However, the last point concerning the possibility of two indexes referring to the same thing—and the related question of how it is possible to decide whether this is indeed the case—requires some additional comment that I will take up in the next chapter.

2 Indexing and Tracking Individuals

2.1 Individuating and Tracking

In the previous chapter I introduced the need for indexical or demonstrative reference to individual things. Postulating such perceptual demonstratives or indexes assumes several sorts of capacities. One is the capacity for *individuating* whatever is indexed or demonstrated. A second is the capacity for keeping track of such individuals—of tracking each one *as being the same enduring thing* despite changes in its appearance and, in particular, despite changes in its location. These two assumptions raise both philosophical and empirical questions and even contradict a great deal of received wisdom in both fields. Consequently I need to explain my uses of terms such as "individuating" and "tracking" or "reidentifying," which are at the heart of the present proposal.

In recent years psychologists have used the term *individuate* to indicate that some part of the world is perceptually separated from the rest by a process that is related to the Gestalt notion of *figure-ground* separation. This sort of parsing of a scene into what perception treats as objects of interest, as distinct from the rest of the undifferentiated world, is one of the most basic operations performed by a perceptual system. In fact, recent evidence suggests that it is performed by the visual system of babies only a few months old (Johnson 2001). But the exact nature of this sort of individuation is not entirely clear. For example, it is not clear whether in individuating something we must also notice and encode or represent particular properties of that thing. Philosophers typically assume that in order to individuate something we must conceptualize its relevant properties. In other words, we must first represent (or cognize or conceptualize) the relevant *conditions of individuation*—otherwise, how could we distinguish the individuated thing from other things in the perceptual field? The concepts that we need in order to do this, according to this story, are called *sortals*.

Sortals are concepts that correspond to countable things, so they include the concepts shoe, table, chair, person, circular disk, and so on, but not water, air, sky, and other things that correspond to "mass nouns," which are not countable (you can say "some water" but not "three waters"). Carving up the world according to sortal concepts is, according to this approach, a prerequisite for individuating the things of the world. Some people believe that very few sortal concepts are available in early infancy; for example, it may be that babies only have one sortal concept, namely the sortal "object" (Xu 1997). According to this view, in order to re-recognize an individual at another instant we need to be able at least to assign it to the same sortal concept.

The idea that identifying (or reidentifying) something as the same individual thing requires conceptualization was vigorously defended by the philosopher Peter Strawson (1959). Strawson argued that such identification requires "the apparatus of concepts," which includes not only sortal concepts, but also the conceptual apparatus of "numerical identity" needed counting, divided reference (distinguishing *this* from *that* entails referring to at least two things at once), and tenses (in order to identify $this_{now}$ with $this_{before}$). I agree with all of Strawson's arguments—individuating and re-identifying in general require the heavy machinery of concepts and descriptions. What I will argue is that FINST indexes give one a special kind of approximation that serves reliably to do the work of individuation and reidentification in our sort of (restricted) world. But what FINSTs provide is not just an approximation. What they provide is indispensable for true individuation. Without a nonconceptual mechanism of the sort provided by FINSTs we would not have the full sense of individual and reidentification. Conceptual identification ultimately requires a nonconceptual basis.

I am going to argue that, notwithstanding the claims about the need for sortal concepts, there must be a type of individuation and a type of reidentification that occurs at least in visual tracking, which is more primitive than the individuation provided by sortals. It is a nonconceptual type of individuation and tracking, and its existence is supported both by empirical arguments (from experimental evidence and from more general empirical considerations) and by philosophical considerations. I will also suggest that this is what we see in operation both in the experimental examples I will present and also very likely in the infant studies of object constancy and infant sensitivity to the cardinality of sets of objects (to be reviewed briefly in section 2.5). Before getting into these philosophically loaded questions, I will offer some empirical demonstrations of what FINSTs can do (an animated demonstration of the experimental materials can be viewed at http://mitpress.mit.edu/thingsandplaces/).

The core idea I will explore in this chapter is the idea of *tracking* or of *keeping track of individuals*, or of recognizing what is sometimes called the *numerical identity* of a thing. Part of what it means to individuate something is to be able to keep track of its identity despite changes in its properties and location. To know that something is an individual is to know that *this* (at time t) is the same thing as *this* (at time $t + \Delta t$), so that when it changes properties or moves in certain ways over time it keeps being the same enduring individual. We know that in general this requires re-recognition. But we also know that the perceptual system does it automatically in very many circumstances without paying attention to the thing's properties (indeed, by explicitly ignoring many of its essential properties). This happens routinely in apparent motion as well as in stereo perception, both of which require solving what has been called the *correspondence problem* (the problem of which individual thing in one display goes with which individual thing in another display), which is just another sort of reidentification. Of course, if the thing being tracked disappears and reappears there is the question of whether it is the same thing, and if so, in virtue of what properties it counts as being the same individual thing. The answer I will give is that in the relevant cases, the nonconceptual mechanisms of the encapsulated visual module determine whether or not two tokenings are tokenings of the same individual thing, and these mechanisms do so, I will claim, without benefit or the heavy equipment of concepts and without powers of reasoning. What properties of the individuals it uses is a separate empirical question to which we may or may not be able to provide a general answer, but the claim is that the properties that determine token sameness or numerical identity may act in a causal manner without themselves being represented. Consequently much will hinge on the mechanism of tracking and on the empirical properties of this mechanism, properties that we can only discover with experimental research. It is this sort of tracking, carried out by an encapsulated perceptual system (which I will refer to as "early vision," after David Marr), that I want to discuss now. My examples will be from vision because more is known about vision (and my own experiments have involved the visual modality) but we will see later that the same story applies equally to (most) other modalities.

Before presenting the experimental demonstrations I might note that the role of tracking has been recognized by a number of people. The place of tracking in the metaphysics of objects was recognized by Smith (1996), and its role in demonstrative identification has been spelled out by philosophers like Gareth Evans (1982). The importance that Evans places on tracking is illustrated by his insistence that "The fundamental basis ... of a demonstrative Idea of a perceptible thing is a capacity to attend selectively to a single thing *over a period of time*: that is, a capacity to *keep track* of a single thing over a period of time" (1982, p. 175). Two further points that this quotation does not address, and which I will argue are equally central, are that (1) such a capacity to keep track must apply to more than one thing at a time and (2) the process of keeping track does not rely on representations of any of the things' properties, including their locations. These two additional points, to which I have already alluded in the previous chapter, are illustrated by experiments in multiple object tracking (MOT), to which I now turn.

2.2   Indexes and Primitive Tracking

In the previous chapter I sketched a theory called *visual index theory* (or FINST theory) which assumes a finite (in fact, numerically small) capacity for indexing certain kinds of individuals. I suggested that the indexing process might be viewed as a process of demonstrative identification and reference, a suggestion that I take up again in this and the next chapter. Such a process could serve the important function of anchoring our perceptions to the world by allowing us to bind a small number of arguments in mental representations to individual distal objects. The existence of such a mechanism suggests that we ought to be able to keep track of a small number of moving items under conditions where we do not (or could not) encode properties that uniquely describe the individual tokens. This observation led me and colleagues to develop an experimental paradigm called *multiple object tracking* (MOT) which has now been studied in hundreds of different experiments and has led to many surprising findings. These findings have far-reaching implications for understanding individuation and other philosophical problems, and so I will devote most of this chapter to describing the experiments and discussing their implications.

Suppose we ask a person to keep track of several moving targets, such as small disks or squares, under conditions where no current property can uniquely identify these targets and distinguish them from identical-appearing moving nontargets. In these studies we refer to the items to be tracked as *target objects* and the nontargets as *distractor objects*, following the terminology used in the psychological study of attention. In a typical experiment, we arrange for the target objects to move unpredictably among

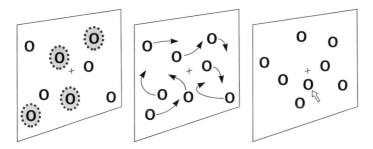

Figure 2.1
Sketch of the multiple object tracking experiment. Items shown with dotted circles around them blink a few times before they begin to move randomly. When they stop, the observer uses a computer mouse to indicate the items that have been designated as targets by having been blinked earlier.

a set of identical nontarget objects, and even to change their visible properties (such as shape or color) at random as they move. If we have a number of FINSTs available and if these become attached to the target objects, then it should be possible to keep track of which objects are the target objects—so long as there are not more targets than the maximum number of available FINSTs. Following this line of reasoning, we devised the multiple object tracking (MOT) experiment as a test of this prediction. In this experiment (illustrated in figure 2.1) a small number of target objects (usually around four) are briefly distinguished from a number of visually identical nontarget objects, typically by blinking the targets on and off a few times. Then all objects move around unpredictably on a screen, the targets traveling helter-skelter among the identical nontargets, for some period of time (say, around ten seconds). At the end of the trial, subjects must indicate which objects had earlier been designated as the targets (they might do so, for example, by selecting them using a mouse, or by judging whether a single flashed object was a designated target).

Although this may sound like a difficult task (especially when the nontargets and targets are allowed to move freely and to pass in front of each other), our volunteers find this task extremely easy to do for four targets and four nontargets moving at speeds that would be reasonable if the objects were real balls in some sort of field game (the actual speeds varied across time and for different experiments, but on average it was such that it would take a moving object 4 to 6 seconds to cross the entire computer screen if it moved in a straight line—which it never does because of the random-walk algorithm used). The basic experiment has been replicated

hundreds of times under many different conditions and in dozens of labo-
ratories, and performance of better than 85 percent in tracking four items is
routinely observed (even young children aged 5 to 8 can track about three
items; see Black and Pylyshyn 2004; O'Hearn, Landau, and Hoffman 2005;
Trick, Audet, and Dales 2003; Trick, Perl, and Sethi 2005).[1] The experiment
is most impressive when actually experienced. The reader is encouraged to
examine recorded animated demonstrations of several versions of the experiment by visiting either http://ruccs.rutgers.edu/finstlab/demos.htm/ or
the book's page at http://mitpress.mit.edu/thingsandplaces/.

Some of the conditions under which this task can be performed will be
discussed later since they illustrate several properties of the indexing and
tracking process that are of theoretical interest; these include conditions in
which objects change color and shape, disappear briefly behind an occluding surface, or simply disappear from view entirely as though the observer
had blinked. For now it will suffice to describe an analysis we carried out on
the first published case of this experiment (Pylyshyn and Storm 1988). In
that study the trajectories of all moving objects were recorded so we were
able to ask whether certain ways of keeping track of the targets could have
been used by subjects in that experiment. For example, one possible way of
tracking the four targets might be to encode and store their instantaneous
locations and to continuously update these by moving attention to each
target in turn. This is not an unreasonable assumption since there is reason
to believe that focal attention is required in order to encode the location
of an object (Saarinen 1996). Such a tracking strategy might proceed by
recording in some form the locations of all targets at the start of the trial
(while they are visibly distinct) and then moving attention sequentially to
each target in turn during the tracking process using their recorded loca-

1. Some published research includes Allen, McGeorge, Pearson, and Milne 2004;
Alvarez, Arsenio, Horowitz, and Wolfe 2005; Alvarez and Cavanagh 2005; Alvarez
and Scholl 2005; Bahrami 2003; Blaser, Pylyshyn, and Domini 1999; Blaser, Pylyshyn, and Holcombe 2000; Cavanagh 1992; Cavanagh and Alvarez 2005; Cavanagh,
Labianca, and Thornton 2001; Culham, Brandt, Cavanagh, et al. 1998; Fougnie and
Marois 2006; Intriligator and Cavanagh 2001; Jovicich, Peters, Koch, et al. 2001;
Keane and Pylyshyn 2006; Ogawa and Yagi 2002; O'Hearn, Landau, and Hoffman
2005; Pylyshyn 1989, 1994, 2004; Pylyshyn, Burkell, Fisher, et al. 1994; Pylyshyn
and Storm 1988; Saiki 2003; Scholl and Pylyshyn 1999; Scholl, Pylyshyn, and Feldman 2001; Scholl, Pylyshyn, and Franconeri 1999; Sears and Pylyshyn 2000; Suganuma and Yokosawa 2002; Trick, Perl, and Sethi 2005; vanMarle and Scholl 2003;
Viswanathan and Mingolla 1998, 2002; Yantis 1992. An up-to-date bibliography is
being maintained by Brian Scholl at http://www.yale.edu/perception/MOT-Papers/.

tions. Because the objects are moving during this updating process the right object might not be at its stored location any longer. But we might nonetheless persevere and pick the nearest object to the recorded location and assume that this object is the target in question. Continuing with such a strategy, we might then update the object's stored location (assuming it was a target) and continue visiting and updating the locations on the list of presumed targets until the end of the trial. Using published estimates of the speed of attention movement we tested this location-updating hypothesis on the actual trajectories used in the experiment (note that this is a conservative test since it ignores the significant additional time that it takes to encode target locations, as well as to disengage and reengage focal attention; Danckert and Maruff 1997). Simulating this strategy on the actual trajectories of objects used in our experiment yields a predicted performance of only about 30 percent under the most conservative conditions—that is, using the highest estimates of attentional speed reported in the literature and even considering the possibility that not just location but also speed and direction of each target are also encoded to enable some degree of prediction of the targets' location. This is far from the 87 percent performance we actually observed with our volunteer subjects (Pylyshyn and Storm 1988). Thus we concluded that targets were not tracked by using their encoded and continuously updated locations.

Other more recent studies also showed that making every object a different color or size or shape does not help tracking (Dennis and Pylyshyn 2002), and neither does changing the objects' colors and shapes randomly during tracking make it worse. In fact subjects are unaware of changes in objects' properties during tracking (Bahrami 2003; Scholl, Pylyshyn, and Franconeri 1999). Thus we concluded that what makes it possible for objects to be tracked in MOT is the existence of a mechanism such as the one we long ago wished we could assume when we envisioned Plastic Man's fingers, the mechanism we call a FINST or visual index.

2.3   What Goes On in MOT?

2.3.1   FINSTs and Object Files

A convenient way to tell the story of what goes on in MOT is in terms of *object files* (Kahneman, Treisman, and Gibbs 1992). Object file theory was developed independently of FINST theory and was published shortly after publication of the initial FINST ideas and MOT. It bears a close affinity to our work—even though the object file research relies on a very different experimental paradigm. But object files provide a useful way to think about

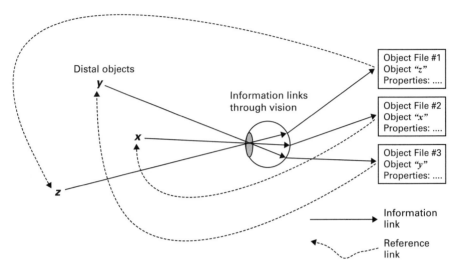

Figure 2.2
Sketch of the structure of the FINST mechanism and its relation to object files and things in the environment. Notice that object files may be empty, as they typically appear to be in MOT.

how FINSTs get used in analyzing a scene, and I will refer to them later in describing the relation between these approaches and the important work by philosophers who have written about individuals.

We can think of an object file as a way for information to be associated with objects that are selected and indexed by the FINST mechanism.[2] When an object first appears in view (or attracts attention because it blinked) a file is established for that object. Each object file has a FINST reference to the particular individual to which the information refers. So, for example, in figure 2.2 the file labeled *Object "z"* contains some information about that particular object—that it is round and green and so on—whatever properties have been noticed about the object. It thus typically contains information about that object that was true in the past—such as that at some time in the past it was blinking and therefore was designated as a target in MOT. The FINST index mechanism is what allows this information to be associated with the *same token element* over time without requiring the object to be reidentified—the identity is maintained by the FINST mechanism that is built into the visual system. Notice that it need

2. In contrast, Kahneman, Treisman, and Gibbs (1992) view a FINST as the initial state of an object file, before any information is filed in it.

not (and most likely does not) have information about the properties that caused the index to be assigned or caused the object file to be created, nor does it necessarily contain information about which properties allow the individual object to be tracked. That takes place within an encapsulated part of the visual system and is a nonconceptual and causal processes (I will come back to this point in the next chapter). What the object file contains is just what was conceptually encoded, in particular the one-place predicates that pertain to that object. (The fact that it is conceptual does not imply that it is either conscious or that it involves concepts of the sort that a person could have—they could be subpersonal concepts that describe the state of proximal patterns.)

For purposes of exposition, an illustration of what the FINST indexing mechanism does is shown in figure 2.2. It shows how a FINST provides a reference link from an object file to an object in the distal environment, and shows that it does so in response to a causal/informational event in the world that captures the FINST reference tokens. Clearly this leaves many details unspecified, many of which will be described later in this book.

2.3.2   The Explanation of Tracking

I have already provided, at least implicitly, an account of MOT in terms of FINST indexes and object files, but it will help future discussion if I do this again in a slightly different way, this time emphasizing the more general implications of this way of looking at things. Here is the alternative account.

When a set of visual objects is blinked or flashed on and off, each of them automatically captures an index, up to the maximum number available (around 4 or 5), presumably according to some priority scheme based on objects' salience. When an index is *captured*, an object file may be created for the object that captured it. The file is initially empty, and may remain empty, depending on whether there is an opportunity or a reason to enter object-specific information into it. As the objects move around, the object file remains attached to its respective object, so long as the object remains in view (actually a bit longer owing to the inertia of the sensory system, but that is a separate story I will not go into here). At the end of the trial when the object stops moving, various scenarios are possible. The simplest is that each indexed object is visited with focal attention and the subject moves the cursor to it (recall that "move attention to *x*" for an indexed object *x* is a primitive operation in our scheme, meaning that any explanation of how it works lies outside our present level of description, presumably falling under an architectural or neuroscience vocabulary).

It appears that nothing is stored in the object files under typical MOT conditions, which suggests that targets are not being picked out under a description—they are not picked out as things that have certain properties or satisfy certain predicates. I have made much of this observation, interpreting it to mean that the FINST link is nonconceptual. But if it is nonconceptual, how can it reidentify an object as one that had earlier been selected as a target? How can it track an individual without conditions of individuation and without the concepts of object and of identity? And how can FINST indexes allow one to subitize, given that counting requires sortal concepts? This is where I believe indexes are of interest to philosophy, and I will return to these points later.

2.4   Other Empirical and Theoretical Issues Surrounding MOT

2.4.1   Do We Track by Keeping a Record of Locations?
We saw in section 2.2 that keeping track of objects in MOT does not depend on recording and updating their locations. But at the same time, location is not irrelevant. After all it is because objects are at different locations that they are considered to be different objects in the first place. And it may be that even though a serial scanning and location-updating process cannot explain MOT performance, some record of objects' location is being retained. It seems at least that when tracked targets disappear there is a record of where they were when they disappeared (Keane and Pylyshyn 2006; Scholl, Pylyshyn, and Franconeri 1999). But a study by Erik Blaser (Blaser, Pylyshyn, and Holcombe 2000) shows that it is possible to track objects (or at least to track one object and ignore another) when the objects in question always occupy the same spatial location and move only in property space.

Tracking through "property space": The Blaser study   Earlier I suggested that people track moving objects without encoding or appealing to any of their properties, including locations. I will return to this claim in subsequent chapters for it represents a departure from intuitions as well as from the received wisdom. But I want to provide one final example of a more general kind of "object" for which tracking clearly does not depend on keeping track of an object's spatial location, because its location does not change during a trial. One might say that the object is tracked as it moves continuously through a property space.

The stimuli for this experiment consist of two rapidly alternating superimposed patches of sine-wave gratings (these patches, called *Gabors*, fall off

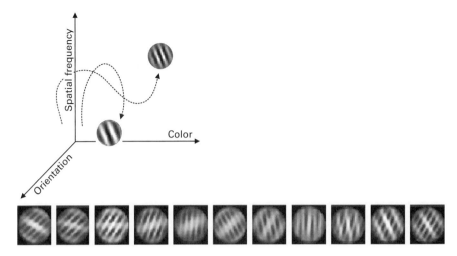

Figure 2.3
The bottom strip shows an example of the sequence of displays used by Blaser, Pyly-shyn, and Holcombe (2000) to demonstrate tracking through "feature space" with-out motion in real space (original displays were in color). The figure at the top shows a typical trajectory that each of the two "objects" follows through three dimensions of feature space.

in intensity toward their edges according to a Gaussian profile, which gives them some desirable technical properties that are not relevant in the pres-ent context). Under these conditions, the superimposed Gabors looked like gratings painted on two transparent surfaces. The gratings varied randomly and continuously over time in their spacing (or spatial frequency), their color (from red to black), and their orientation. Observers were asked to se-lect a particular specified grating and to "follow" or track it over a period of time, indicating at the end of the trial which one they had been tracking. An example of the "trajectories" through feature space of these two objects and the actually display sequence (without color) are shown in figure 2.3. Subjects were also given other less obvious tasks to perform in order to show whether they had successfully tracked a particular one. For example, they were asked to make a pair of judgments about two changes that occurred on these gratings (sudden small jumps in color or spacing). We found that not only could people track one of these spatially fixed patches, but they also showed evidence of treating them as single objects (e.g., two judgments were made faster if they pertained to the same "object" than when they involved different objects, a technique for showing the object-specific nature of attention to which I will return in chapter 3). Thus it seems clear that people can track objects even if the objects are not moving through space, that is, under conditions where their spatial locations do not serve to individuate them.

2.4.2   Can We Select Objects Voluntarily?

Top-down and bottom-up (or interrupt-driven vs. test-based) selection   I have assumed that selection of items is data driven. In other words, properties of the objects capture or *grab* indexes on the basis of some item-specific properties that set priorities for indexing. But many investigators who have used the MOT task assume that participants in these experiments can choose when and whether to index particular items. In fact in some cases targets are indicated by color differences rather than by flashing. The reason I have assumed that indexes are basically captured by certain objects is theoretical: If indexes are the most primitive preconceptual contact that the mind has with things in the world, then the visual system is not in a position to decide what to index.

Consider what is involved in this issue. In Pylyshyn 1984 (chap. 6), I discuss the first line of causal contact between the world and mental representations—the mechanism that converts patterns of energy arriving at the sensors into symbolic codes. Such a mechanism is generally referred to as a *transducer*. To prevent a hypothesized transducer from subsuming all of perception (as happens in James Gibson's "direct perception"; see Fodor and Pylyshyn 1981), and thereby losing its explanatory value, severe constraints must be imposed on how any hypothesized transducer can operate. Among these constraints is the requirement that a transducer (as opposed to the entire perceptual system) be *data driven*—that its operation depend only on incoming information as opposed to on the visual/cognitive system. A data-driven mechanism is triggered by (or is responsive to) the arrival of an information-bearing signal from the world rather than a query posed by the visual system. In computational terms it is based on an *interrupt* rather than on a *test* applied by the perceptual system (e.g., a conditional "if-then" operation). We sometimes refer to this as bottom-up as opposed to top-down control. But it should be noted that regardless of the details of the empirical data on the operation of a system that represents information about the world, such a system *cannot be entirely top-down*. At some point the world must cause certain effects on the perceptual system—which is to say, it must impose itself onto the system willy-nilly. Even a top-down system that checks for the presence of certain potential or hypothesized properties can only check for information that has made it into symbolic form, that is, information that has been transduced in a data-driven manner. A system cannot literally reach out into the world to check on properties unless the properties are among those that are able to affect the system causally, which means in a bottom-up manner. This is also true in the case of real computer systems; any if-then test that is computed can only be done on some already transduced signal (often a flag that is set by an interrupt).

Voluntarily enabled selection Not surprisingly, we were able to demonstrate experimentally that observers can voluntarily select targets to track, even when the selection requires focal attention (Pylyshyn and Annan 2006). For example, when the items are numbered, people can select items numbered 1 to 4 and track them, while ignoring items numbered 5 to 8. Then we looked more carefully at how long it took to select targets from among the eight items. In one of our conditions a bar flashes on the disks that subjects had to track. We compared how long this flashing cue had to be present with how long it had to be present if the task was to track the disks that did not have a flashing bar (the complement set). Assuming that the flashing bar automatically attracts FINST indexes, we expected that for a given flash duration the track-flashed condition would be better than the complement (track-unflashed) condition, which is exactly what we found. We also presented a condition in which a horizontal bar flashed on four of the eight disks and a vertical bar flashed on the remaining four disks, and vice versa. The task was to track the disks that had horizontal bars (or sometimes the ones that had vertical bars) and ignore the disks that had vertical bars (alternatively, the ones with horizontal bars). Again we found that when the selection criterion required attention (track flashed-vertical among flashed-horizontal) the cue had to be present for longer than when the selection criterion was automatic (track disks with flashed bars among disks without flashed bars). Moreover, when the number of targets was increased (from 3 to 4 and then 5) the amount of additional time required was also greater. All these results suggest that although we can select items voluntarily, such selection takes more time because the items have to be visited one at a time with focal attention.

This is an instance of a general principle: Automatic functions often require, or at least can be affected by, voluntarily applied enabling conditions. For example, perceptual phenomena typically depend on direction of gaze—few phenomena work when the critical part of the stimulus is not foveated. Often the phenomena depend not on gaze but on focal visual attention. For instance, the automatic perception of a line drawing as a 3-D figure (as in the Necker cube) is affected by the locus of attention (and may account for why some people mistakenly feel they can influence which version of the ambiguous cube they see merely by a act of will; see, e.g., Churchland 1988). Some of these effects of focal attention are surprising. For example, certain effects of masking one pattern by another presented briefly at the same location (and for slightly longer than the original pattern) are observed only when the pattern is attended (Di Lollo, Enns, and Rensink 2000). The automatic stereovision system can also be sensitive to the locus of observers' attention (Frisby and Clatworthy 1975). It is also known that certain features can be filtered by early (preconceptual) stages of perception, as though a "switch" can be set to prefilter certain properties (the earliest theories of attentional selection were in fact explicitly filter theories; e.g., Broadbent 1958). Certain automatic effects in auditory phonetic recognition (such as the categorical perception of phones) occur only when observers are set for a linguistic stimulus, as opposed to music or an arbitrary noise (Best, Studdard-Kennedy, Manuel, and Rubin-Spitz 1989).

These are not cases of the cognitive penetration of perception (of the sort discussed in Pylyshyn 1999), because there is no rational content-dependent influence. Rather, these are cases where the functioning of an automatic mechanism (or perceptual module) can be enabled by a voluntarily controlled setting. What happens during voluntary selection of targets in MOT is, I believe, a case of an automatic data-driven function being enabled by a voluntary act of focusing attention. In vision, automatic processes such as "singleton" feature selection may depend on the local uniqueness of certain properties. What focal attention may do is define an area over which the uniqueness is computed. This proposal is consistent with evidence that when attention is directed to a particular location, a unique target ("singleton") near the site of the focal attention is more likely to capture attention than one more distant (Mounts 2000). In any case this suggests a plausible account of how voluntary selection can occur in a way that is compatible with the independently motivated requirement for an automatic mechanism that captures reference indexes (i.e., "grabs FINSTs").

The empirical evidence concerning individuation and tracking is rich and often surprising. In the remainder of section 2.4 I describe two findings that challenge our understanding of what goes on in tracking and which also have implications for the philosophical issues concerning nonconceptual representation, individuation, and the tracking of identities.

2.4.3   Tracking without Keeping Track of Labels

One early finding concerns the failure to recall the *identity* of targets while tracking. Our story of how we track multiple moving objects in MOT using FINST indexes claims that an index keeps referring to the same individual object throughout the experimental trial. In doing so it keeps track of the identity of each individual target during this period. In other words, it knows that a particular individual object X_i is a target because it was visibly distinguished as a target at time t_1 and is the same individual now as it was at time t_1; therefore it must be a target. If this story is correct, then if the object had been labeled with label L_i at the start of the trial and if we can show that under conditions of the experiment subjects can recall the four pairings X_1–L_1, X_2–L_2, X_3–L_3, X_4–L_4, then subjects should be able not only to identify the targets as targets but also to provide their labels. But in fact people are very bad at recalling targets' labels even when they correctly identify them as targets (labels were either numbers affixed to the disks or just the distinguished locations of the disks in the corners of the display at the start of each trial; for details see Pylyshyn 2004). How can that be? In order to track an object it is necessary to be able to trace its identity back to a prior state when it was known to be a target, which ultimately means it must be traced back to the beginning of the trial when it was visibly distinguished as a target. So how can one not also remember its name, which represents a very small additional memory load that we can show is well within the subjects' memory capacity? The latter is shown by the fact that the disk-name pairs can be recalled nearly perfectly so long as the tracking and label-recall involves different objects.[3] (An example of the sort of display used can be viewed at http://ruccs.rutgers.edu/finstlab/demos.htm or the book's page at http://mitpress.mit.edu/thingsandplaces/.)

According to the above logic, if all targets were tracked perfectly we would expect the labels to be recalled perfectly as well. But tracking is not perfect, and switching the identity of a target with that of a nontarget is recorded as an error in tracking, while switching the identity of a target with that of another target does not affect the tracking score. Thus the

---

3. For those interested in the experiment, it goes something like this (details in Pylyshyn 2004). A (static) set of randomly placed numbered disks is presented and subjects are told to try to remember their numbers. This is followed by the usual tracking task involving *different* disks without labels. Then the first set of disks (the ones that had not been tracked) is presented again in their same fixed locations— this time without labels—and subjects are asked to recall their labels. In this condition recall of the labels was nearly perfect, showing that the tracking task in and of itself does not interfere with the simple recall of four pairs of objects and their labels.

reason for the failure to keep track of labels might be traced to the fact that distribution of errors is nonhomogeneous. I propose such an account in Pylyshyn 2004. If the likelihood of a target being mistaken for another target is higher than the likelihood of a target being mistaken for a nontarget, this would explain the observed difference between tracking performance and labeling performance. But why should the likelihood of these two types of confusions be different—why should targets be more often confused with other targets than with nontargets? The answer I suggested in that paper is that during tracking an attempt is made to eliminate the items which might cause confusion (i.e., the nontargets) by a process of inhibition. Such a process has been observed in many situations and is thought to be invoked under conditions where there is a task-specific need to keep certain items in a display from attracting attention (or, in our terms, from grabbing an index). Such an assumption might explain the asymmetry, but it raises an even more interesting issue: how can items that are not being tracked be inhibited unless either everything that is not a target is inhibited or the nontargets are also being tracked? This question is discussed below, as it has far-reaching consequences for the correct view of individuation and tracking.

2.4.4   Nonconceptual Individuation without Reference?

As many philosophers have pointed out, true individuation requires concepts and conditions of identity. But the earlier discussion suggested that some functions that require concepts in general may have nonconceptual solutions, at least in particular cases. One such example concerns computing identity in apparent motion and stereovision when solving what is known as the correspondence problem. The correspondence problem is the problem of computing the identity of distal causes from distinct proximal (i.e., retinal) perceptual clusters. In other words, it is the task of treating two temporally or spatially distinct tokens of local features as arising from the same remote object. This is a ubiquitous problem in vision science and is especially clear in computing apparent motion (where temporally and/or spatially disparate objects or flashes are seen as a single moving distal object) and in stereovision (where two distinct objects, one on each retina, are seen as arising from the same feature in a 3-D scene, a prerequisite for computing their retinal disparity and thus their distance in depth). These (and other) cases of correspondence computations exhibit important properties which suggest that they are computed by special mechanisms in the encapsulated early vision system that do not use conceptual properties of the object tokens. Moreover, there is reason to think that these mechanisms are different from the FINST mechanism in a way that bears on the puzzle of inhibition of moving nontargets, raised above.

Neither tracking nor correspondence computation is very sensitive to the local featural properties (e.g., color or shape have little effect on the correspondence matches in apprent motion; Kolers and von Grunau 1976) of the objects in question (with perhaps the exception of a few properties such as their spatial frequency or the polarity of the luminance of the objects—black on gray versus white on gray). In both cases the process appears to work best when there are distinct individuals as opposed to smoothly varying luminance functions. But a major difference between these processes is that the correspondence computation in apparent motion and stereovision does not appear to be limited in capacity the way that MOT is. In fact correspondence may be established more readily when there are more items to be placed in correspondence.

For example, displays that contain more dots are more easily interpreted in the so-called *kinetic depth effect* (Wallach and O'Connell 1953), an apparent motion display in which perception of a three-dimensional surface in motion appears from a properly arranged sequence of dots, or in random dot stereograms (Julesz 1971), in which a field of random dots, presented to the two eyes so that there is a relative location disparity between them, produces a perception of a dotted surface in depth. In these cases it appears that computing correspondence between pairs of dots is not a numerically limited process the way that visual indexing is. This suggests that individuating objects and putting pairs of them in correspondence may be distinct from individuating and referring to objects, a process that must occur for successful tracking in MOT. Recall that at the end of a MOT trial, subjects must select particular individual objects as targets, for example by moving attention to them and then moving a cursor to each in turn. In the correspondence examples, no information about which object was which is needed over and above what is required for pairing them. Moreover, the pairing can be done on the basis of spatially local information—it is a computation carried out with what is called "local support."[4] This suggests that we may need to distinguish the process of feature-clustering and individuating from the process of picking out and referring to objects.

The need for such a distinction has also come up in connection with some surprising findings in recent studies of MOT. Because these findings

4. The criterion of local support is important insofar as functions meeting this criterion may be computed by a network of cellular automata, which, in turn, makes them good candidates for being a function of early vision (Ullman 1976).

suggest that individuating and computing clusters of features that belong together is different from the process of tracking, I will describe one of these experiments for concreteness.

As mentioned in the previous section, we had reason to believe that target–target confusions (where the identity of one target is confused with the identity of a different target) are more common than target–nontarget confusions and that this might be due to nontargets being kept out of contention in MOT by a process known as inhibition. Inhibition is a quite general phenomenon in perception. For example, it has been shown that objects that have just been attended are less likely to be immediately attended again (i.e., within about 300 to 900 ms), even if attention is summoned there by a flash. This phenomenon, referred to as *inhibition of return* (Klein 1988), is thought to help us in searching through a set of candidate visual objects (as in the "Where's Waldo?" game). This kind of inhibition has also been shown to be associated with objects as opposed to (or in some cases in addition to) locations and to move with moving objects (Tipper, Driver, and Weaver 1991). There is also some evidence that multiple moving objects might be inhibited in this way in the course of searching through them for a specified target (Ogawa, Takeda, and Yagi 2002).

To examine whether nontargets were inhibited in MOT we carried out a number of experiments (described in Pylyshyn 2006) using a method that involves presenting a small probe dot during a MOT trial. Performance in detecting such a dot has been used as a measure of both attention and inhibition (Watson and Humphreys 1997; Watson and Humphreys 2000); performance in detecting the dot is better on attended items and worse on items that are being actively ignored. We presented probe dots not only on targets and nontargets, but also in various places in the empty space between them. We found that, as expected, detection of the probe dots is poorer on nontargets than on targets. But surprisingly, detection in empty space is about the same as on targets (when compared with a control condition in which subjects merely watched for probes without tracking). This result (which has recently been replicated; see Flombaum, Scholl, and Pylyshyn 2006) suggests a puzzling conclusion, namely, that the inhibition attaches to moving nontargets without affecting the space through which they move. In other words, it looks like inhibition is *tracking* the nontargets. But according to the present view, nontargets could not be tracked in MOT using FINST indexes because these indexes are limited in number and, by hypothesis, are all being used to track the targets. So how could the inhibition "track" the nontargets?

The jury is still out on whether there is an alternative way to explain these findings (e.g., it may be that what is being inhibited is anything that moves but is not a target). Let us accept the above analysis for the sake of argument, since it raises an interesting possibility. It raises the possibility that keeping inhibition attached to moving nontargets involves the mechanism that is responsible for solving the correspondence problem—that it is carried out by a mechanism that automatically and nonconceptually puts together the sequence of proximal tokens into the percept of an enduring individual, as it does in apparent motion and stereovision. Unlike the FINST index, however, this mechanism merely collapses a sequence of time slices of proximal clusters but does not provide a reference to them. According to this analysis there are two distinct functions involved in tracking in MOT. One consists in individuating moving items and collapsing them over time and space according to the correspondence principles, thereby constructing perceptually enduring individuals. As we saw in the case of apparent motion and stereovision, this aspect is not numerically limited and is computed based on spatially local information (it follows the principle of local support). The second function is the one I referred to as demonstrative reference—it consists of providing a conceptually unmediated way to refer to the individuals, using FINSTs. This function is numerically limited, allowing reference only to about four objects. The first function applies to all moving objects in the field of view; the second applies only to objects that have been selected as described in section 2.4.1 (i.e., the targets).

Although this story remains provisional and somewhat speculative, it does suggest that an account of individuating and tracking may be more complex than most people have assumed, and that the question of the existence of nonconceptual counterparts to individuating and tracking may be both more nuanced and ramified—and also more interesting—than one might have expected. That's why empirical evidence remains essential in developing ideas about how the mind connects with individual things in the world.

2.5 The Infant's Capacity for Individuating and Tracking Objects

Before discussing the philosophical implications of such experiments I should mention that the FINST framework, together with the idea of object files (Kahneman, Treisman, and Gibbs 1992), has provided a way of understanding another sort of tracking: infants' tracking of individual objects and their sensitivity to the cardinality of sets of objects that are moved about and hidden behind a screen. The ideas discussed above have been used in analyzing these fascinating findings (Carey forthcoming; Carey and Xu 2001). These studies use the "violation of expectation" method in which infants' looking times are taken as a measure of whether the infant's expectation was violated by the display. The basic finding is that (contrary to Piaget's claim that infants do not have object constancy at a young age) infants as young as 6 months understand that if you hide a toy behind a screen and then place another toy behind the screen as well, then when the screen is removed there should be two toys (there is even evidence of object constancy in 3-month-olds; Baillargeon and DeVos 1991). This is shown by the finding that if there is only one toy when the screen is removed, the infant looks for a longer time, which is interpreted to mean that the result was unexpected. The same is true when a toy is seen to be removed from behind a screen where two toys had been placed earlier—infants look longer if there are two toys rather than one. A large number of experiments have been carried out using not only the "looking time" method but other methods as well (e.g., after how many found items does an infant stop reaching into a bag looking for more; Van de Walle, Carey, and Prevor 2000). They indicate that infants can respond to the cardinality of sets of three or fewer (see the review by Krojgaard 2004).

Later studies have shown even more subtle effects. For example, experiments have shown that infants respond correctly to the cardinality of two identical items only if they saw both at the same time before they were hidden, but respond to two different items if they were seen one at a time before being hidden (perhaps indicating that two identical items seen one at a time are interpreted as one item seen twice). The findings keep refining the abilities of infants. For example, infants under 10 months of age were shown a red disk being removed from behind a screen so the infant could see it before it was replaced behind the screen. This was followed by showing a green disk being removed and then replaced. The finding was that in this condition infants expect two objects (two different colors = two individual objects). But interestingly, the infants were indifferent as to whether the two objects that they saw when the screen was removed were both red or one was red and the other green. In other words they used objects' colors to individuate them and to infer that there were two, but they failed to use the objects' colors in forming expectations and recognizing anomalies until they were over 10 months of age (Tremoulet, Leslie, and Hall 2000), or in some cases 12 months of age (Xu, Carey, and Quint 2004). Alan Leslie distinguishes between what he calls "individuating" and "identifying." The latter, but not the former, presumably requires that the relevant properties be entered in the object files. This is very similar to the distinction I have been making between selecting and encoding, or between causal properties and properties that are represented.

More recently there has been evidence that infants *can* use other properties such as basic-level kinds (Xu, Carey, and Quint 2004) and distinct faces (Bonatti et al. 2002) in determining cardinality and in recognizing anomalies in the properties of items. These studies confirm that, as I claimed earlier, one must distinguish between properties that cause indexes to be grabbed and properties that are represented (and stored in object files). The way properties get used in various tasks is rather complex as well. Studies have shown that infants do not treat piles of sand poured onto the stage as individuals: They do not respond to the cardinality of objects that were poured (Huntley-Fenner, Carey, and Salimando 2002)—and adults too are poor at tracking objects that move from place to place in a MOT experiment if the movement is like pouring or wormlike slinking (vanMarle and Scholl 2003). Nor do infants respond to the cardinality of objects if they see the objects (made of blocks) taken apart and put together again before being placed behind the screen (Chiang and Wynn 2000).

Although the ideas of FINSTs and object files are used in explaining these results, some people have interpreted the demonstrations as showing that infants have the sortal concept *object* which they use to individuate (Xu 1997; but see the contrary opinion of Ayers 1997; Hirsch 1997; Wiggins 1997). The question of whether infants have the concept of object is an interesting one, but it does eventually run into the need to ground that concept in experience (by "ground" I mean connect the concept with its instances, not *learn* or acquire the concept, which may well be innate). For example, it has been suggested that the first sortal concept that an infant has is the concept *object* (as part of what is called their "core knowledge"), which is the concept of something that is "bounded, coherent, three-dimensional, and moves as a whole" (these criteria were introduced by Liz Spelke in Spelke 1990, so it is sometimes referred to as a "Spelke object"). But of course if that's what an object is for an infant, then infants must also have the concepts "bounded," "coherent," "three-dimensional," and "moves as a whole," in which case the Spelke object could not be their first concept. If, on the other hand, the Spelke object is not defined in terms of other concepts, then it cannot apply to all and only things that are bounded, coherent, and so on. So what determines the extension of the concept?

Once again, the distinction between causal properties and properties that are represented is crucial. On the view proposed in this book, infants start off with an architecture that determines their sensitivity to certain properties—including many abstract properties (such as "proto-cause" and perhaps something like "proto-Spelke-object") that are largely coextensive with the conceptual equivalents, but which cannot be identical to these conceptual properties. They are neither conceptual *definienda* nor *definientia*. They are constituents of thoughts only in the limited way that indexicals or names are constituents; they contribute only reference to the content of complex thoughts. By contrast, some properties do get encoded in the form of predicates, since predicates are properties of indexed things, so FINSTs are logically antecedent to predicates. In other words, "Red" is a predicate that can be bound to things selected by FINST indexes, which results in $Red(F_1)$ being stored in F_1's object file, that is, the file corresponding to the demonstrative referent of index F_1. I will argue that it is a general property of conceptualizations of the perceptual world that only indexed objects can serve as arguments of predicates, and consequently, only properties of selected objects are conceptually encoded.

2.6   Summary and Implications for the Foundations of Cognitive Science

2.6.1   Review: Nonconceptual Functions and Natural Constraints
By hypothesis, indexing and tracking in the context of MOT are nonconceptual functions carried out within the modular visual system—a system that may or may not have representations (such as the primal sketch or $2\frac{1}{2}$-D representation described in Marr 1982).[5] Yet indexing and tracking appear to contradict the prerequisites of individuals, particulars, and identity discussed by Quine, Strawson, and other philosophers. According to Quine (1960), you can't think about particulars in the world without what

5. For now I leave open the question of whether the early vision system that implements indexes has representations of any kind. The evidence I have reviewed suggests that no representations of object properties are used in tracking. Moreover, any representations in this part of the system are encapsulated from the cognitive system (Pylyshyn 1999). The question of whether at this level it uses concepts is to some extent terminological: If it has concepts they are what some (Dennett 1978; Haugeland 1978) have called *subpersonal* concepts, not the sort of concepts that form part of the thoughts that we, as human agents, may have—not the sort of concepts that we would recognize as *our* concepts, were they conscious. Such subpersonal concepts may, for example, be codes for proximal properties involved in perception, such as edges, gradients, or the sorts of labels that appear in early computational vision (Marr 1982), or parsing trees in language understanding/generation.

he calls "an apparatus of individuation," by which he means sortal concepts and identity and maybe divided reference and tenses. Strawson also considers individuating and reidentifying to be essentially conceptual functions. He writes in his book *Individuals* (Strawson 1959) that "the introduction of particulars ... involves a conceptual complication: it involves the adoption of criteria of distinctness and ... criteria of reidentification for particulars of the kind in question" (p. 203; see also Keane 2004). And so it does. Early vision does not have the power of predication and does not have count nouns, sortal concepts, or the capacity for past-tense reference (also part of Strawson's criteria for individuation) and consequently cannot identify or reidentify individuals as the same individual encountered previously. Yet under certain conditions (viz., the conditions that allow indexing and tracking) FINSTs do allow us to individuate and even to reidentify certain individuals: They allow us to maintain the identity of tracked objects as enduring individuals, and they even play a role in our ability to recognize the cardinality of a set of objects when it is no greater than about four (though assigning an actual *number* to the set clearly requires the concept of number). Once we have indexed an object we can keep track of it (within some broad range of conditions). And with the mechanism of object files we can also accumulate past-tense information about the objects. And the visual system can do all that without the heavy apparatus that is required in principle.

How is this possible? It is possible because wired into our early vision system by evolution is a mechanism that provides a type of identity that is not conceptual. This should not be surprising; vision provides many nonconceptual functions that are, as a matter of fact, extensionally equivalent to conceptual categories *in our sort of world*. For example, early vision has mechanisms for constructing 3-D (shape) representations from 2-D (retinal) images, despite the fact that the mapping from 3-D to 2-D is in principle not reversible. This irreversibility had been taken by some vision scientists as proof that constructing a 3-D representation could only be done by framing hypotheses based on general knowledge of the world. But vision does this without concepts and without any knowledge of what makes something a real physical 3-D object or what objects are likely to be in its visual field on any particular occasion (see the discussion in Pylyshyn 1999). It does so in virtue of constraints built into the visual system (other related constraints are discussed in section 5.2). It constructs a representation that is generally correct given that the perceived world meets certain general constraints that tend to hold in our sort of world (or our ecological niche).

By "our sort of world" I mean a world where, for example, our visual field is such that the vast majority of image features (features in the proximal or retinal image) have the property that close neighbors tend to arise from object-features that are at similar distances from the observer. The reason this constraint holds is that in our sort of world projections of continuous surfaces onto the retina tend to greatly outweigh in area the discontinuous edges. This depth-continuity constraint is used in determining which image features in one eye should be associated with which features in the other eye in computing stereo disparity. Similarly, in our sort of world the majority of image features tend to arise from the surface of rigid objects and therefore tend to move together when the object moves. Consequently, in solving the correspondence problem mentioned earlier, the visual system tends to give preference to pairings that preserve such continuity, that is, where the distance and direction of the correspondence pairs are similar to those of its neighbors (a natural constraint used in the model of apparent motion developed by Dawson and Pylyshyn 1988; see also Dawson 1991).

Another powerful constraint is that edges that are aligned or form a vertex in an image are also aligned or form a vertex in the distal scene (barring accidental coincidences). These "nonaccidental" image properties are used in the recognition of scene properties because the likelihood that they arise by chance is very low in our kind of world, and when they do arise, they can easily be diagnosed by a small movement on the part of the observer. Also in our sort of world the light tends to come from above so that shadows fall below the features that cast them, a fact that influences whether certain shadings are interpreted as convex or concave (as mounds or holes). (For these and other examples, see Pylyshyn 2003, chap. 3.) Other such constraints are discussed by Hoffman (1998), who refers to them as "intelligent" solutions to the problem of vision, though they are all applications of general constraints that are built into the visual system as opposed to inferences from conceptual knowledge. They are all examples of how a nonconceptually based system, operating in a well-defined niche (which may include most humanly habitable worlds), can mimic a system that uses concepts.

Although geometrical properties are the more natural ones if we are considering natural constraints, vision also provides nonconceptual mechanisms for much more abstract properties. For example, it provides a mechanism, available even in 6-month-old infants, for recognizing causal sequences (this is the mechanism that was initially studied in adults by Michotte and explored in infants by Leslie 1982). Luckily for us, our visual system (and presumably the same is true for other perceptual modalities) provide us with functions that are not just approximations to these essentially conceptual skills, but approximations that almost always work in our kind of world. And the ones that are internalized are not just the more frequently seen patterns. Perhaps surprisingly, commonly observed physical properties, such as simple prohibition of interpenetration of solid objects, don't seem to be internalized as natural constraints. Alan Leslie (1988) discusses an example based on the Pulfrich double pendulum illusion (see Wilson and Robinson 1986) that makes this point in a dramatic way. Suppose two side-by-side pendulums are set swinging out of phase (so that one is just starting its motion to the left when the other is starting its swing to the right). If they are viewed through neutral-density (gray) filters such that the filter over one eye is darker than the one over the other eye, the pendulums will be seen to swing in a circular (or elliptical) path in depth rather than back and forth in a plane. The reason for this illusion is thought to be that the weaker signals going to the eye with the dark filter result in slower visual processing in that eye, which in turn results in the apparent circular or elliptical path. In Leslie's example, he notes that the consequence of this Pulfrich illusion is that the pendulums are seen as going *through* one another. Unlike many illusions this one can be seen in full close-up reality; there is no doubt to the observer that the bottles at the end of each wooden pendulum are solid sand-filled detergent bottles, yet they are clearly seen as interpenetrating one another.

Another example is the Ames trapezoidal window demonstration. When a trapezoidal frame is rotated about a vertical axis it is seen not as rotating, but as oscillating back and forth. This illusion is quite powerful. But if a solid bar is tied at right angles to the rotating axis, it will be seen (correctly) as rotating in one continuous circle. But now the two percepts together result in the observer's seeing the bar passing through the trapezoidal window even though both are solid. So it seems that although many natural constraints are built into the visual system, they tend (with a few exceptions like causality) mostly to be optical-geometrical rather than physical-mechanical constraints. It could have been otherwise (and if it had, it would still receive a perfectly logical evolutionary explanation), but as a matter of fact, it isn't.

This idea of natural constraints is quite powerful. Yet I will suggest in chapter 4 that it does not seem to play much of a role in explaining how mental imagery works. As you watch your mental image rotate, slide, twist, expand, get cut up, be superimposed on other images, and so on, what you see is just what you expect to see—exactly what you intended to happen. Nobody has produced examples of phenomena that seem to reveal constraints of the cognitive architecture that are specific to mental images, the way such constraints are revealed in vision.[6] Part of the reason for this, I believe, is that mental images are really not images so much as types of thoughts, and thoughts do not easily reveal built-in constraints. This is not to say that there aren't any—there must be thoughts that a dog or a cat or a chimpanzee (or, for that matter, a cosmologist) can have that you can't, but it's not easy to imagine one (exactly—because that would require imagining what for you is unimaginable!). As Fodor (1980b) has colorfully put it: *"From in here* it looks as though we're fit to think whatever thoughts there are to think.... It *would*, of course, precisely because we *are* in here. But there is surely good reason to suppose that this is hubris bred of an epistemological illusion. No doubt spiders think that webs exhaust the options" (p. 333).

2.6.2 Summary: Why Are FINSTs Needed?

I want to end this chapter by providing a quick preview of why the FINST mechanism I have described is important to cognitive science. FINSTs give us nonconceptual access to what I have called a *thing* or a *sensory individual* or *visual object*, or, in the context of FINST theory what I sometimes refer to as FINGs (from FINSTed THINGs). Because the representation is not conceptual, these sensory individuals are not represented *as* objects or as *X*s for *any* possible category *X*. They are just picked out transparently by a causal or informational process without being conceptualized as something or other. Early vision picks out and indexes a small number (4 or 5) of such sensory objects, roughly the way you might pick out a fish by placing a baited hook in the water—it happens primarily at the initiative of the objects; we say it is data driven. Selecting a subset of individuals in this way allows the cognitive system to encode and accumulate predicates about them, which, in the case of unary predicates, it places in the object file for that visual object. And as long as there are not more than four or five of these individuals the visual system can treat them as though it had a concept of "individual object." But it's important to remember that the

---

6. "What?" I hear you say. "How about imagining an object described by basonic string theory that has 26 dimensions?" "Okay," I reply, "as soon as you show me what it looks like I will imagine it. That's what imagining, in the sense of 'visualizing,' means—it means having a visual experience. There are of course capacity limitations in mental imagery, but these appear to be the same sorts of limitations that apply elsewhere in cognition (e.g., limits on the number of chunks or units that can be attended to at any one time).

early vision system does not have the concept "object" or any other concept (except maybe the demonstrative token *this* if you want to count that as a concept on the grounds that it can partake in thought), so it cannot infer from the fact that it is tracking X that X cannot go through walls or even that there is an X, the way you could if you were tracking something like a planet or a baseball (from which you could infer that there is such a thing as a planet or a baseball). Part of our project in postulating FINSTs is that we need to get our cognitive mind to select something before we cognize the something in terms of a concept such as "the object X." Otherwise the question arises: In virtue of what is that an X?—which starts us on the slippery slope of asking the same question about each of the conditions for X-hood. Question: In virtue of what is that an object? Answer: Because it has mass and moves through smooth continuous trajectories in space. Question: And what does it mean that it has mass, and so on? That question requires that we have the concept *mass*, and how do you ask about its trajectory unless you have the concept *trajectory*—and so on recursively. The recursion has to end somewhere, and where it ends might as well be something for which you have at least some independent motivation and, if you are lucky, some empirical support. That's where FINSTs come in.

Another way to say why a mechanism such as a FINST is important is that even if the early vision system somehow *had* the full conceptual apparatus of individuation and identity it still could not use that apparatus to connect to the world unless at some stage along the processing chain there is a causal leap from things in the world to concepts. You can't go on building concepts from other concepts without eventually bottoming out in a purely causal/informational connection (including, possibly, connections with the cognitive architecture—for more on the question of what could serve as a causal/informational connection, and whether it needs to appeal to the object's location, see section 3.3.1). All of this may seem like heresy in the face of the important philosophical work of Strawson, Quine, and others, and its ramifications could be far reaching. Although philosophers may continue to understand "individual" as a construct that essentially involves concepts, it should not be forgotten that it must ultimately rest on a nonconceptual mechanism such as the one I have been describing. In discussing the potential value of FINST indexes to philosophical issues a few years ago I made the following remark, to which I still subscribe:

While it is clear that you cannot individuate objects in the full-blooded sense without a conceptual apparatus, it is also clear that you cannot individuate them with only a conceptual apparatus. Sooner or later concepts must be grounded in a primitive causal connection between thoughts and things. The project of grounding concepts ... in perception remains an essential requirement if we are to avoid an infinite regress. Visual indexes provide a putative grounding for basic objects—the individuals to which perceptual predicates apply, and hence about which cognitive judgments and plans of action are made.... Without such a preconceptual grounding, our percepts and our thoughts would be disconnected from causal links to the real-world objects of those thoughts. With indexes we can think about things ... without having any concepts of them: one might say that we can have demonstrative thoughts. (Pylyshyn 2001, p. 154)

3 Selection: The Key to Linking Representations and Things

3.1 Selection: The Role of Focal Attention

We have been discussing the connection between the world we perceive and mental representations. This topic has a way of returning again and again to the notion of *selection*. Selection is a central topic in contemporary cognitive science and, as we shall see, it is also the place where empirical cognitive science comes in contact with a series of problems in the philosophy of mind. Selection enters the empirical discipline via the study of what has been called *focal attention*. From our perspective the study of attention should also be where we find clues about what the visual system picks out for further analysis. Clearly focal attention and what I have been calling indexing are very similar. On the face of it the major difference would appear to be that we have several (perhaps 4 or 5) indexes that work independently not only to select but also to provide a reference to things in the world. Perhaps if we examine the experimental literature on visual attention we may find some evidence about what sorts of things can be selected and also what selection is for.

The general view in psychology is that attention is the mechanism by which cognition is able to make selections from among the various aspects of the perceived world, and that the ability to make selections is at the very core of how we interact with the world (Patrick Cavanagh refers to attention as the mechanism that "exports vision to the mind"; Cavanagh 1999). This, however, leaves a great deal unsaid and raises questions that are at the heart of our present concern.

(1) The first question that the notion of selection raises is: *Why*? Why should the mind select and what role does selection play? The usual, and probably universally accepted, answer is that we must select simply because

our capacity to take in information is limited. Being incapable of taking in everything, we must perforce select, and we do so by applying what Donald Broadbent, one of the founders of modern information processing psychology, described as a *filter* (Broadbent 1958). That the mind is limited and therefore has to be selective is unquestionably true, but it is far from being the whole story about the function of focal attention. (Even the part of the story that it correctly points to is grossly incomplete. If the mind is limited, along what dimensions is it limited? And if it has to select, on what basis and along what dimensions does it—or can it—select?)

(2) It has also become clear that selection is needed not only to keep relatively unimportant or irrelevant information from clogging the mind, but also for reasons that have nothing to do with the mind's capacity. It would be needed even if we were like the Martians in Heinlein's cult science-fiction novel *Strangers in a Strange Land*, who can "grok" the entire perceptible world in one swallow. We would still need it because in order to analyze and encode certain properties of the world we have to distinguish some parts of the visible scene from other parts; in particular, as Gestalt psychologists pointed out in the twentieth century, we must distinguish a focal figure from a background, or distinguish between a *this* and a *not-this*. Since perception makes such figure-ground distinctions for both moving and stationary things, it implies that more than just selection is occurring; it implies that perception identifies the thing selected as an enduring individual independent of its instantaneous location. This in turn suggests that there is a mechanism in perception that allows us refer to things in some way and keep track of their continuing identity. Thus focal attention may be thought of as a mechanism by which we pick out and refer to things we perceive (as Campbell 2004 argued). FINST theory postulates a generalization of focal attention to multiple things (although FINST indexes are different from focal attention in a number of important ways). As we saw earlier, we need to select several things at once in order to detect patterns among them. Thus the need to *individuate and refer to* things provides a second reason why we have to select items and why focal attention is a central concern in any discussion of how the mind connects with the world through perception. But there is yet another reason why we have to select certain sorts of things with attention—and indeed why what we select has to be things rather than places.

(3) The third reason we need selection has been explored in both the experimental psychology literature and the philosophical literature. It is the fact that properties—or whatever finds expression as predicates—come in

certain sorts of bundles or groups. The question of how our perceptual system manages to decode these bundles of properties has come to be called the *binding problem* (a term associated with the work of Anne Treisman; see, e.g., the review in Treisman 1988). When properties are properties of the same thing or the same sensory individual they must be marked somehow as *conjoined* properties, not merely as properties present in the scene. The earliest stages of vision cannot simply report the presence of properties. They must, in addition, provide some way to preserve the information that certain properties belong to the same sensory individual, so that we can distinguish between, say, a scene containing a green circle and a red square from a scene containing a red circle and a green square, or between a large striped animal coming toward us from a small striped animal going away from us, as well as all other combinations of these features. Indeed, the requirement holds across modalities, so that the information must be in a form that enables us to distinguish between a green object that goes "quack" and a red object that goes "moo." The problem of providing this information in the right sorts of bundles—the binding problem (what Jackson 1997 called the "many properties problem")—is both crucial for our survival and important in understanding how vision connects with the world. Although I reserve discussion of this problem until I examine Austen Clark's analysis in section 3.4, I mention it here because we will see that the solution involves object-based selection in a crucial manner.

3.1.1 Allocating and Shifting Attention: The Role of Objects and Places

In recent years experimental psychologists have distinguished two ways in which attention can be allocated in a visual scene. One way, referred to as *exogenous* attention allocation, depends on events in the world; it is said to be *data driven*. This form of attention allocation begins with an event in the visual scene that *captures* attention automatically without the intervention of volition or of cognition more generally. Some event—most notably the appearance of a new object in the visual field—captures attention (though other sorts of events, such as a sudden change in luminance, will do as well; see Franconeri, Hollingworth, and Simons 2005). The other way of allocating attention occurs when you are searching for something and sweep your attention across a scene. It is called *endogenous* or voluntary attention allocation. A simplified demonstration of both types of attention switching is illustrated in figure 3.1. Attention that has been allocated by these two means differs in a number of subtle but important ways. Exogenous or automatic attention allocation is the more important form of

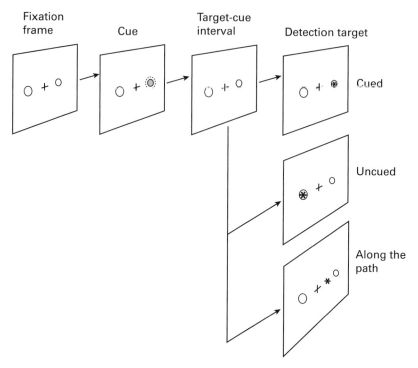

Figure 3.1
Illustration of how attention may be exogenously captured by a sudden brightening, shown in the second panel. Performance on a detection task (fourth panel) is better at the cued location than at the uncued location and, at intermediate times, is also better at a location along the path between fixation and the point to which attention is moving. For endogenous attention movement the subject is told (or shown by the appearance of an arrow at the fixation point) which direction to move his or her attention. (Based on Posner 1980.)

attention shift. It is more rapid and reaches a higher level of facilitation than attention that is shifted voluntarily. Voluntary shifts of attention are easily disrupted by the automatic exogenous pull of visual events occurring at the same time (Mueller and Rabbitt 1989; Rauschenberger 2004).

An important finding comes from a series of experiments and mathematical analysis by Sperling and Weichselgarter (1995). These authors have made a persuasive argument that, at least in the case of automatically shifted attention, the locus of attention does not actually move continuously through space. The apparent movement may instead arise because of the distribution of activation over time and space when attention is captured and switches from one thing to another. According to this analysis, the pattern of apparent motion may arise because the degree of attentional activation gradually decreases at its starting location and gradually increases at its target location. When these two spatiotemporal distributions are summed at intermediate locations it results in an apparently moving activation-maximum. Because voluntary shifts typically do not have a target event to which they are automatically drawn, it remains possible that they may sweep through intermediate positions. Although the data are not univocal on this question, it is plausible that when you move your attention voluntarily in a certain direction, you *may* sweep the locus of your visual attention through intermediate *empty* locations (the so-called *analog movement* of attention).

I would caution against taking this as proven, however, since Jonathan Cohen and I have shown that when people try to move their attention through an empty region in the dark (extrapolating the motion of a visible object that disappears behind an occluding surface) they probably do not move their focal attention through a continuous sequence of empty locations (Pylyshyn and Cohen 1999). This conclusion is based on the finding that subjects perform poorly at continuously tracking with their attention the location where the invisible object is at any moment, whereas given a series of visible marks along the invisible path they do much better. Thus we concluded that their attention normally jumps from one visible feature to another using a highly precise *time-to-contact* estimation skill (for more on the latter, see Tresillian 1995). This conclusion is also supported by experiments by Gilden, Blake, and Hurst (1995) showing that when a subject tries to track the imagined continuous motion of an invisible object, the temporal pattern one gets in an adaptation experiment (when the imagined motion crosses an area adapted to motion) is consistent with the hypothesis that the attention movement consists of a series of static episodes rather than of a continuous movement.[1] So movement of attention may not be continuous even if this movement is endogenously or voluntarily generated.

1. What Gilden, Blake, and Hurst (1995) found is that imagined (i.e., attentive) motion in the direction of the adaptation was sped up while imagined motion in the opposite direction to the adaptation was slowed down. Although this seems plausible, given the waterfall illusion, it is not what actually happens when a perceived object moves through a motion-adapted region. With real moving elements the motion is always slowed down regardless of which direction the adapting motion had been in, presumably because of the fatigue of motion detecting neural circuits.

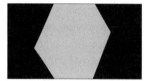 

Figure 3.2
Task used by Baylis and Driver (1993) to illustrate single-object superiority. The task
was to judge whether the left or right vertex was higher. Judgments made when the
vertices were seen as part of a single figure (because of instructions as to where to
focus) they were faster than when the vertices were perceived as belonging to two
different figures. In subsequent studies (Baylis 1994) the effect of other stimulus properties was ruled out.

3.1.2   Attention Selects and Adheres to Objects

A great deal of research in the past twenty years has convinced psychologists that viewing selective attention as location based is either incorrect
or at the very least only a secondary part of the story of attention allocation. Increasing numbers of studies have concluded that we attend to
what I have been calling *things* (what the psychological literature refers to
as "objects") rather than empty places. Evidence for this came initially
from demonstrations of what is called *single-object advantage*. When a pair
of judgments is made, the judgments are faster when they pertain to
the same perceptual individual, even when all geometrical properties are
controlled for, as shown for example by the experiment illustrated in
figure 3.2.

There is also evidence that the effect of attention tends to spread from
where it is initially attracted to cover an entire larger object that subtends
that initial attractor. For example, when attention is attracted to the highlighted end of a bar it then spreads to the entire bar. This spread does not
simply terminate at an edge, but proceeds through what is perceived as the
entire bar even if the entire bar is not explicitly indicated by a contour but
is created by an illusory process called "amodal completion," as shown in
figure 3.3. Thus it is the bar as a perceptual whole object that determines
how attention spreads. This suggests that the principles of attentional
spread are modulated by the way that objects are parsed at some earlier
or concurrent stage in vision. Thus the clustering operations mentioned
earlier determine what constitute the units of attentional selection. Not
surprisingly, they also correspond to the way objects are perceived in qualitative experience. This does not show that attention is directed to phenomenal objects (as some have suggested); rather, it is the other way

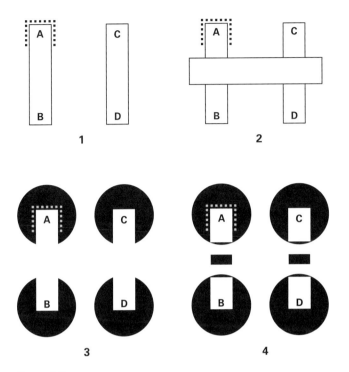

Figure 3.3
When attention is drawn to one end of a bar (marked A) by a cue (e.g., the brightening of the contour, indicated here by dotted lines), its effect can be observed at the other end by the faster detection of a probe at that location (marked B), while the equally distant location on another bar (marked C) is not enhanced. This is true so long as A and B are perceived to be on the same bar (which they are in panels 1–3, but not in panel 4). (Adapted from Moore, Yantis, and Vaughan 1998.)

around: phenomenal objects follow the clustering pattern established by the parsing of a scene into objects by attentional selection.

Even more relevant are studies showing that attention *moves* with objects being attended. A variety of phenomena of attention—including attentional enhancement (in the form of *priming*) and the negative effect of attention on the ability to reattend to the same thing a short time later— show that attention appears to stick with objects rather than remain at the attended location. The first case is illustrated by studies by Kahneman, Treisman, and Gibbs (1992), which show what is referred to as object-specific-priming-benefit (OSPB). In such studies the time to make a judgment about the identity of a pattern, such as a letter, is shortened when

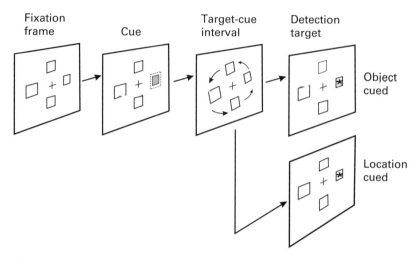

Figure 3.4
When attention is captured exogenously by an object and then disengaged, it takes more time to reattend to that object. This *inhibition of return* appears to move with the attended object (Tipper, Driver, and Weaver 1991).

the letter occurs in the same object (typically a box frame) in which it had previously occurred (there is even evidence that such priming may last up to eight seconds; Noles, Scholl, and Mitroff 2005). A similar phenomenon has also been found with MOT displays, of the sort described in chapter 2, where objects that are tagged by blinking show attentional facilitation even if no explicit tracking is required (Haladjian and Pylyshyn 2006). The second case is illustrated by the phenomenon called *inhibition of return*, wherein attention is slow to return to something that was attended some 300 to 900 milliseconds earlier. Figure 3.4 illustrates an experiment showing that inhibition of return appears to move with the formerly attended object, rather than affect the place that had been attended.

There has also been a suggestion in some of these studies that location may also be inhibited in this case (Tipper et al. 1994). But the locations in question in these dissenting findings are typically either nonempty or in a simple relation to indexed objects (e.g., halfway between two objects). It is doubtful that a location in a uniform unstructured field (what is called the *ganzfeld*; see Avant 1965) can be selected or inhibited—indeed after a few minutes of staring into a ganzfeld people tend to get disoriented and cannot even look back to some location they had just attended. Attention appears to be unable to get a grip on an entirely empty location (failure to find inhibition at empty locations was also reported recently using multiple object tracking; see Pylyshyn 2006).

Visual attention is a much-studied phenomenon and a great deal of evidence is available, of which I have presented only a few illustrative examples (a few more studies are described in chapter 5). From our perspective what is important is that there is considerable evidence that sensory objects attract and maintain focal attention and that the evidence for the more commonsense notion that attention can be allocated to empty spaces is far from univocal.

3.2   Selection and Demonstrative Reference: The Role of FINSTs

In chapters 1 and 2, I presented the outlines of a theory of visual indexing called the FINST theory. According to this theory, things in the world capture (or *grab*) one of a small number of available FINST indexes, which thereafter are available for referring to the things whose properties were the cause of the capturing. In describing matters in this way I emphasize the role of an index as a *reference* mechanism. Indexes act like pointers in computer data structures: they provide a reference to some sensory individual (the nature of which has yet to be specified) without thereby encoding any property of the individual that is indexed.

The parallel between pointers in a computer and FINST indexes is quite exact and helps to clarify what is being claimed, so it deserves a brief aside. The terms *pointer* or *address* are misleading in that they both connote a location. In fact neither refers to an actual location. When we use the term "pointer" we are referring to a different level of abstractness from that of physical locations. Moreover, a pointer does not pick out a location in any kind of space, in even the most extended sense, including some sort of "functional space," since such a "space" does not have the minimal properties of a metric space—as I will argue in chapter 5. A better way to view a pointer is as a name or a singular term. But the question still remains: what does such a singular term refer to? I claim that in the case of FINSTs it refers to what I have been calling *things* or *Fings*, meaning sensory individuals, or visual objects—not *places where things are located*, but individual things themselves. At the end of this chapter I will return to the question that people often ask: Why don't I simply claim that they refer to physical objects? And why do I insist that the indexes do not select things by pointing to places where things are located? More on this presently.

3.2.1 Causes and Codes

We have a strong intuition that when we detect a particular color, texture, or shape in a visual scene, we detect it *as being at a particular location*. Indeed we feel that we can't detect a property without also detecting its location. There are two questions at issue here that need to be kept separate. One is the question of which properties enter into the causal link between the things in the world and the mechanism that does the primitive picking out—or in our terminology, which properties cause indexes to be grabbed. Another is the question of which properties are encoded (i.e., represented) and made available to the mind when an index has been assigned.[2] Another way to put this is in terms of the Kahneman and Treisman theory of object files, introduced briefly in the previous chapter: we can ask which properties cause an object file to be created and which properties are encoded and entered into the file. These can be—and very likely are—different properties. The distinction is reminiscent of Kripke's (1980) distinction between the properties used in fixing the reference of a term, and those that make up its meaning.

The puzzle of how some property can cause the capture of an index without itself being encoded may be exacerbated by the fact that in a modern computer it seems as though any signal that affects the operation of the computer serves as an input and therefore is encoded. But if you look in detail at how the input to a computer is processed you find a clear distinction between reacting and encoding. When you press a key on the keyboard two things happen. One is that there is an *interrupt*—a high priority signal is sent to the processor that tells it to stop what it is doing and attend to the interrupt (there are many possible types of interrupts—in Windows, the one from the keyboard is usually called IRQ1 or Interrupt Request 1). Getting an IRQ1 signal tells the computer that a keyboard event has occurred but it does not tell it which key was pressed (or released, since both cause interrupts). At that point nothing has actually been encoded, but control is passed to an *interrupt service routine* (ISR). Only then does the computer

---

2. There is also a third distinct question that I will not discuss: Which properties are responsible for the object being tracked, i.e., for maintaining the index binding? Evidence suggests that properties such as color, size, and shape are not used in tracking; if objects have distinct colors, shapes, etc. tracking does not improve, and changes in these properties during tracking are not even noticed (Bahrami 2003; Scholl, Pylyshyn, and Franconeri 1999). On the other hand, the speed of objects' motion, how close they come to one another, and probably the rate at which they change direction does appear to affect ease of tracking, though these too do not appear to be encoded.

determine which key had been pressed. I mention this process because the two stages (interrupt and test) correspond respectively to the stage at which a FINST index is captured (grabbed) and the stage at which certain properties of the thing that caused the FINST assignment may be encoded and stored in its object file (see section 2.3.1). These are independent stages, and one can take place without the other. Another example of the distinction between index assignment and property encoding was discussed earlier (in section 2.5) when I described the study by Tremoulet, Leslie, and Hall (2000) in which they showed that infants under ten months of age could use a property (color) to individuate objects and form an expectation as to *how many* things there are behind a screen, while they do not use the same property to recognize *which* objects are behind the screen.

There are two kinds of properties that make certain information-carrying states representations or codes. The first are *extrinsic:* these are the relational properties in virtue of which the codes are about something or other. It is through this semantic "reaching-out" character of codes that the organism is able to maintain epistemic contact with the world—to refer to things, to select and track things, and to bind the codes to things in the world. People have recognized two types of semantic relations in which codes participate: those that encode in terms of conceptual categories, making it possible for the codes to serve as constituents of thought, and those that, although they have representational content, do not function in rational thought. Codes of the second type are sometimes referred to as *nonconceptual*; they encode in terms of codes that do not function in thought. They may also represent in terms of categories, but the categories are not accessible to the rational cognitive system of the viewer. They may represent in what are sometimes called *subpersonal* modes. For example, they may represent properties of the proximal stimulus or properties useful for motor control or other actions (e.g., moving attention). I will have more to say about such nonconceptual codes in the next chapter (where I will propose that they are extremely limited—in fact that they consist only of the direct reference to objects made by FINST indexes).

The second type of properties that determine whether the information-carrying states are codes are *intrinsic*. These are properties in virtue of which the codes take part in computational processes. Such codes have to be instantiated by properties to which the system, *qua* computational process, is sensitive. In other words they have to be instantiated by properties that function to make the system work as a computer or a mind. Not every property to which a system reacts is a code, only those that affect its computational states in the relevant way—knocking the computer over or replacing one of the memory chips, for example, does not count as encoding information (for a more detailed discussion of this point, see Pylyshyn 1984).

3.2.2   Conceptual and Nonconceptual Representations and Quasi-representations

(1)   Conceptual representation   The term "conceptual" is used a great deal in discussions about mental representations, though its use has usually relied on the intuitive notion that it is closely related to language. A conceptual representation is one that is in principle expressible in language because it encodes the world in terms of individual concepts. Concepts, in turn, are very much like lexical items: They are individual symbols that represent categories and that take part as constituents in combinatorial systems that express thoughts, beliefs, goals, and other typical cognitive states. This much is easy since they are the clear cases that are recognizable as thoughts, beliefs, and other "propositional attitudes." But what about the encoding of such properties as those that are needed in theories of visual processing? These include properties of the proximal image, including edges (and their properties such as spatial frequency—whether they are sharp or gradual, their orientation, polarity, type—concave, convex, occlusions, cracks, etc.); properties of surfaces (such their depth profile and type—e.g., convex or concave—their texture, the 3-D orientation of tangents and perpendiculars at points on their surface); values and patterns of lightness, shadows, velocity profiles, orientation of median axes in 3-D, presence of geon types (which are the basic constituents of shapes, at least according to some theories; see, e.g., Biederman 1987); and others, as well as comparable properties in the auditory modality (e.g., temporal patterns of fundamental, harmonic, and aharmonic frequencies, apparent location of sound sources, phonetic content).

The proprioceptive modality probably offers the greatest array of properties that we use every minute of our waking day but cannot describe, both for lack of terms and because we are not conscious of them. There are countless proprioceptive signals that allow us to maintain our posture and balance, to walk upright, to avoid obstacles while moving, to reach for things, and carry on all our mechanical commerce with the world. These are generally not conscious—in fact in most cases they do not produce any noticeable sensations (do you sense the contractions and expansions of your muscles as you sit without slumping?). Some though certainly not all of these sorts of sensory inputs may be represented—stored for future use or processed to predict a future state of the world or of your body, or to plan a sequence of actions. However we think of concepts, much of this information is not conceptual. These are properties which, if they are represented at all, are represented subpersonally in terms that have meaning only to subpersonal computational mechanisms and not to whole persons. Moreover, not every sensory property is represented. Some sensory information is represented and some not; some is represented in terms of categories that could potentially be available to cognitive processes (we could in principle reason about them) and some not. For example, if you are a linguist you might reason about phonemes and NPs or VPs, though not in the same way that these subpersonal concepts are processed within the language-parsing system. The boundaries between nonconceptual and conceptual on the one hand and between conceptual-personal and conceptual-subpersonal on the other hand are all distinctions that we can appreciate from clear cases but for which we cannot provide operational criteria. The same is true of the distinction between representations whose contents are consciously available and those whose contents are not available to introspection. I will have more to say about that distinction in the next chapter.

(2) Nonconceptual representations and nonrepresented properties In recent years it has become clear that there is a great deal of information of which we are not aware, which serves purposes other than object recognition and belief fixation. Among the information that is causally efficacious is information relating to the locations of features and their distances relative both to other features and to the organism itself ("feature" usually means any sensory property, but more typically a basic, spatially local property). This information plays a role in defining feature-clusters and other Gestalt-like groups, and in pairing space-time features to create the perception of apparent motion. There is also clear evidence that such information can serve with remarkable precision in shaping our actions, both voluntary and involuntary (e.g., it allows you to keep your balance while walking).[3] It is also clear that information about *location* plays a central role in many such unconscious processes. Does this entail that the location

3. A remarkable example of how much we rely on unconscious proprioceptive information in walking and maintaining our posture is provided by cases of patients who are essentially deafferented and have no proprioceptive input. They can, with great difficulty, replace the proprioceptive information with visual information but only with extremely arduous training and persistence. See the description of one such patient by Cole (1995).

of features is *represented*, as claimed by many philosophers who speak of these processes as constituting a form of nonconceptual representation? Austen Clark (2004) claims that it does—that perceptual grouping of features on the basis of their proximity to one another, as occurs when we construct feature-clusters, requires encoding the location of the features in question.

The notion of nonconceptual representation was introduced largely to acknowledge not only that there is information that is unlikely to be conceptualized (since, for example, we are not aware of it, or it never enters directly into beliefs or other cognitive states), but also to accommodate information that is extremely fine grained and that appears to be functional in at least the sense that it includes discriminable sensory differences, yet is very unlikely to be conceptual (or even conceptualizable). The category of nonconceptual representation covers many different kinds of cases (see, e.g., the essays in Gunther 2003). This includes information that clearly is relevant to our actions (such as reaching and grasping or walking) yet is below the radar of our awareness and our rational thoughts. Moreover, it often involves such precise magnitudes that it does not seem as though we could in principle conceptualize and reason about it (consider, for example, when we hit a golf ball, or throw a basketball into a net, or play a piece on the piano). There are representations that we do not want to call conceptual only because they do not involve the sorts of categories that people are aware of or could be made aware of. One example of this is that of representations computed in the course of a visual analysis—that involve, for example, such categories as edges and their orientations, boundaries between light and shadow, types of textures, surface orientations at a point, and other properties of the retinal stimulus that we as perceivers do not reason about, but which the encapsulated vision module has to compute over (Fodor 1983; Pylyshyn 1999). These are the sorts of categories that show up as labels in Marr's "full primal sketch" and "$2\frac{1}{2}$-D" representation. They are in every respect like conceptual representations except the categories are subpersonal and not available outside some modular process.

The most widely cited evidence in favor of the assumption that there is a type of representation that is nonconceptual appeals to the apparent differences between the contents of conscious experience and the contents of thoughts.[4] This manifests itself in at least three ways: *First*, it is clear that

4. For more on the role of conscious contents in relation to forms of representation, see chapter 4 (e.g., section 4.1), as well as the discussion of representation of space in section 4.4 and chapter 5.

we can consciously distinguish among finer differences (e.g., finer grada- tions in hue) than we could reasonably assume we have concepts for. *Sec- ond*, there is a degree of independence between a proximal stimulus (i.e., retinal pattern) and a percept, and this needs to be explained. Take, for ex- ample, the way an ambiguous figure (such as the Necker cube, shown in figure 4.1) changes between distinct appearances even though both the proximal stimulus and our beliefs about the figure remain the same. What is it that changes? According to one view what changes is how we represent the figure in nonconceptual form. Because this way of understanding non- conceptual representation rests on certain views about the contents of our conscious experience, I will leave an expansion of this topic for the next chapter. *Third*, there is reason to think that the content of experience— the full fine-detailed information that we experience—is available for a very short time before it either fades or is encoded conceptually. The idea that detailed nonconceptual information is available briefly is consistent with many findings in the experimental literature that provide evidence for what is often called *iconic storage*. For example, Sperling (1960) found that a great deal of visual information is available for a fraction of a second after the information input (i.e., the illuminated display) has disappeared. This so-called iconic store does not contain conceptualized information (in fact it is commonly referred to as *precategorical* store). Such information is available for any visual process that itself does not take more than a few hundred milliseconds, including processes that encode information con- ceptually. Although this third option does constitute a type of nonconcep- tual storage, calling it a representation may be misleading insofar as it need not involve any encoding, but may arise merely from inertia or hysteresis on the part of sensors. It may lack the signature properties of representa- tions: it is arguably just a geometrical projection of retinal stimulation (at least according to one view, championed by Sperling), so it cannot misrep- resent, and its content (what it represents) does not enter into any general- izations (see (3) below for more on these criteria for being a representation).

My concern at this point is primarily with the question of whether certain spatial properties such as location and distance are encoded (repre- sented) early in vision and whether they can serve as the basis for primitive selection. For this purpose we should recall that there is a substantial differ- ence between the claim that certain properties, such as the locations and distances between objects in the world, play a *causal* role in a visual pro- cess, and the claim that these properties play a role by virtue of being *repre- sented*. Objects are always at some location or other, and the effect they have on a perceiver may depend on where they are, but the locations they are at (even relative to one another) may or may not be represented. The same is true of the location of objects on the proximal stimulus (e.g., on the retina) or further up in the nervous system, such as patterns of activity on the retinotopically organized fibers leading from the eye, or in the primary visual cortex, which is largely retinotopically mapped. Since these locations are past the sensors, are they necessarily representations? If so, what is the essential difference between the way that distance in the world affects perception and the way that the corresponding distance on a neighborhood-preserving (i.e., homeomorphic) anatomical mapping affects perception (for ease of reference I will refer to the results of such mappings as "neural layouts" or NLs)? We can say that such neural layouts *register* (rather than represent) spatial properties. They help to illustrate the general theme that there are many types of representations, ranging from conceptual, through subpersonal, to informational states that are better referred to as registrations rather than representations. In the next subsection I will examine neural layouts to see if they warrant the conclusion that spatial properties are always represented in NLs since locations appear to be roughly preserved on a maplike surface.

(3)   Are neural layouts always representations?   Intuitively it seems that a neural layout (a layout of activity in the cortex that is a homeomorphic mapping of some other spatial domain, such as shown in figure 4.4) carries information about location in a special way that makes it a maplike representation (I will have more to say about maplike representations and their role in navigation in section 5.4.2). The intuition is that any projection of spatial information onto a neural layout (NL) is automatically a representation since it preserves spatial locations (at least to a first approximation). This intuition derives from the fact that such an NL resembles a canonical map or picture and could (if spread out) be used by a person to navigate or to recognize patterns. However, the layout need not be used in this way.

  Whether we call any retinal or other neural layout a *representation* is partly a question of terminology, and NLs usually do carry information about something in the world to which they are causally connected. As mentioned above I prefer to call that type of mapping a *registration* of information—spatial properties are registered rather than represented in NLs. What does matter is not the terminology, but the distinctions we need to make with respect to the role NLs play in explanations. If we use the term "representation" to refer to any information-bearing state, then we will still need to distinguish another, stronger sense of representation. The main distinction we still need is that between states whose representational *con-*

tent plays a role in explanations and those in which the content (if any) does not play any role. If we gain no explanatory advantage by specifying *what* an NL represents, then nothing is gained by treating the NL as a representation. The fact that the NL looks like a map—even if places on the NL correspond to places in the world—is still not enough for it to be a representation in the strong sense.

There are several specific requirements that should be met for something to count as a spatial representation in the strong sense. We need to show not only that locations, distances, and directions in the NL correspond to the same properties in the world but also that they determine the organism's behavior vis-à-vis those represented places. In other words, we need to show that these properties of the NL function to represent properties of the world for the organism. One indicator that they function in this way is if at least some generalizations concerning behavior require appeal to the represented domain as opposed to the pattern of the NL itself. Some principles governing NLs might well be captured solely in terms of properties of the NL with no regard to what they may represent. The principles for forming clusters of features and most Gestalt grouping principles may well be of this sort. These principles (at least as understood by people like Kohler and Wertheimer) are expressed over properties of the proximal stimulus or over neural fields in the brain,[5] but not over locations, distances, and directions in the world.

One way to see this is to reflect on the fact that unless the function of the NL is to represent spatial properties for the organism, it would not be possible for the NL to *misrepresent* something. The possibility of misrepresenting is a signature property of representations—a retinal pattern cannot misrepresent the visual world since optics does not make "mistakes." Similarly, it is meaningless to ask of an NL in which frame of reference it represents an

5. Processes operating over NLs typically respond to spatially local properties of the NL—they operate over "local support." The principles of operation of such processes are *prima facie* expressible over nonconceptual neural properties. Recently there has been an increase of interest in applying dynamic systems theory to modeling the mind. Since such theories are generally not representational (and not computational in the sense discussed in Pylyshyn 1984) there is little chance that they will explain cognitive processes. But they may find application in the sort of nonrepresentational processes that transform NLs or registrations, derive Gestalt clusters, solve the correspondence problem in certain cases, and even carry out tracking (examples are found in Koch and Ullman 1985; Pylyshyn 2003, appendix 5A). Thus theories that postulate spatial registrations may be appropriate for the sort of neural field processes envisioned by Wolfgang Kohler (1947).

object's location, since by itself it does not represent an object as located anywhere. But in the strong sense of representation, where the NL functions to direct movements or to identify objects, it *does* matter how its spatial relations are represented. In that case an NL may represent some locations with respect to a head-centered frame of reference, or as being to the left of another location, or as being more than an arm's length away; and for purposes of determining actions *it matters how the location is represented* (or what it is represented *as*). Without this strong sense of representation, with only a direct object-to-NL mapping, there is no possibility of misrepresentation, and thus it is misleading to call the NL a representation or a map.[6]

It's important to keep in mind that this discussion is about *explaining* regularities in vision and behavior. So the answer to the question at hand—whether an NL is a spatial representation—is that it depends on whether one must refer to the geometrical properties of the represented world in providing explanations. For example, do the principles (such as principles of clustering or of correspondence) that have to be cited refer to properties of the NL or properties in the world? Suppose, for the sake of argument, that the clustering algorithm applies only over distances on the neural lay-

---

6. I am leaving out a lot here. What makes a terrestrial map able to misrepresent is that this sort of map typically is constructed with the intention that certain of its features correspond to certain features of the relevant terrain, and the map has to be interpreted with these intentions in mind. Thus there is ample room for the intended correspondence to fail and for the map thus to misrepresent. These degrees of freedom are absent in the case of NLs unless we assume that the map is interpreted by some process that allows a possibility of misinterpretation. Sometimes it is tempting to assume an interpreter, and at other times it is tempting to assume a design purpose for the NL—and sometimes it makes sense to talk of a "map" even though there may be no NL, as in the case of insect navigation (see section 5.4.2). Talk about the design purpose (what the NL is *for*) is sometimes helpful, even though strictly speaking there is no agent who designed the representation-using system, because it ties together a variety of otherwise unconnected properties of various mechanisms. In fact our understanding of "natural constraints" rests on assumptions about the purpose of some of the mechanisms, and Marr (1982) motivated his analysis by asking what various visual mechanisms were *for*. Dretske (1981) suggests another way in which an information-carrying state might misrepresent, a way based on learning: If the system has been exposed to pairs of properties and internal states, it could learn which features of the environment the states represent and thus could be in a position to misrepresent those features. These are all questions that I will not get into, beyond arguing that there is more to being a map than homeomorphism.

out, which, in turn, is a homeomorphic transformation of activity on the retina.[7] In that case nothing is gained by saying that these distances represent properties in the world, since by hypothesis the distance on the NL is all that is relevant to explanations involving distances and those are indifferent between whether it represents a visual angle, a 2-D distance on the retina, a 2-D distance far away from the observer, or a distance in 3-D oriented at the appropriate angle from the viewer to project onto the line on the NL. Therefore, it is not a representation in the strong sense; it does not represent the property *as* something in the world, notwithstanding that, if spread out on a flat surface, the pattern of activity looks like a map. But since it carries some information about spatial locations we say that it *registers* spatial properties.

(4) When should we postulate representations? The purpose of postulating representations is to provide explanations and to capture generalizations that would not be captured without reference to the contents of such representations—to what they represent. But sometimes (as in the hypothetical NL discussed above) the function of information-carrying states can be fully described without reference to contents. It could be that principles such as, say, those involved in clustering or apparent motion can be fully explained without reference to any representational content of the states involved. In discussing the way information might be carried by an NL, I noted earlier that an explanation might sometimes be stated in terms

7. These examples are for purposes of illustration; I am not prejudging the empirical question of whether the principles of clustering or of pairing features to solve the correspondence problem apply only to proximity on the NL. If they apply to distal properties then the present argument would not work—but then again neither could we claim that the NL is the basis for the clustering or correspondence solution, since we know at least that V1 (or any other NL) is prior to processes that provide 3-D information (prior to the constancies). There have been conflicting claims over whether 3-D properties are relevant to apparent motion; some investigators maintain that 3-D distance is relevant (Attneave and Block 1973; Wright, Dawson, and Pylyshyn 1987) and some that it is not (Ullman 1979). Recent years have seen many reports of 3-D properties being relevant to what seem like early processes, such as popouts in search (Enns and Rensink 1990; Rensink and Enns 1995) or even multiple object tracking, where it seems that speed in the distal world, rather than on the retina, determines the performance in MOT (Enns and Franconeri 2006; Liu, Austen, Booth, Fisher, et al. 2005). These suggest that such processes are postconstancy or postdepth analysis and therefore do not involve (only) places on the NL (in V1). But this is an empirical question that requires further research.

of the physical (or connectivity) distance between places on the layout (or individual units of an NL—indeed such networks have been proposed, including one in the appendix of chapter 5 of Pylyshyn 2003), in which case nothing is gained by treating such clustering processes as operating over codes or representations since nothing hangs on whether or not we take such distances as representing distances in the world.

The above discussion reflects a general preference toward a conservative use of representations in theories.[8] Recently I have argued that we should not postulate representations if no explanatory advantage is gained by such a postulate. In Pylyshyn 1991 I suggested that in general the preferred explanation is one that relies on assuming the least general mechanisms compatible with the evidence—in other words on mechanisms that are constrained in the patterns of behavior that they are able to accommodate. There is nothing unusual in this idea. Given a body of evidence we generally prefer the explanation with the fewest degrees of freedom or the fewest ad hoc assumptions. But considering all the relevant evidence we have, our account will always require *some* assumptions or principles postulated to account for the evidence at hand—those are the degrees of freedom we have for taking account of the evidence in giving explanations and in predicting future observations. There is, of course, always the problem of individuating and counting assumptions. But however we do that, we give extra weight to the least general assumptions or, in the case of a computational theory, to the weakest or most restricted mechanism compatible with the observed behavior. Explanations based on representations are the most general—with them we can construct a Universal Turing machine that can emulate any mechanism.[9] So we prefer to appeal to less general mechanisms, based on fixed structures, as opposed to the highly malleable

8. Devitt (2006) recently coined the term "Pylyshyn's razor" to refer to the principle that we should try to minimize the power of the explanatory mechanisms to which we appeal, and that therefore we should not postulate representations where more restricted forms of architecture-based (nonrepresentational) mechanisms would do. I have argued for such a principle in various places (Pylyshyn 1984, 1991, 1994, 1996). See also note 10, this chap.

9. It has not always been recognized that the universal Turing machine (UTM) is just another TM. What makes it a UTM rather than the nth TM is the way we view the symbols on its tape. A UTM comes into being only when we (the observers) interpret some of the symbols on its tape as representations—in particular as representing the identity or the program of another TM, the one whose behavior the UTM is simulating.

representations. This leads to the principle that we try to account for as much as we can based on what I and others have called the *architecture of the system* (Pylyshyn 1980) before postulating representations.[10] An explanation based on properties of the architecture not only appeals to a more constrained mechanism, but (unlike the more powerful representation-based explanations) also makes a specific commitment about what functions one should find in the neural substrate. Of course there is a tradeoff; the weaker the power of the postulated mechanism, the less likely it is that it will be adequate to account for the evidence as more and more evidence is accumulated. This is why in cognitive psychology one is forced sooner or later to attribute more and more functions to representations.

3.3   Problems with Selection by Location

I return now to the topic with which I began this chapter, the question of whether we select places or objects. Notwithstanding the evidence for object-based attention, both psychologists and philosophers tend to view location as the primary property in terms of which selection occurs, and therefore as the property through which the mind addresses things in the world. This view is consistent with the informal observation that if you want to look at something or touch something you need to know where it is. There have also been several studies (reviewed in Pashler 1998) showing that in most cases where an object is correctly identified, its location can also be reported correctly, from which many investigators (e.g., Pashler 1998, pp. 97–99) conclude that location is the basic property used for recovering other properties. For example, there is evidence that the way one finds a combination of color and shape (i.e., when searching for a conjunction of these two properties) is by using one of these features (e.g., color) to find its location and then to use its location to test for the second conjunct (e.g., shape) at that location (Pashler 1998). Mary-Jo Nissen (1985) tested this view directly by examining the probabilities of finding various combinations when searching for conjunctions of properties. She showed that when searching for a target with a specified color and shape,

10. This is also closely related to other razors. De Morgan's cannon says that one should not postulate higher-level psychological functions, or functions associated with organisms higher on the phylogenetic scale, when lower psychological functions would fit the evidence. It is sometimes considered a special case of Occam's razor, a general principle that we prefer simplicity in theories, where simplicity is an essential though undefined commodity.

the probability of finding the right color and of finding the right shape were not independent, suggesting at least that there is some way these two interact in the search for their conjunction. Nissen then showed that the probability of finding a given color and the conditional probability of finding a particular shape given that attention is focused on its location were independent, lending support to the hypothesized two-stage process (e.g., to determine whether the conjunction of properties P_1 and P_2 is present, (1) find property P_1, get location L_1 of P_1, (2) switch attention to L_1 and check whether P_2 occurs there).

Of course in all these cases, where objects do not move, being at a particular location and being on a particular object are perfectly confounded. Moreover, it is quite reasonable that priority may be given to location *once the object has been selected*. There is considerable evidence for the claim that location is treated as special among the various *conceptualized* properties of selected objects. Indeed, our work on multiple object tracking has shown that when objects disappear, the location of targets is retained better than any other property of the targets (Scholl, Pylyshyn, and Franconeri 1999). We have also shown that the disappearance of tracked objects for half a second, and perhaps even much longer, does not disrupt tracking if the objects reappear where they had been when they disappeared, thus showing that the location of disappearance must have been retained in some form (Keane and Pylyshyn 2006). But our assumption is that the disappearance itself causes locations to be conceptualized and stored in memory. It's not clear if in this case the relevant memory is the object file that was associated with that object at the time of its disappearance, or if it uses some other sort of memory such as visual short-term memory. If it's the former it would suggest that an object file can exist, at least for a short time, even if it is not connected to an object.

3.3.1   A Note on the Role of Location in Selection and Tracking
The proposal that we select and track visual objects based on the continuing individuality of the objects (what philosophers call their "numerical identity") has sometimes been looked upon with suspicion, as though what were being proposed is some sort of magic wherein an object is mysteriously picked out and tracked without any physical connection. There may be two reasons for this suspicion. One is that every object is in fact at *some* location and when one selects it one is selecting an object that happens to be at a particular location (though not necessarily selecting it *as an object at that location*—see note 12). Thus there is the usual temptation toward the intentional fallacy here as in other cases of representation (in

this fallacy, properties of the referent of a representation are mistaken for properties of the representation itself—a case of the use-mention error). In fact not only is an object at a location when selected, but it may even be selected *because* of its location, since one clue that there are several individual objects is that they are at different locations. As I pointed out in section 3.2.1, many properties of objects may contribute causally to the object's being selected. But that does not entail that any of those properties is encoded or represented, or that any properties that are represented play a role in keeping track of the identity of individual objects. The claim that a certain property may cause a particular item to be selected (or may grab an index) yet not be encoded is also a claim that some find puzzling.

When an index is grabbed by some individual, the process presumably involves a causal chain that eventually causes sensors to respond to a local region of the proximal (e.g., retinal) stimulus. Such sensory processes respond to stimulation at particular location(s) and are sensitive at least to a local distance metric since presumably one of the things they do is compute a cluster of local properties based in part on their proximity to one another. But it is a separate question whether properties such as the size of the cluster or its retinal location are *represented*. It should be clear that there is no requirement that such metrical information be *encoded* and entered into an object file in order for an index to be captured or an object file to be created. Whether it needs to be represented in some other sense is a separate question that I will consider next, and to which I will return in chapter 5 when I consider the issue of how spatial properties might be represented.

Some people are suspicious about the object-selection principle because they have trouble imagining how information about the properties of an object can be encoded without the observer's knowing the objects' location, and how an object can be tracked without the observer's keeping track of where it is. Before looking more closely at the MOT case, let's consider this question somewhat more broadly. There clearly must be a causal information stream coming to and/or from the object for a FINST to be assigned or for the object to be tracked. A FINST assignment often occurs when a new object comes into view, but it can also occur when there is some other sort of transient (e.g., the object briefly becomes brighter). Can a FINST index be assigned if the location of the transient is not known? If you think about the various current technologies that select things, you see that there are many ways that selection can occur, other than by using information about the location of the selected object. I have already given the example of a pointer in a computer which selects (and retrieves) the referent of a particular given symbol, say, "*x*" (in computer science such a symbol may be referred to as a name or a variable or a pointer). It does this without knowing where the referent of "*x*" is (and indeed, in a modern multitasking computer there is no specific place where the referent is located for more than a few milliseconds at a time). It is able to do this because of the architecture of the computer, which means that the explanation must be given at a different level or in different—noncomputational—terms (e.g., electromechanical in the case of a computer and its hard disk, neurophysiological in the case of the brain).

Other ways of selecting things requires identifying information to be transferred between the "*x*" and its referent and/or the other way around. This is the case with cell phones, which find the phone you are calling without knowing where it is. Other selection methods use different ways to identify the referent of "*x*"; a tuning fork can be found by emitting its specific tone, a piece of metal can be found by using a powerful magnet (as people who have gone into an MRI room with keys have discovered). None of these uses location as *the way of selecting* its target, so selecting without using a location should not be too mysterious. What is essential for accessing a target is simply some way of identifying it, which is why it is essential that the FINST mechanism track the relevant object and maintain its identity from the time when it first grabbed an index (when it was visually distinct at the start of an MOT trial).

The minimum function needed for an object to have the right kind of causal or informational link with a symbol token is that there be some causal or nomologically supported *dependency* between the object and its associated symbol token (this is similar to the informational view of reference as developed by Dretske 1981). What kind of dependency? Any simple causal connection will do. One candidate is an object's appearing in the field of view (under the right background conditions of lighting, size, location relative to the fovea, speed of motion, and so on), causing a symbol token to appear in the appropriate part of the early vision system. To a first approximation, a symbol might be tokened in the early vision module while, and only while, the object is in view (it's an approximation because the symbol will actually persist for some minimal time after the object fades—a qualification that needs some spelling out). The symbol is unique to that token object on that particular occasion only (unlike a name, you can't use the token to think about the object in its absence). If the object moves around, nothing changes in the symbol token; whatever relation it had with the object, such as the above dependency relation, remains. Nothing about such a dependency mentions location (except in the general background conditions).

Such a dependency relation establishes a causally supported symbol–object pairing, which is an important beginning. But is clearly not enough for the purposes of the FINST theory. The FINST proposal requires that once a dependency relation is established, an information channel opens up, so that, for example, some operation performed on the symbol token has consequences that depend on properties of the object. For example, if the symbol is in the appropriate relation to the system architecture (e.g., if it is placed in a certain register) some other designated register will change contents depending on the color (or shape or any other sensory property) of the associated object (a possible neural net implementation of a similar function is provided in Pylyshyn 2003, appendix 5A). This, in effect, allows a function to be executed that returns a property of the relevant object, which is another way of saying that the index can be used to bind the argument of a function or predicate to the object in question. Mental functions don't normally reach out and channel information to things in the world; rather, they channel information to representations. Yet once the right kind of dependency relation holds between an object and a symbol token (i.e., once an index has been established) it can, in effect, be deployed to query the object. Whether this way of putting it is the most perspicuous remains to be seen. But the idea is that some such minimal functionality is necessary for the information link between object and symbol token to serve the sort of function postulated in this discussion.

The basic requirement for indexing is that there be a channel between symbol and object—a way for some part of the visual system to "communicate" with the particular object (e.g., send a signal to it, or test it for certain properties). Which part of the visual system is involved and the detailed story on how it "communicates" with the particular object are questions likely to have only a neural-physical-optical account, which is to say that it may well be part of the fixed architecture. Indeed, as noted earlier, this is the sort of function for which neural networks of the connectionist sort are particularly suited. In fact the proposals mentioned earlier (Koch and Ullman 1985; Pylyshyn 2003, appendix 5A) do provide a way of sending a signal to certain salient objects. These networks are interesting mainly because they show that a signal can be sent to "the most active neural cluster" without ever specifying *where* that cluster is—at least not in a way that could be used outside the neural layout. If we accept the view presented in the previous section, that NLs need not be representations in the strong sense, this means that a strong sense of representation of location is not needed to establish an access channel between symbol tokens in early vision and selected objects.

Consider how the selection process works in some of the experiments discussed earlier that were motivated by the FINST theory. Data reported by Burkell and Pylyshyn (1997) show that distance between items does not affect search, and data on subitizing (Trick and Pylyshyn 1994b) show that precuing the location of items to be enumerated does not affect subitizing, which we interpreted as suggesting that accessing indexed (FINSTed) objects in search or enumeration tasks does not require having to locate them first (though with larger numbers of objects it does). In addition, data on MOT suggest that the tracking system either does not have location (or direction) information or, if it does, it does not (or cannot) use it with any precision in tracking (e.g., Franconeri, Pylyshyn, and Scholl 2006; Keane and Pylyshyn 2006 showed that when objects disappear behind an opaque occluding surface and reappear shortly after, they are not tracked better if they reappear at predicted locations going in predicted directions). The tracking process is assumed to use indexes to bind the target objects to some internal symbols or object files. This includes binding a target to the argument of the process that can switch attention to it. To execute MoveAttention(x) the hardware that carries out the command needs to be able to actually bind x to the object and thus to move attention to it. Just as we don't know in detail how attention shifts, so we do not know in detail how binding occurs. If we can think of attention allocation as akin to moving a spotlight, as many people do, we can think of tracking as involving a causal chain centered on the target. In fact there are several proposals for how an attention beam can be kept centered on a moving object (e.g., Kazanovich and Borisyuk 2006 propose a neural model). The problem is well studied in computer science with both hardware (Gul and Atherton 1989) and software implementations (Shapiro 1995). Most of these involve clustering or edge-finding processes, which use information about relative location of features (typically based on a neural layout), but this information is used only locally and thus need not be available outside an encapsulated module, the way that routines in some programming languages have local variables whose values are unavailable outside the running routine.

Finally, just as we need to distinguish between interrupts and tests, so we need to distinguish between memory (which stores encoded information) and a mechanism's inertia or hysteresis or decay time. One of the MOT findings is that objects can be tracked even when they disappear for a short time (a fraction of a second). We can think of this as requiring memory, and therefore as storing an encoding of object properties (such as location, speed, and direction of travel), or we can think of it as just being within the time constant of the mechanism. After all, we do not find it a theoretical challenge that people can track moving objects in MOT despite the fact that the screen is refreshed every 17 or 34 ms, so why is tracking over longer periods of invisibility a problem? The tracking mechanism may be complex and it may have various constraints built in, just as the rest of the visual system has such built-in constraints. For example, one of the empirical findings concerning tracking briefly disappearing targets (Scholl and Pylyshyn 1999) is that when a target goes behind an occluding surface it is tracked better if there are occlusion and disocclusion cues, as there would ordinarily be if the target moved behind an opaque surface and reappeared on the other side. So clearly even though the tracking mechanism computes simple functions that do not require access to general knowledge, there are natural constraints built in that determine the conditions under which it tracks best. In these we see a role for some local spatial and temporal integration (an apparent "quasi-memory"), although in every case what is involved is short-term or temporally local and spatially local computations, so it is compatible with the view that indexing does not require an encoded memory for location in order to enable tracking.

More important theoretical implications of whether selection is by location, by property, or by individual object emerge in connection with a problem that I have already mentioned, known as the *binding problem* or the *many-properties problem* (the term used by Jackson 1997), which I take up next.

3.3.2   Selection and the Binding Problem

Sensory properties come in certain kinds of bundles, and one of the challenges for early vision is to make information about this bundling available for subsequent conceptual encoding. As I mentioned at the beginning of this chapter, this is one of the main functions served by *attentional selection*. The bundling I speak of is simply the fact that given that properties belong to things, it is important that the combination of properties that belong to the same thing be somehow indicated. What the earliest stages of vision must do in order to permit the subsequent conceptual description of a scene is present the information in such a way that properties that belong together, or are associated with the same tokens in the scene, are somehow flagged as such. Many mechanisms that have been proposed as part of early vision fail to do so. Consider, for example, the early "Pandemonium" model of Selfridge (1959), or its modern "connectionist" descendants, or the purely hierarchical views of initial encodings in which simple property detectors (simple cells) send activity to complex cells, which send activity to hypercomplex cells, until (at least in the minds of some theorists)

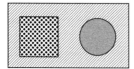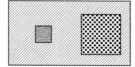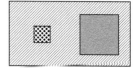

Figure 3.5
The early visual system must report information in a form that makes it possible to discriminate these figures composed of identical sets of shape, texture, and size properties but in different combinations. Specifying how it does so is called the *binding problem*.

ultimately something like the "grandmother cell" was activated, leading to recognition.

These proposals detect properties independently and leave it to subsequent stages to put them together into object descriptions. But it is not enough to indicate, for example, that certain properties such as redness or greenness or triangularity or squareness are present in the scene, because then higher centers of conceptual vision would not be able to tell that, say, the red goes with the triangle and the green goes with the square, or vice versa. The problem that this raises turns out to be completely general and rather deep, and is discussed in various forms by Strawson, Quine, Kaplan, and others. How does early vision circumscribe and report the information in a display such as in figure 3.5 so as to preserve the information that in the first two frames it is the large square that has black dots and that the circle and small square are finely textured gray?

The answer given universally to this puzzle, both in psychology and in philosophy, is that vision represents properties such as shapes and textures by their location in property-specific neural layouts called *feature maps*. The story is that it is the fact that *dotted* on the texture map is at the same location as *square* on the shape map and *large* on the size map that puts them together—and it is this that allows vision to distinguish the three objects in figure 3.5.

Treisman and Gelade (1980) postulate an additional "master" map that puts features together by allowing the locations on the feature maps to be kept in registry and that allows focal attention to be moved across the scene independently of features, but in registry with feature maps. There is empirical evidence that discriminating objects on the basis of a conjunction of properties may require the application of focal attention. The story about how this happens can be told in terms of *feature integration theory*, or FIT (Treisman and Gelade 1980). According to this theory, in order to find the small dotted square among the three figures shown here, one makes use of two feature maps and a master map—all of which are part of the early vision system. Figure 3.6 shows the feature integration theory applied to a group of colored shapes (shown in the figure as different textures). The stimulus in this example is registered on three maps. The *shape map* shows that there is a rectangle at one location, the *color (or texture) map* shows locations of the different textures, and the *orientation map* shows the location of the different orientations. Each of these maps is coordinated with a master map that does not show the features, but does provide a way to control the search through the feature maps. So to locate the large dark horizontal ellipse, one checks the *shape map* for an ellipse. Then one checks the color or texture map for the texture. To solve the binding problem one simply finds the place where both matches occurred. One does this either by using the master map to guide focal attention to places and then checking the properties that correspond to those places at the distinct feature maps, or by finding one of the conjuncts and checking its location for a feature on another feature map.

But there is a problem with this analysis, and indeed with any analysis that does not recognize the central role played by objects. To see why this is so, consider how to encode, say, the large square in figure 3.5 as being at some particular location on the shape map. One is immediately faced with the problem of how to locate that shape so that it provides the appropriate cross-reference for locating a color. The square is not at a precise punctate location so one has to locate it at a region (Clark 2000 does recognize the role of regions in a way that FIT does not, though it does not help resolve the problem discussed here). If a fixed-size region is chosen, then if the region is too small, it will not distinguish the small square from the large one in figure 3.5. If it is too large, it will not distinguish between the square and the circle, and if it does, it will not be in a position to determine what texture that region has since it will include both the texture inside and the texture outside for at least some of the shapes. So the region has to be just right in both size and shape—a requirement that assumes that the object in question has already been selected! The problem is that there is no precise place where squareness is located, and without a precise place for squareness there is no place to look for texture on the texture map. There is even evidence that what counts as the border for purposes of attentional selection depends on the perceived object—the same border may sometimes serve as the boundary of selection and sometimes not (see figure 3.3). This problem will not be solved by an easy fix, such as allowing the region to fill out to some border, because what counts as the relevant border is the

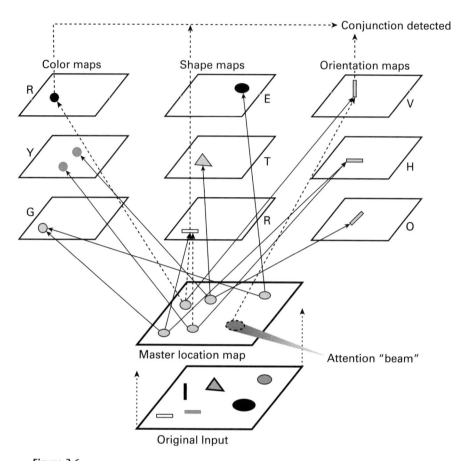

Figure 3.6
The feature integration theory assumes a master map for coordinating and conjoining properties by their spatial co-occurrence (after Treisman and Gelade 1980). A conjunction is deemed to occur when a property is detected and marked on its particular map and attention confirms that the second property exists at the same location.

outside edge of the object whose shape is represented, or by letting location be a probability distribution, as Clark suggests is his more recent paper (Clark 2004). Since objects do not have to be spatially separated, no strategy that depends on assigning a virtual location will work. For example, if one object is *inside* another the feature conjunctions cannot be distinguished without considering which object they apply to and where the boundary of the object in question falls.

The problem goes even deeper than just collocating shapes, orientations, size, colors, or textures. The binding problem has to be solved not only for simple 2-D shapes, but for 3-D objects, and even for *sets of moving objects*. In fact, Alvarez, Arsenio, Horowitz, and Wolfe (2005) and Cohen and Pylyshyn (2002) found that search for conjunctive features can be carried out over targets during multiple object tracking without any decrease in tracking performance, and Trick, Audet, and Dales (2003) found that tracking did not impede subitizing (enumerating four or fewer moving tracked items). What is likely going on in that case is that people select moving objects (using FINSTs) and then, having selected them, they apply their focal attention to those objects to note their color or texture or any other property or combination of properties.[11] The same is true of regions defined in terms of both space and time. The relevant spatiotemporal region is the one traced out by a moving object, not one defined in terms of spatiotemporal coordinates that do not depend on prior detection of an object. Moreover, as noted earlier, perception must provide the information in a form that enables us to conjoin properties across different modalities.

3.3.3   Selection and the Causal Link

The second problem with selection by location arises from the requirement that the link between world and mind be one in which it is primarily the world that initiates the connection—the functions of early vision or sentience are data driven or, as we say in computer science, interrupt driven. The possibility that under certain conditions attention might be directed to empty locations (e.g., as it is scanned from place to place under endogenous control) does not help the problem of connecting the world with the mind, because *empty places do not have causal powers and therefore cannot*

---

11. In MOT subjects generally do not notice such intrinsic properties as color or shape. We assume that this is because such noticings—such property encodings—do require unitary attention, which is in short supply during tracking (for reasons we are still examining). As we saw earlier, tracking objects does not use the contents of the object files and so is independent of such property encodings.

have an effect on mental states. Only *things* at locations can cause a mental event. You can't bind an index to an empty location, so you can't evaluate a predicate over it (in the next chapter I will consider whether you can move your eye or your limb to a specific empty location).

3.3.4 Selection as Nonconceptual Access

The third problem with selection by location may be the most general and telling of all. If empty places were to be selected—say, as consequence of the observer's voluntarily scanning attention from one object to another—it would not address the question of how the mind connects with the world. For that the relevant question is: What is selected *nonconceptually*, that is, without the benefit of a description or encoded properties? What is selected in some specific situation may *in fact* be a location (say, some space between two objects through which attention is scanned), just as it may in fact be a speck of dust, the edge of a table, a chair, or the capital of France. But because the selection is nonconceptual, even if we happen to select an instance of a *P*, we do not select it under the category or concept *P*.[12] So although an empty location might just happen be selected under some circumstance, it cannot be selected *as a place*, since this sort of selection is selection under a concept. At the primitive level under consideration here, what is selected is merely indexed or demonstrated and not conceptualized in any way. The reason for insisting on this stringent constraint is that nonconceptual contact must occur *some-*

---

12. There is an important distinction to be made here. Suppose careful research shows that property *P* is necessary and sufficient for an index to be assigned. In that case the index carries the information that what is indexed has property *P* (in the sense of Dretske 1981). Then one might ask (as Jeff Engelhardt did in a class on this topic): Is this not a case of indexing under the category "*is P*"? Note that *P* will almost certainly be a disjunction of properties, quite likely a disjunction of very many properties with nothing in common other than that they attract indexes (i.e., they need not have a definition independent of the FINST mechanism). But more important, there is a difference between selecting all and only things that are *in fact P* and selecting them *as Ps*. In the former case the selection could be made on the basis of any property that is reliably correlated with *P* (e.g., is nomologically connected with *P*) so that if *P* includes "having a local maximum in brightness" the selection is equally correctly described as based on the property of, say, "emitting electromagnetic radiation that does not occupy more than a 5° visual angle." On the other hand, selecting things *as Ps* would select only those things represented as being *P*, and if they are not represented they could not be selected in this intentional way. The difference might be described as one between *de re* and *de dicto* selection.

where and selection is one of the most promising candidates, for reasons discussed earlier. But when such selection does occur it must not select an *x* represented as *P*, or select *x* because it satisfies some description $P(x)$, that excludes selection of a place represented as a place; that would be selection under a concept, namely, the concept of place. This means that even selection by an indexical locative such as *here* will not do since that would be selection under the concept of location.

Thus the proposal that selecting locations serves as the primitive basis for sensory contact with the world falls short of providing the required foundation. What is needed is just what FINST indexes provide: a numerically limited mechanism for picking out and preconceptually tracking the enduring identity of things. Because of the causal-connection requirement, the thing in question will more often than not be an actual physical object, although it is not encoded as such, which is why I refer to it interchangeably as a visual object, a proto-object, and a thing (or FING).

3.4   Feature Placing and Sentience

The attempt to understand the primitive connection between world and mind inevitably brings us to the philosophical literature on individuals and on sentience—the sensory contact with the world. Although those who speak of sentience frequently have in mind conscious sensory contact, it is possible to remain neutral on the question of whether one must be conscious of every such contact. To insist on including only conscious access would force us to leave out very many important facts about sensory content that remain below the radar of consciousness.

Austen Clark has recently brought together the literature on individuals —particularly the seminal work of Peter Strawson—and empirical research on perception and attention (as well as some ethologists' writings on animal perceptual orientation). Because Clark's goals—understanding the sensory processes that precede conceptualization—are close to my own, I will summarize some of his views (Clark 2000, 2004). In the end I will conclude that although the work is well conceived and insightful, Clark's acceptance of Strawson's "feature-placing" principles runs him into problems, some of which I have just reviewed: feature placing assumes that our initial contact with the world concerns *features at locations*, and therefore, that location encoding comes into play very early in the sensory process.

For Clark, sentience is a matter of the sensory experience we have before that experience is encoded in terms of predicates, which he takes to be constitutive of conceptualization; therefore, to understand sentience is to provide an account of what goes on prior to conceptualization. It is clear that what Clark means by sentience is pretty much what I have been referring to as what is accomplished by the early vision module—that organ of vision that operates independent of cognition.[13] (Incidentally, Clark's use of the term "experience," like mine, does not presuppose that all sensory experience is necessarily conscious.)

According to Clark, experience is represented, but not conceptualized. So what exactly is the content of such representations? Clark answers by citing Strawson's "feature-placing language," a language weak enough to encompass only the representational capacity of sensations and nothing more—so it is devoid of concepts or predicates and cannot represent particulars or token individuals. It is important to Clark that these representations be impoverished. They do not include predicates of any kind, since those are clearly conceptual. Nor does it include identity, multiple or "divided" reference (distinguishing *this* from *that*), or tenses (distinguishing *now* from *then*). Clark summarizes his view as follows:

The hypothesis that this book offers is that sensation is feature-placing: a prelinguistic system of mental representation. Mechanisms of spatio-temporal discrimination ... serve to pick out or identify the subject-matter of sensory representation. That subject-matter turns out invariably to be some place-time in or around the body of the sentient organism.... (Clark 2000, p. 165)

there is a sensory level of identification of place-times that is more primitive than the identification of three-dimensional material objects. Below our conceptual scheme— underneath the streets, so to speak—we find evidence of this more primitive system. The sensory identification of place-times is independent of the identification of objects; one can place features even though one lacks the latter conceptual scheme. (Ibid., pp. 144–145)

This feature-placing mechanism serves some of the same functions on Clark's theory that indexes serve on our FINST theory; in particular, they allow us to make primitive demonstrative reference.

Sensory processes can pick out, select, or identify space-time regions of finite extent. If they could not, many of our demonstrative identifications would fail. Seeing

13. In this Clark differs from Peacocke, for whom the preconceptual content of perceptual experience, referred to in the case of spatial content as a scenario, is more fine grained than usually associated with early vision. Peacocke (1992) makes it clear that his "scenario content" is not the same as the representations posited, say, by Marr (1982). I will return to this idea in the next chapter. Scenario content appears to be equated with the content of the conscious experience of space.

which one, hearing which one, and so on all devolve upon capacities of spatio-temporal discrimination. Sensing sameness of location provides the primal form of identification. Language and world come closest to direct contact in the face-to-face encounters of demonstrative identification. This is also the venue where the rational soul and the sensitive soul must meet. (Ibid., p. 145)

Although there is much in this picture with which I agree (including the emphasis at the end of the last quotation on "demonstrative identification"), I think the basic idea of feature placing as a way of characterizing nonconceptual selection is mistaken. There are many arguments against the appeal to feature placing in the context of sentience (many have been made by, e.g., Keane 2004, and the authors of the special issue of *Philosophical Psychology* [2004, vol. 17, no. 4]), but the arguments against the view that region-selection constitutes the basis for demonstrative identification and for initial selection presented in the previous section are, I believe, decisive. Feature placing requires that the early sensory system deliver information that is roughly equivalent to filling out the two arguments in the propositional frame "Property *P* at location/region *R*." Thus the frame requires that a location be specified when any feature is encoded. Clark does not indicate whether either of the two argument positions can remain empty, and thus whether a region of empty space can serve in this specification. Empty space seems to me to be ruled out by the requirement that whatever is selected must be able to serve as the causal antecedent of a perceptual event. The arguments given in the previous section seem to rule out the feature-placing frame as the basis for preconceptual sensory representation, because no selection of a region can be made unless one has made a prior identification of the object in question—it is always the boundary of the object that determines what region is relevant.

Clark's theory of sentience is important because it lays out some of the boundary conditions that such a theory must meet, and it updates earlier work of Quine and Strawson with empirical results on vision and visual attention. All these writers, however, find themselves appealing to *location* as a way of solving the binding problem. Quine correctly recognizes that just specifying that several properties are present (i.e., specifying that the conjunction of properties is present) is not enough to bind the properties in the right way. If they are to be conjoined properties we must in addition make sure that they are "superimposed" (Quine's term) and then bind them by using existential quantification, stating that $\exists(x)(P(x) \wedge Q(x) \wedge \cdots)$, the way I did in chapter 1, note 4. Quine even says (1992, p. 29) that in doing this "an object has been posited," which sounds like he has embraced our position. But that is not quite so, for an object is conceptual, whereas we are dealing with nonconceptual entities (as we must if we are to have a bridge from the world to conceptual representations). For Quine, as for Strawson, we cannot pick out an individual without the apparatus of concepts, particularly sortal concepts. This is where one has to bite the bullet and accept that there are things that are individuals, in the sense that they endure and can be continuously identified over certain space-time trajectories, but are not objects in the full physical sense (they could not be in the extension of the concept *physical object*, since that would require appeal to some physical theory within which the natural-kind concept is defined—and in any case an unlimited number of physical objects cannot even be seen since they are too small or too big or hidden from view). What we pick out and track are not mental representations but things, which most of the time turn out to be objects in our sort of world.

3.5   What Do FINSTs Select? Some Consequences of the Present View

The claim that we nonconceptually select whatever captures a FINST is a claim that has some rather surprising consequences. FINST selection is a transparent context—we do not select something as a member of some category or as falling under some concept. When I select, say, the rabbit before me, I do not select it under the concept "rabbit" (i.e., as a token of the type "rabbit") or any other concept. The FINST does not distinguish between selecting a rabbit, a rabbit's properties (such as its fur, shape, movement, color), a set of undetached rabbit parts, or any other *coextensive* category, because the selection is not based on a category at all. But if I do not select it under one of those concepts then there is a real sense in which I don't know *what* it is that I have selected (i.e., what type of object it is) even though I know *which* object it is. I have sometimes referred to the thing selected by a FINST as a FING (a term subsequently adopted by Carey and Xu 2001). Since I explicitly reject the condition that selection must be conscious (and in that I differ with many philosophers), it follows that one needn't even have a conscious experience of what one has selected.

Some may find this is a rather surprising position. Indeed, John Campbell has proposed that conscious experience of the referent of a demonstrative is essential for knowing what we are demonstrating: "We need the notion of consciousness in explaining how it is that we have knowledge of the reference of demonstrative terms" (Campbell 2002, p. 136). This may be true for using a demonstrative term in speaking, but in the case of a perceptual demonstrative such as a FINST, we typically do not have conscious experience of its referent unless we apply focal attention to examine it (the issue of the appeal to conscious contents more generally is discussed in chapter 4). It is only at that point that we may conceptualize it. If the FINST is to serve as the first link in the chain between the world and our concepts, then we can't initially "know" the referent. This is the price we have to pay if we are to understand how our conceptualizations can be grounded in causal contact with the world. If we knew what we were selecting, then what we select would fall under a concept. In terms of the previous discussion (section 1.3.2), the selection would constitute a *test* (or a judgment) that applied the concept, rather than what FINST assignment must be, an *interrupt* in which the selection causally imposes itself on our perceptual system (hence I frequently speak of FINSTs being captured or grabbed by the perceptual world).

Here is another way to think of the question being raised in this chapter. What does the early vision system—the modular encapsulated system that does not reason from general knowledge of the world, but merely operates mechanically on the inputs from the world—deliver to the mind? Clearly this modular vision system does not deliver beliefs of the form "there is a truck coming from my left"; it delivers something much more primitive. Exactly how primitive this message is has been the subject of a great deal of philosophical analysis, including the work of Quine and Strawson cited earlier. It is also the focus of Austen Clark's study of sentience. I suggest that it is even more primitive than what can be expressed in Strawson's feature-placing language that Clark adopts (the claim that our initial representation has the form "Feature F at location L"). According to the view I have proposed, what it delivers may be expressed (roughly) in terms of a demonstrative such as *"this"* (although the evidence suggests that there may be four or five such distinct demonstratives: $this_1$, $this_2$, $this_3$, $this_4$). In other words it delivers a reference to a selected sensory individual (call it x) to which the argument of a predicate can be bound, so that properties may be subsequently predicated of x—presumably starting with such predicates as $Object(x)$ or $Location(x, L)$.

Of course there must be some empirical constraints on what can in fact be selected in this way. For example, what is selected must have the causal power to capture a FINST index. Moreover, there is evidence that not just any well-defined cluster of physical features can be selected and tracked—some, like certain arbitrary parts of things, may not lend themselves to being selected and tracked by FINSTs (e.g., in Scholl, Pylyshyn, and Feldman 2001, we showed that the endpoints of lines cannot be selected and tracked), and others may be selected but because of the way they move cannot easily be tracked (e.g., vanMarle and Scholl 2003 showed that objects that appear to liquefy and "pour" from one place to another or that stretch and slink in wormlike fashion can't be tracked). The exact nature of the physical constraints on primitive selection and tracking are empirical questions that we and others are investigating. As scientists we may carry out research to determine the sorts of properties that tend to grab FINSTs. Since these are primitive causal connections, we may not be able easily to specify what these connections are connections to in the general case; they could be connections to any possible link in any causal chain that ends with the appropriate stimulation of the retina (but see below). The category "whatever attracts our attention" may not be a natural kind. Whatever we may discover to be possible properties that cause the assignment of a FINST index, the index itself does not deliver that property or category as part of its function: It just delivers a reference to the primitive selection, to a FING, the way that focal attention might deliver a selection, except that it does it for four or five individuals. According to the view presented here, it is this selection that enables a reference to the selected FING. Moreover, if the FINST was captured by a property P, what the FINST refers to need not be P, but the bearer of P (the FING that has property P). A FINST refers to something that has properties with the causal power to capture it, even though it need not refer to those particular properties (e.g., it might refer to the object that has a unique brightness without referring to its luminance at all). This is the same as my earlier point that there is a distinction between properties that fix a term's reference and the properties that are constitutive of the term's meaning—a distinction that Kripke relied on in his theory of the reference of proper names.

Notice, however, that unlike Kripke's case of fixation of the reference of proper names, where one can appeal to an initial "dubbing" in fixing the referent, the grabbing of a FINST does not involve an intentional act. Since, according to the present story, establishing a FINST is entirely a causal process, the question arises, which link in the causal chain determines what is selected? Not the one intended by someone. In vision, for example, the chain includes the light leaving some light source(s), being reflected from some surface(s), passing through the cornea of the eye and stimulating the rods and cones of our retina. Why not say that the light source or some element of texture of the reflecting surface, or the specks of dust in the air through which the light passed, is what the FINST refers to? I claimed that when properties are encoded, they are encoded as properties of particular FINSTed things—they are represented as $P(x)$ where P is the property-type and x is the thing referred to by the FINST. So it matters which causal link is associated with what the FINST refers to, since that is what the property P

is predicated of. Insofar as selection is a causal process, one might take the position that asking what is causally selected is no different from asking which link in the chain is the cause of the firing of the relevant rods and cones—all links are equally part of the causal story. But that isn't true of referring. There has to be some unique thing that is referred to. As soon as we have a predicate that specifies a property, some particular unique thing is *represented as* having the property in question. So what determines the particular link in the causal chain that has the predicated property? There are several views on this question, which I will not discuss here. It is one of the "big questions" about how reference is naturalized and is beyond the scope of this monograph.[14]

Whatever a FING is, it clearly does not meet the requirements for individuals as understood by Strawson, Quine, and most other philosophers. This selection does not come with conditions of individuation, the mechanism of identity and tenses, and so on. That's because FINGs are not true individuals in the general sense; they are what the visual system gives us in order to bootstrap us into relevant causal contact with the world. This is similar to the situation that faces us in many other logically indeterminate functions such as the visual perception of 3-D shapes from 2-D images, and many other areas of vision, where early vision appears to reflect the natural constraints of our kind of world so as to accomplish apparently conceptual tasks using wired-in concept-free and inference-free methods (examples of such "natural constraints" were discussed in section 2.6.1 and will be developed further in section 5.2.1).

14. Among the candidates for answering the "which link" question are those that appeal to the conscious content (mentioned earlier), a functional role theory (specifically cited in connection with the problem of FINST targets by Levine forthcoming), which says that the referent is determined by the role the FING plays in psychological processes such as inference and action. Another possibility (recently suggested by Fodor, forthcoming, chap. 9) is that counterfactuals may rule out all but the correct link in the causal chain. This proposal works because the reference for which we are trying to give an account is a visual reference, so only currently visible things are relevant and only links in a causal chain to the FINST from some initial but currently visible cause have to be considered (which excludes the big bang, and the switching on of a light earlier, among other things; but it allows the light source if it is visible). Such a chain must pass through some property of the referent. Which property? The answer cannot be determined solely from that one chain—it needs another parameter. According to Fodor's proposal (which he calls a triangulation), if we consider counterfactual causal chains that end with the same FINST but have a slightly different perspective (a slightly different viewer location) then if the chains intersect they will intersect at the link that is the referent of that FINST.

There are many examples where the perceptual system seems to be wired (presumably through evolution) so that it represents information about the world in a way that is constrained so that our representations tend to be veridical most of the time, not in general, but in the kind of world in which we happen to live (our ecological niche). Other examples include such properties as causality and space. Causality, it turns out, is interpreted by the visual system of very young infants who are unlikely to have a working concept of cause—their visual system simply puts into the same category a class of events which we adults would count as exhibiting causality. For example, babies are finely tuned to distinguish between possible causal events such as a moving object hitting another and causing it to be launched into motion, and very similar events in which the timing or the spacing is incompatible with a causal account (Leslie 1982; Leslie and Keeble 1987).[15] This, of course, is not the *concept* "cause," which is a difficult concept even for philosophers to analyze, but it is a perceptual category that is close enough to serve in our kind of limited experience outside of science and philosophical inquiry. Let us call these sorts of categorizations *proto-concepts*, because they may serve as the primitive (and possibly innate) non-conceptual *precursors* of later concepts. Other such proto-concepts may include the abstract category *object* and even *animacy* (Scholl and Tremoulet 2000; Tremoulet and Feldman 2000).

15. Luca Bonatti has argued that infants are sensitive not to causality as such but to continuity in motion, and that a better account of the data can be provided based on principles of object tracking.

4   Conscious Contents and Nonconceptual Representation

4.1   Nonconceptual Representation and Perceptual Beliefs

In the previous chapter I introduced the idea of nonconceptual representation as a form of perceptually derived representation that does not involve concepts and therefore does not enter into beliefs and thoughts (and probably also memories, since they typically involve inferential reconstructions). Nonconceptual representations have been widely discussed in philosophical circles for a number of reasons. One reason concerns the basic problem that we have encountered in several places earlier in this book: the need for a way to get information from its distal causes through proximal effects (e.g., the retinal image) to perceptual beliefs, the latter being conceptual by definition. The interface is thought to involve a type of information-bearing state whose content is more concrete and detailed than is the content of beliefs, but which nonetheless qualifies as being a form of representation because it carries information about some state of affairs in the world. This form of representation does not represent the visual scene in terms of conceptual categories but is more iconic and uninterpreted.

   The primary evidence cited in favor of such a form of representation is the disparity between appearances and beliefs (the hallmark of perceptual illusions) or between the panoramic, uniformly fine-grained nature of our conscious visual experiences and the relatively abstract, categorical, and variable-grained nature of our thoughts, beliefs, and recollections. Moreover, the mapping between the proximal stimulus and how the scene appears to us is not fixed, which itself needs to be explained. For example, when we look at an ambiguous figure such as a Necker cube (shown in the left panel of figure 4.1), *something* changes over time as we watch, and that something is not the physical stimulus, nor is it generally thought to be our beliefs about what we see. It is what we usually refer to as the *appearance* of the figure or how we consciously experience it. Since the content of our experience seems to be distinct both from the proximal stimulus (the optical projection of the figure on our retina) and from what we believe about the figure, this suggests that we need another vehicle of representation for that type of content.

When we examine a visual scene, the content of our experience is very different from what we know to be the information that enters the visual system. The evidence is clear that the incoming information is highly incomplete and has a narrow scope (it is literally a moving peephole no more than about two degrees of visual angle) compared with how we experience it (this point will be discussed later in connection with the special case of the experience of space). But the experience also seems intuitively different from what we might plausibly capture in terms of the vocabulary of concepts we are likely to have. The argument from the richness of experience compared with the relative poverty of our conceptual resources depends both on how we characterize experience and on what we think are the conceptual resources of the mind. But even without considering the fine points of what are reasonable bounds on our conceptual apparatus, it seems clear that we are unlikely to have as many distinct concepts for, say, colors, as there are colors that we can discriminate. Certainly if we consider the number of color terms in known languages we find that the number is actually very small (languages have no more than about 11 monoleximic words; see Berlin and Kay 1969). Yet we can distinguish well over a million different colors (Halsey and Chapanis 1951), so it is unlikely that we encode each of these as a separate concept or code. (Of course there are many more concepts than there are words. But since each word corresponds to some concept, it seems reasonable that each concept is at least a *potential word* in some language. A million different colors is far more than the total human vocabulary, so it seems unreasonable to suppose that every discriminable color could have a corresponding concept.)

Notwithstanding such plausible arguments for nonconceptual representations, there are several questions that need to be considered and several tacit assumptions that need to be exposed before the hypothesis that there is a nonconceptual representation of the sort generally accepted in philosophy can be taken as established. The most contentious of these is the assumption that the content of this nonconceptual representation is the same as the content of conscious experience. This view assumes that the content of conscious experience corresponds to a level of representation in an information-processing or functional analysis of the cognitive system. In other words, it assumes that the content of conscious experience is a natural kind for purposes of psychological explanation. I take up this and other issues in the next few sections.

4.2   The Role of Conscious Experience in the Study of Perception and Cognition

Cognitive science, and particularly vision science, has had a deeply ambivalent relation with the phenomenon of conscious experience. On one hand, the way things appear or what they look like has always been an important, if not the primary, source of data, at least for vision science. When one thing looks bigger in one condition than in another or looks to be moving faster under one condition than another, or when colors appear different under one lighting condition than another, these are considered primary data to which theories of vision are expected to respond. On the other hand, the content of a person's experience has also proven to be one of the most misleading sources of evidence, because it is not neutral with respect to the theories that the subject holds, be they scientific or folk theories. Moreover, which explanations appear most natural is highly sensitive to the way we describe our experiences, and conversely, the way we describe our experiences (even to ourselves) depends to a large extent on what tacit theories we hold.

The way we describe our perceptual experiences often caries with it the implication that the content of the experience itself *explains* observed phenomena—that the occurrence of experience X causes experience Y which then explains some ensuing behavior. There are more or less benign versions of this sort of what might be called intentional causation (also sometimes referred to as psychological determinism; Hochberg 1968). An important and essentially irreproachable version of this thesis is the appeal to the tight coupling that holds between how a part of a scene is experienced and how other parts of the scene tend to be experienced (see Epstein 1982; Rock 1997). For example, if you see the edge of a Necker cube marked x (in figure 4.1) as being the top front edge of the figure, then you are likely to see the face of which it is a part as the top face (as in the second panel); but if, instead, you see the edge marked y as being the top front edge, then you will see the face that it bounds as the top edge of the figure and the appearance of all the other edges will change so the interpretation of the figure remains coherent. When the percept changes (as it does in ambiguous figures such as in the first panel) the couplings force the interpretation of related parts to change accordingly. This fact has been the basis for a successful technique in computer vision called *constraint propagation* (see the

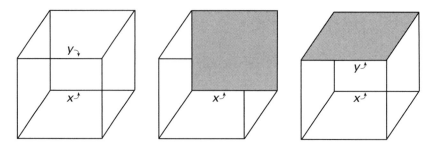

Figure 4.1
The way we see edges is intimately connected with the way we see the faces those edges bound. These appearances (or "ways of seeing") form a tightly coupled system. If our percept of one part changes, the appearance of other parts change systematically in order to maintain the coherence of the whole. Panels 2 and 3 show the two versions of the ambiguous figure in the first panel. Notice how the interpretation of an edge is connected to the interpretation of the faces it bounds and that both interpretations change together when the ambiguous percept in the first panel "flips."

work on the "blocks world" that culminated in the successful system devised by David Waltz, described in, among other places, Pylyshyn 2003, chap. 3; Waltz 1975). (It is also the basis of an approach to models of reasoning using constraint satisfaction; Tsang 1993.)

When we speak of labels on the representation of a scene, or indeed when we speak of what a pattern is seen as, we are speaking of the contents of a perceptual representation. In most cases such contents are assumed to be conscious; hence we are speaking of the contents of a perceptual experience. But what exactly *is* the content of a conscious perceptual experience? The content of a belief is relatively clear, because beliefs are individuated in part by their contents—that is, we identify a belief by what it is about, or we may treat beliefs that are about the same thing as the same belief (I am ignoring for now the fact that beliefs can differ in ways other than in their content, e.g., their form). But what about the content of a conscious experience? The situation here is not at all straightforward.

4.2.1 The Contents Question

The role that conscious experience can play in vision science depends on our understanding of what such experience reveals. Our first impression is that what conscious experience reveals is both private and obvious to the person who experiences it: if you see something or other, then what the experience reveals is just *what you see*. But if you try to say what that is, you find it is far from straightforward. Indeed there is a long chapter in the history of psychology of the late nineteenth and early twentieth centuries, where that question was at the forefront of discussions of what psychology is and what it should be (Titchener 1912; Washburn 1922).[1] The *introspective method* was taught as an objective way to study the contents of conscious experience by turning the mind on itself in a disciplined analytical manner, freeing it to report its own conscious contents, as opposed to reporting properties of the object of our perception (inadvertently being influenced by what one knew about the objects of perception was known as the *stimulus error*). In the end the method failed to provide the foundations for a science of conscious experience, although conscious experience itself continues to be a growing concern in both psychology and philosophy.[2] It is not my purpose here to discuss introspection or to look at the fascinating history of the study of consciousness in psychology. I wish only to point out some of the problems raised by the use of conscious contents as a source of evidence for building theories of perception.

There are two sets of questions about our conscious awareness. One is what might be called the objective scientific question: What are we entitled to conclude about perception from certain perceptual experiences we have? The other, logically prior question is what the content of our perceptual experience is: What is the thing about which questions of interpretation can be raised? This question is independent of methodological issues concerned with how one should interpret reports of "how something looks." The question even applies to one's understanding of the content of one's own conscious experiences. The question—*what do I experience when I look at this stimulus?*—is fraught with problems. One might reasonably take the position that to ask what we experience is already to take a theoretical stand, namely that the content of the experience is transparent to the person who experiences it; it is part of what Sellars (1956) called "the given." There has been a considerable amount of philosophical discussion of this question. The assumption that one is the infallible arbiter of the content of one's conscious experience has serious problems, particularly if one takes

---

1. For original writings from this era, and earlier, see the interesting website "Classics in the History of Psychology" maintained by Christopher D. Green at York University, Toronto, Canada: http://psychclassics.yorku.ca/index.htm/.
2. The Association for the Scientific Study of Consciousness (ASSC) has become a major scholarly society with a large annual meeting where, among other things, the relation between brain and consciousness is discussed and neuropsychologists report various fascinating brain damage syndromes in which patients exhibit disconnects between behavior and conscious contents. See http://assc.caltech.edu/index.htm/.

it to have conceptual content—that is, to be the experience *as of* something or other.

Consider what we experience when we look at a scene. Suppose I look at the wall of my room; what is the content of my conscious experience? If I try to describe what I am experiencing I find myself describing the things in the room and their visible properties (such as color, texture, or location). My conscious experience is the experience of the things that I perceive (possibly also what these things remind me of and what feelings they may arouse, but let's confine ourselves to the perceptual experience itself). How exactly can I describe what I experience? Does it consist of all the properties that are in the scene, or only those that I notice? Do I experience only what is present in the incoming information, or does my experience also include what the visual system "fills in" and what I infer? For example, do I experience the uniformity of the color and lightness of the wall which, as it happens, I know is not in fact uniformly illuminated? Is the uniformity of lightness and color constancy that I am describing an inference or a direct experiential content? The lightness you perceive is known to depend on your perception of the location and arrangement of the surfaces in question (Gilchrist 1977). Also in a typical scene it is rare that I see all of any object because most things will be at least partially occluded by others, even though I do not notice these occlusions unless they are brought to my attention. It thus appears that the content of my experience includes postconstancy and post-filling-in information, and therefore, my experience relies on more than just the information coming from my eyes.

Let's continue with this example. There is a picture on the wall. Do I experience it *as a picture* or do I experience what the picture depicts—or both? There is also a calendar on the wall which I see and which is therefore part of my experience. Since I forgot to change the page at the end of last month it shows the wrong month. Do I experience it *as a calendar*, and do I experience it *as* showing the wrong month? Ordinary informal talk is unclear on such issues. If I do experience it as a calendar showing the wrong month, then other people looking at the wall are unlikely to have the same experience as I do unless they know what I know about the calendar. I look down at my desk and see a sculpture that serves as a paperweight (or perhaps vice versa, depending on how you feel about such pieces). I see it as a three-dimensional object that has not only a front but also a back and sides and parts that are hidden or occluded by other parts. Do I experience only the front, or only the parts that are not occluded, or do I experience the back and the hidden parts as well? I do not see the back in the sense that I receive no optical information from it, so how can it be part of my experience? Some writers in the Gibson "direct perception" tradition claim that we *see* the back of 3-D objects as well as the front because both are part of the experience of what Alva Noë (2004) calls the *perceptual presence*, which is different from our *knowledge* of the back of a perceived object. This may actually be the more common view. For example, Block (1995) says that if you are looking at a row of buildings and then find out that they are mere fronts of a movie set, the content of your conscious experience changes. According to Block, the visual experience as of a façade is different from the visual experience as of a building. If that is the case, then conscious content is clearly cognitively penetrable, which affects the role it can play in a perceptual theory. It cannot, for example, serve as the imput to vision, as what some philosophers call the "given."

Many also say that what we see, our perceptual experience, is *viewpoint independent*, which implies that we represent it as a solid without giving special status to the surface that faces the viewer. By contrast others insist that what we see is just the front of 3-D objects, and thus that what we see clearly depends on our viewpoint. David Marr's theory of vision explicitly provides a middle ground by proposing what he called a "$2\frac{1}{2}$-D sketch," which is a representation in depth of only the visible surfaces. Which of these is the content of our experience? For Gaetano Kanizsa (Kanizsa and Gerbino 1982), the perceptual reconstruction of occluded contours is an automatic and cognitively impenetrable stage in the process of seeing (I have also defended this view in Pylyshyn 1999). According to this view, what we experience when we see is not the incoming information but is a complex output of our early vision system together with some inferences, perhaps from other parts of the scene or perhaps from our knowledge and expectations of what is in the scene. Is all this part of our conscious perceptual content? It is certainly what we mean when we report what something "looks like," so at least in the everyday sense it is part of our conscious content. Where do we draw the line? In Pylyshyn 2003 (chap. 1) I give examples to illustrate that the everyday nontechnical sense of "what something looks like" is very broad and includes visual puns of the sort popularized by Roger Price in what he called "droodles" (see http://www.droodles.com/).

In several thoughtful essays, Fred Dretske (e.g., Dretske 1993, 2006) adds to the perplexity for those who would appeal to the content of conscious experience in building theories of vision, by arguing that we may not always be aware of the content of our experience. That's because, according to Dretske, there is a difference between being conscious of things and being conscious of facts. That one is conscious of something is itself a fact of which we may or may not be conscious. Dretske gives the example of looking at a wall made of hundreds of orange bricks. Given enough time to scan the wall, does our experience include the experience of *each* of the bricks? Dretske claims it does, because if asked whether there was a blue brick among the orange ones we can confidently answer *no*. Dretske claims that this implies that we saw (and experienced) *each* of the bricks since the information that there was no blue brick depends on having been conscious of the properties of each brick.[3] Yet if asked we might, quite reasonably, claim that we were not conscious of each of the bricks. According to Dretske that just shows that we need not be aware of the conscious content of our perception. Other philosophers have also spoken about the difference between phenomenal and nonphenomenal consciousness (e.g., Lormand 1996), thus further complicating the problem of using conscious contents for theory construction.

There are many examples of our being unaware of information that was readily perceivable and that, by other criteria, was in fact perceived. The question one might ask of each of them is whether they are cases in which we are not conscious of the information, or cases in which we are conscious of the information but were unaware that we were conscious of it. Examples include various cases of apparent functional "blindness." One of the best-known examples is referred to as *change blindness*. In these demonstrations subjects are unable to report the change between two alternating briefly presented pictures even though the difference between the two pictures is clearly visible when attention is drawn to it (Simons and Levin 1997; Simons and Rensink 2005). Another example is *inattentional blindness*, in which subjects fail to see a clearly visible feature that occurs at precisely the point where they were visually fixated while they are attending to a more peripheral item (Mack and Rock 1998). Another such example that is extremely persuasive and puzzling involves watching a movie with several players who are passing a ball around while the subject is required to count the number of passes. In this example many subjects are unaware of a person dressed in a gorilla suit who walks right through the middle of the scene (Simons and Chabris 1999). These types of blindness appear to

---

3. In this example, however, judging that there were no blue bricks is likely an *inference* of the form: (1) If there had been one clearly visible blue brick I would have seen it; (2) I did not notice a blue brick; therefore (3) there was no blue brick. Thus it does not entail that information from each brick was perceptually (consciously) available, only that the perceiver believes that if there had been a blue brick he would have seen it. This is known in the computational inference field as *negation as failure* and is entailed by the *closed world assumption* that is part of the logic programming language Prolog. (See entry in Wikipedia.org.)

involve a failure of information to reach consciousness even though the information is in some sense clearly taken in since it is located on the fovea directly in view. In fact, Dretske (2006) claims that the lesson we should take from such examples is precisely that one can be conscious of something and at the same time be unaware that one is conscious of it.

The distinction between consciousness of things and consciousness of facts is similar in spirit, and might perhaps even be subsumed under, the distinction between *phenomenal consciousness* and *access consciousness* advocated by Ned Block (1995). According to Block, there are two functions of consciousness that should be distinguished: the purely phenomenal function (characterized as "what it is like to be in that state") and the access function (characterized as states in which information is "poised to be used as a premise in reasoning,... the rational control of action ... and speech," Block 1995, p. 230). These are referred to as P-consciousness and A-consciousness, respectively. These two functions are not only conceptually distinct but also may involve different neural mechanisms (Block 2005). According to this view it is possible to have a vivid phenomenally conscious experience that does not "broadcast" information to other mental processes, and thus it is possible to have functional access to information that is accompanied by little or no phenomenal experience. Although Block often talks as though these were two forms of consciousness, he means a "phenomenal aspect" or "phenomenal content" in contrast to "representational aspect" or "representational content" of consciousness. Although these two aspects nearly always occur together they are conceptually separable, and in some cases empirically separated, as when one or the other is damaged by brain lesions. As we have already seen, various types of "blindness" demonstrate information access without phenomenal consciousness. Cases of phenomenal content without access (without representational content) are more difficult to find inasmuch as the best evidence for phenomenal content takes the form of verbal reports which *ipso facto* constitutes evidence for informational access.[4] The best example may come from split-brain patients who are able to carry out certain tasks

---

4. Rosenthal (2005, pp. 191–192) argues that it is hard to reconcile cases of P-consciousness without A-consciousness with the understanding of P-consciousness as "what it would be like" to be in that state, since there is no way to be in that state unless one is aware of it—i.e., without there being some A-conscious aspect we can use to identify those states. This debate is of interest for an understanding of the nature of conscious states, but it does not bear on the current point which is concerned with what we can learn about perception if we set "conscious content" as an explanandum.

without being aware of why they are making the choices they make (discussed in section 4.3.2 below).

Another quite different view of consciousness is provided by David Rosenthal (2005), who argues that consciousness consists of being the target of "higher-order thoughts" (HOTs) or of having noninferential (unmediated and typically unconscious) thoughts about one's thoughts. This view, like other views about what it is to be conscious, deals with issues that are beyond the scope of the present discussion. I mention the HOT view, however, because although it is certainly very different from those of Dretske or Block, it does have room to encompass the distinction between conscious experience and awareness of conscious experience or between P-consciousness and A-consciousness. As long as you think that thoughts about thoughts are a real possibility and recognize that they (sometimes) underwrite conscious contents, you might consider cases where thoughts about thoughts do not yield conscious states, and also cases in which conscious states can arise from thoughts about other sorts of mental states besides thoughts (e.g., desires, acts of will). Because all three views allow for a certain degree of independence between qualitative experience and information-processing functions, all these options allow the possibility of being conscious of something without being aware of what you are conscious of, or of phenomenal consciousness without access consciousness and vice versa.

My point here is not to advocate a particular way of interpreting the notion of conscious experience, but merely to point out that while the content of experience is important for building theories of perception, it is encumbered with many problems. At the very least the examples above show that whether something is or is not part of the content of our experience is not self-evident, so experiential content is not something we can take at face value merely on the grounds that since it is *your* experience you alone are the authority on its content. In addition, there is no reason why you should be able to say what the theoretically relevant aspect of the experience is and, even worse, you can also get this wrong—as we will see in other examples I will provide below.

4.2.2   Conscious Experience and Public Report

Reports by subjects of what something looks like are even more problematic since what people report in an experimental setting is known to be affected by many factors, including what subjects think the experimenter wants (such compliance effects have been called *experimenter demands*), what they believe the task to be (which have been called *task demands*) as well as subjects' general beliefs and utilities. Every response requires making a decision that may involve weighing the costs (including embarrassment) of different sorts of errors, particularly errors of commission versus errors of omission. For example, work on subliminal perception or "perceptual defense" shows that accuracy in reporting whether one has "seen" a briefly presented word is different for taboo words than for neutral words equated for frequency of occurrence (Freeman 1955). These are typically not cases of subjects being disingenuous, but of making rational choices—choices that can be traced to processes described by models of decision making, such as utility theory and signal-detection theory. Sometimes signal-detection theory can separate contents from reporting biases in a fairly direct way by providing different measures for *response criteria* (the parameter usually written as β) and for *sensitivity* (the parameter $\mathbf{d}'$) in experiments involving thresholds. This is done by taking into account not only the correct responses, but also the relative rate of errors of omission and errors of commission. If the subject has a bias to report seeing something independently of whether there was a signal, then both the hit rate and the rate of errors of commission will increase. Such a bias would be useful if the signal were present on most of the trials or if the utility of detecting the signal was high (e.g., if it signaled danger). If, on the other hand, the subject has a conservative bias, then the hit rate will be lowered but the rate of errors of omission will also increase. This sort of bias would be useful if the signal were present only rarely. These tendencies can be used to separate response bias from the availability of conscious contents (Snodgrass 2002). Experimental psychology has learned that sincere reports of conscious contents have to be evaluated in relation to other sources of evidence and in the light of developing theories.

Consider, for example, the problem of interpreting such findings as those reported by Wittreich (1959). A well-known illusion is that when people walk across the floor of a specially designed room called the Ames room (shown in figure 4.2) they appear to change in size.[5] Wittreich confirmed

5. It does not reveal a magician's proprietary trick to tell you that the room is actually distorted, having been constructed with one side much lower and shallower than the other. The design specifications are such that rays drawn from a peephole to every visual feature—i.e., corner and vertex (the room has windows)—bear the same visual angles to one another as they would in a regular rectangular room. Thus when viewed through the peephole all the visual cues in the Ames room are identical to those that would have been available in its corresponding phantom rectangular room. Of course it is not possible to build a distorted room such that the illusion persists as the viewer moves inside the room, though this could (almost) be

Figure 4.2
From a fixed peephole vantage point the Ames room seems like a normal rectangular room, but people in the room look to be different sizes depending on where they stand. (© The Exploratorium, www.exploratorium.edu, used with permission.)

this observation, but he also found that this did not happen when the people were well known to the observer—for example, the observer's spouse— even if these people were accompanied by a stranger, whose size did appear to change! Notwithstanding the presumably sincere reports made by the subjects, there remains the question whether to interpret this finding as showing the malleability of judgments of the content of conscious experience, or of the operation of the visual system itself. The problem is not that subjects are disingenuous, but simply that the lines between what we report and what we believe with great conviction, as well as between what we report to others and what we report to ourselves, are not so clear. If, as many have supposed (e.g., Block 1995; Dennett 1991), part of conscious content is what vision (or imagination) reports to the rest of the mind,

---

done in an electronic virtual reality room (the reason for the qualifier is that VR displays cannot reproduce all cues exactly; in particular, since objects are not actually located at different depths but on the same 2-D surface, the eyes do not focus at different depths, which results in some conflicting cues).

then what it reports may be different from the information that it actually possesses. In other words, there may well be a partial dissociation between the content of our conscious experience and the information that is passed on to other stages in mental processing. Sometimes we can show this fairly directly by comparing measures from which the reporting bias has been mathematically factored out, as we do when we use the signal-detection measure d' rather than percent correct. Such measures not only separate what information observers have from what they report to an experimenter, but also from what observers report to themselves—that is, what they are aware of. More often than not, general questions such as this are ultimately adjudicated according to whether a theory that takes certain observations at face value simply misses underlying (causal, functional) principles.

Focusing on the conscious contents of perception has also encouraged *direct perception theories* (such as those of Gibson 1979), which claim that perception allows us to directly access ("pick up") information about properties of the world that are prominent in our experience, such as the property that things have of being suitable for certain purposes—from being eaten to being sat upon (suitability is referred to as having certain "affordances"). James J. Gibson has argued, quite reasonably, that we see not patterns of light and shadow and patches of color, but familiar things such as tables, chairs, and people. Moreover, we never see just the front surface of objects; we see entire objects and we see them as particular things, such as our car or our spouse, or as having certain affordances, such as being graspable or edible. Although the urge to shun visual representations led Gibson and his followers to embrace what is essentially a behaviorist position, they were right to claim that perception eventuates in the extraction of abstract properties rather than low-level sensory patterns ("sensations"). The moral of this observation should have been that what we see is a reconstruction of the properties of distal objects: we never experience the preconstancy proximal stimulus. But in direct realism theories (for various modern versions, see Smith 2003) this is not the moral that is drawn. Rather, these observations are taken to be an indictment of the view that perception begins with properties as described by physical science and constructs a representation of a scene (perhaps in some cases with the aid of inference from general knowledge). Instead, they are taken as support for the radical view that the world should be redescribed according to the categories of experience, which are assumed to be the starting point of perception; these are the categories to which perception is inherently attuned and which are "picked up" the way a tuning fork picks up the notes in its immediate environment. To make this picture work Gibson also had to deal with the problem of misperception, which, in turn, led him the view that theories should be applied to perception in an "ecologically valid" environment (for a critical discussion of these ideas, see Fodor and Pylyshyn 1981; Pylyshyn 1984, chap. 6). Although it is not usually put in this way, it is the temptation to see the categories of conscious experience as the primitive bases for (or inputs to) perception that has been one of the siren calls of direct realism.

Notice that the position I have been describing in this book bears some similarity to Gibson's. I too do not believe that we should take the starting point of vision (the nonconceptual first steps) to be sensations, if by sensations we mean consciously experienced colors, shapes, textures, and so on (or whatever the primitive sensations turn out to be). Rather, the starting point should be nonconceptual, in particular it should be nonconceptual demonstrative references to proto-objects or FINGS.

4.3   What Subjective Experience Reveals about Psychological Processes

In this section I will move quickly through some evidence showing that attempts to infer the nature of psychological processes from the evidence of conscious experience have led us into blind alleys in a number of areas of psychology. I will conclude that the problem arises when one views the content of conscious experience as anything but fallible evidence, which has to be assessed in comparison to evidence from psychophysics and neuroscience.

4.3.1   The Illusion of Conscious Will

The conscious experience of deciding and of willing an action has been called "the mind's best trick" (Wegner 2002, 2003). Daniel Wegner has reviewed a great deal of evidence that points to there being large and frequent discrepancies between how and when we have the experience of willing some action and the actual causal antecedents of the action. The research comes from many different phenomena and reveals such things as the following.

(1)   The experience of willing an action and the actual decision to act can be dissociated   It has been shown by neurophysiological evidence that the experience of willing an action comes at least 0.3 seconds and maybe even longer *after* the effective decision for the action has occurred (these experiments are reviewed in Libet 2004).

(2)   The experience of personal agenthood or authorship of actions can occur when actions are controlled by someone else   This is shown in a variety of experiments but can be seen most dramatically in the so-called rubber-hand illusion, in which by the use of mirrors, the experimenter's (or someone else's) hand is optically located where the subject feels his or her hand to be, and the manipulation of the seen hand's fingers is done by the experimenter. In this dramatic illusion, the movements of the hand appear to the observer to be his or her own actions. The illusion persists until some major discrepancy occurs (e.g., the faux hand is withdrawn while the subject's hand remains in place).

(3)   The experience of other-controlled action can occur when the action is that of the experiencer   This is the converse of the rubber hand illusion and has been demonstrated in many controlled experiments, but also occurs frequently in such settings as dowsing ("water witching"), Ouija boards, and other "spirit" manifestations where it has been shown that the subject is unwittingly doing the controlling.

A critical aspect of perceived agenthood comes from the timing of events. Just as we experience causality between objects in such demonstrations as Michotte's tunnel, so we experience ourselves as the cause of some action when the timing is appropriate. Recall that in the Michotte demonstrations, if an object disappears behind an opaque surface (an occluder) and an object appears on the other side at an appropriate time, the experience is one of a single object disappearing and then reappearing on the other side of the occluder; or if an object collides with a stationary object which begins to move and the timing is appropriate, the experience is that the collision by the first object causes the previously stationary object to begin to move. The same sort of perception of causality appears to work where the first event is the *experience of willing* and the second is some *visible action*; then, with the appropriate timing, the subjective experience of will is perceived as being the cause of the action.

The conscious experience of will is not exactly the same as the conscious experience that arises in visual or auditory perception—it is not a sensory experience or a sensation—but it is a conscious experience nonetheless. The person who has the experience reports the clear *perception* that he or she has initiated an action (or in some cases that he or she did not initiate an action and therefore that someone or something else had done so). These are just the sorts of experiences that make their way into the corpus of data that lend support to one or another theory of perception; they are the "experience *that*" something or other has occurred, or the *"experience as"* of something or other. So the point here is the same as it was in other cases where the contents of conscious experience are used in building theories of perception: The opportunity for being misled by illusion remains.

4.3.2 Conscious Experience, Interpretation, and Confabulation

Closely related to the illusion of conscious will are cases where observers falsely report the *reasons* for their observed behaviors or the steps they go through in reasoning. The answers people often give to *why* and *how* questions are based on their conscious experience of their mental processes. The most egregious cases of mistaken reports of psychological processes arise in the case of reports of reasoning with the aid of mental images, and I will spend some time on this special case later in this chapter. Other cases arise when people are asked to report why they said or did something. Among those investigators who made the most of reports of how and why subjects made certain moves in playing a game like chess, or in solving slow and deliberate problems such as problems in logic, were Allan Newell and Herb Simon, whose work on problem solving appeared in an important book (Newell and Simon 1972). In those studies they made a great deal of use of "thinking out loud" protocols, in which subjects indicated what they were thinking as they attempted to solve a problem, as well as why they were considering various options. Even though the problems chosen for analysis were ones that were solved slowly and deliberately and made little use of prior knowledge, Newell and Simon still found that they had to fill in and refine the recorded protocols in various ways. One problem was that subjects rarely disclosed all the moves they considered or the reasons they had for considering and rejecting them. A large number of these intermediate "states of knowledge" went unreported and had to be inferred from other states that were mentioned and from the rational demands of the problem-solving process. Even among the states that were reported, many had to be discounted because they played no obvious role in the reasoning path (called a "problem behavior graph") but seemed rather after-the-fact reconstructions (much the way that recollections are typically reconstructions, as shown in the classical work by Bartlett 1932). The best such problem-behavior paths were inferred by including additional sources of evidence, such as eye movements, that proved to be more reliable indicators of what the subject was focused on at various points in time. Thus even under the rather favorable conditions of slow, deliberate, and frequently conscious problem solving, the reports of conscious states required a great deal of reconstruction by the theorist. In other words, the reports were treated as fallible sources of evidence.

In social psychology, the idea that we are extremely poor at expressing the processes and causes of our behavior by introspecting our conscious thoughts is well known (Nisbett and Valins 1987; Nisbett and Wilson 1977). Although we think we know why we do things or why we make the choices we do, the evidence shows the contrary (as we already saw in the studies of the experience of conscious will in section 4.3.1 above). The reasons we give ourselves and others are more often than not fabrications based on intuitive folk psychology theories. In addition, the methodology of asking people what they are aware of thinking in the course of planning some action is clearly unsuited for studying such processes as understanding a sentence, where almost none of the process is available to conscious scrutiny. In very many cases subjects have no information or conflicting information about their mental processes, and when forced to provide reports they simply manufacture ("confabulate") explanations and rationalizations as best they can.

There has been a great deal of interest in recent years in widespread observations of confabulation, in which people provide descriptions of their mental processes when they do not have the relevant information. Particularly relevant cases are those in which people do not have access to information about why they made a particular choice (verbally or manually) yet they nonetheless provide a coherent story for why they did what they did (see, e.g., Hirstein 2005). Confabulation is quite frequently reported among patients with dysfunctions that prevent them from accessing the correct information for one reason or another. For example, it is often found in patients with large scotomas (blind regions in their vision) that prevent them from receiving information from large parts of the scene. People with these scotomas are often unaware of having blind spots, yet they (incorrectly) report patterns in the region of the scotoma (in fact everyone has a blind spot where retinal fibers leave the eye, though most are unaware of it). There are also some remarkable cases of blind people who insist that they are not blind (denial of obvious impairments is known as *anosognosia* and the special case of blindness is sometimes called *Anton's syndrome*). These patients guess at what they are shown, and then confabulate elaborate explanations of why they misidentify things by sight or why they bump into things (Hirstein 2005; McDaniel and McDaniel 1991). Conversely, there have been patients who exhibit an even more astounding capacity to make some *correct* judgments of the location and shape of patterns in their ostensibly "blind" field, while insisting that they can see nothing there. These are the famous cases of what is called *blindsight* (Bornstein and Pittman 1992; Weiskrantz 1995). Blindsight and other types of agnosias have attracted the interest of students of consciousness because they demonstrate the dissociation of functional vision from conscious visual experience.

An important point in all these examples is that subjects are perfectly sincere in what they report; they do not feel that they are making up answers even though they could not have known the true (and rational) basis for their answers. There are very many things that we do not know but are not aware that we do not know. The contemporary study of what is called *metacognition* is in part about that. Just as we have the *tip-of-the-tongue* phenomenon where we feel we almost have the word we are looking for, so there is the *feeling-of-knowing* (or the feeling-of-not-knowing) which often convinces us that we either know something that we do not, or that we do not know something that is just below the conscious horizon (for examples of this sort of phenomenon, see the collection of papers in Metcalfe and Shimamura 1994). When we think we know something that we do not know, we often engage in confabulation—we make up a plausible story.

4.3.3   Failures of Conscious Access: Split Brains and Split Visual Systems

Confabulation is most clearly illustrated in so-called *split-brain* patients—patients in whom nerve fibers (called the corpus callosum) that normally connect the right and left half of their brain are either congenitally missing or were surgically severed to ameliorate severe epileptic symptoms. In these patients, experiences that occur in one hemisphere are not available to processes in the other hemisphere. Since information from the right half of each retina goes to the left hemisphere, control of the right hand is from the left hemisphere, and most language functions are in the left hemisphere, it is possible to set up experiments in which half the brain has the information and the other half has to make a response. Michael Gazzaniga has studied these patients extensively and has reported cases where information is presented to the mute right cerebral hemisphere where it is used to make a right-hemisphere controlled response (say, a pointing with the left hand). The patients are then asked *why* they made the response they did. In these cases the left hemisphere that has language must respond—but it does not have access to the relevant information, since it was the right hemisphere that received the visual information and made the response. In such cases the left (linguistic) hemisphere generally confabulates an answer. Confabulation in split-brain patients has been described extensively (see the summary in Gazzaniga 1995; Gazzaniga 2000).

One example that Gazzaniga gives is the case in which different pictures were shown to the two hemispheres of a split-brain patient (referred to as patient PS). The left hemisphere was shown a picture of a chicken claw while the (mute) right hemisphere was flashed a picture of a snow scene. Then an array of pictures was shown to the subject that included a chicken and a shovel, and the patient was asked to choose one related to the pictures he had seen earlier, making one choice with each hand. The patient chose the shovel with his left hand (controlled by the mute right hemisphere which saw the snow scene) and the chicken with his right hand (controlled by his linguistic left hemisphere which saw the chicken claw), even though the patient could not report seeing the snow scene (since it had been shown to the mute right hemisphere). When asked why he chose the chicken and shovel he (or rather his left hemisphere) replied, "Oh that's simple. The chicken claw goes with the chicken and a shovel is needed to clean out the chicken shed." To account for the way that the speaking hemisphere takes on the task of providing a rationale for the apparent inconsistency, Michael Gazzaniga has proposed a theory that credits the left hemisphere with the task of integrating information, both information that it possesses directly (if it is a left-hemisphere function) and information it gathers indirectly by observing some of the behavior controlled by the mute right hemisphere. There were also puzzling examples in which the linguistic left hemisphere was able to give the right answer to something that had been shown to the right hemisphere. Upon careful analysis, it turned out that the left hemisphere had observed the response made by the right hemisphere (in one case it had heard a sound that allowed it to figure out that the left hand, controlled by the right hemisphere, had touched a brush) and inferred what it had seen, but was unaware that the verbal response was related to this information.

These examples are relevant to the question of what reports of conscious states are about and what they imply with respect to their use in building theories of visual processing. In the split-brain cases, the left hemisphere (which has language and therefore answers the *why* question) faces a conflict between what it experiences and what it infers from watching the actions of the left hand (controlled by the mute right hemisphere), leading to a guess of what might have happened—that is, a confabulation. Yet patients report that their phenomenal experience in answering the questions in these strange cases is the same as their experience in cases where things are normal (i.e., when both hemispheres have the relevant information).

Many of the split-brain examples involve a conflict between two different sources of knowledge (in the two cerebral hemispheres), but there are also many cases where there is no conflict, just the failure of consciousness to access the information that in fact determined an action. This arises frequently under conditions where the motor system is able to act on the basis of information that is unavailable to the conscious recognition system, because of a brain injury that prevents the information from reaching the part of the visual system responsible for sensory consciousness. An outstanding example of this is the famous case, studied by Milner and Goodale (Goodale and Milner 2004), of patient DF, who, because of severe bilateral damage in the ventral part of her visual-motor cortex, could not recognize the simplest patterns but could react appropriately and accurately to the same information when executing actions such as adjusting her hand orientation and grasp size while reaching for the article that she was unable to identify or even describe.

This independence of vision for conscious experience and vision for action occurs because the visuomotor system resides largely in the dorsal part of the brain—the part that feeds information from the eye through posterior parietal cortex to the motor system—whereas the conscious recognition system consists primarily of activity in the ventral part of the visual system (which routes information through inferotemporal cortex). In many experiments reported by David Milner and Melvyn Goodale (Milner and Goodale 1995) it was shown that in both animals and humans, the part of the nervous system that is in the dorsal visual pathway works differently from the part that is in the ventral pathway. Dorsal processing works rapidly, is more responsive to magnitudes (size, distance, location), and is relatively insensitive to the sorts of visual illusions in which visual context results in an inaccurate experience of size, distance, or motion. For example, if a subject reaches to grasp a circle whose apparent size is altered so it appears larger than it really is by virtue of being surrounded by smaller circles (or made to look smaller by being surrounded by large circles), which occurs in the Ebbinghaus or "size contrast" illusion, the grasp-control process is not fooled by the illusion but sets the grasp to the correct size (Aglioti, DeSouza, and Goodale 1995). In another example, a subject reaches for an object that is displaced during the saccadic eye movement that precedes the arm movement. Because of saccadic suppression, the subject is unaware of seeing any change in the object's location, yet the (dorsal) reaching system seamlessly corrects for the displacement (Goodale, Pelisson, and Prablanc 1986).

Studies by Wong and Mack (1981), subsequently confirmed by Bridgeman (1992) using a different methodology, showed that the information available to consciousness can be put in direct conflict with the information used by the motor system. The Wong and Mack study involved a luminous dot and frame shown in the dark. The target and frame both jumped in the same direction, although the target did not jump as far as the frame. Because of induced motion, the target appeared to jump in the opposite direction to the frame. Wong and Mack found that the saccadic eye movements resulting from subjects' attempts to follow the target were in the actual direction of the target's motion, even though the perceived motion was in the opposite direction. However, if the response was delayed, the tracking saccade followed the perceived (illusory) direction of movement, showing that the motor-control system could use only immediate visual information, even though the conscious experience is the same in the two cases. In all these demonstrations the conscious percept differs from the information that the motor system uses in determining actions.

4.4   The Phenomenal Experience of Seeing

A note about organization: In the remainder of this chapter I address the general problem of what to make of our conscious experience of space and of other properties of mental images. Since these topics constitute a central application of the ideas on selection and perceptual demonstratives (FINSTs), I treat them in some detail. However, for expository purposes I have divided these topics into two parts. The present chapter emphasizes the role of conscious experience in driving theories in these two areas. The next chapter addresses the same problems from the perspective of spatial representation, discusses some conditions that a theory of spatial representation should meet, and offers an alternative account to the one generally given in the mental imagery literature. The account I offer is not a general theory of spatial representation, but an account that deals only with the spatial properties of one sort of spatial representation, namely, the representation we construct when we reason about spatial patterns and relations, which I call *active spatial representation* or ASPAR. Consequently the discussion of representation of space and other properties of mental images is split between the two chapters.

The conscious experience we have when we imagine something (as when we have a "mental image") is strikingly like that of seeing something. It is this aspect of the experience that makes it problematic as a source of evidence about the nature of our mental representation. That's because the experience we have is that of seeing a perceived world and not of our mental state. As with other conscious contents discussed earlier, our visual image is actually the result of many different mental processes, including our perceptual-motor skills, our concurrent perception of things located around us, and inferences we draw from our beliefs about the properties, location, and likely behavior of objects we are imagining. Our experience is typically of a stable panoramic layout of spatial locations, some of which are empty while others are filled with objects, surfaces, and features that stand in some spatial relation to one another. This is the very phenomenology that leads people to postulate an inner replica of the perceived world and to suppose that this replica constitutes the experiential content of our mental image—a panoramic display that fills the world around us (Fred Attneave called it "cycloramic" since it appears to cover 360 degrees of view; Attneave and Farrar 1977). If we assume that the content of experience must somehow arise from a representation that encodes that content, and that the representation is constructed from the information we receive through our senses, then there is a problem about how such a representation could possibly come about, given the poverty of the incoming information. The incoming information consists of a small peephole view from the fovea (no more than 2 degrees of visual angle or about the width of your thumb at arm's length) that jumps about several times a second, during which we are essentially blind (the information available to the brain is a familiar story and has been described in detail; see, e.g., O'Regan 1992). So the gap between our visual experience and the available visual information requires some explanation. There are many ways to try to fill the gap (some of which will be discussed in the next chapter), but the natural way, given the form of the experience, is to try to build an internal facsimile that corresponds to the contents of the experience. In other words, we find ourselves postulating a process that takes account of eye movements and constructs an inner picture in synchrony with these eye movements, along the lines shown in figure 4.3.

But as we now know, this theory is patently false—there is no inner replica or picture of any kind in our head, neither literally nor in any other nonvacuous sense capable of explaining how we represent spatial information in perception and thought. The mistake of reifying the spatial experience in this case is reminiscent of Kepler's worry (mentioned in chapter 1)

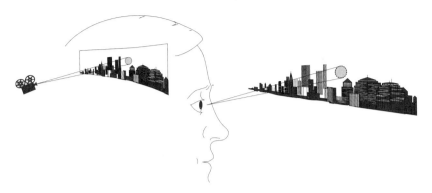

Figure 4.3
The intuitive view of the content of our experience of seeing. According to this view
an inner display is constructed by a process that "paints" the display in synchrony
with the eye's scanning of the visual world, thereby achieving a panoramic and
filled-in picture of that world, similar to how we experience it (from Pylyshyn 2003).

about how we can perceive the world veridically when the retinal image is
upside down. Just as Kepler and his contemporaries spent many years looking for a place in the brain where the image was reinverted, so also have
many vision scientists searched for a place in the brain where the fragmentary incoming visual information is completed or filled in. The experience
of visual perception suggests that vision provides a dense manifold of panoramic information, so theorists have searched for where such a detailed
representation might occur in the brain. The answer is *nowhere*: There *is*
no reconstructed detailed representation such as shown in figure 4.3. (The
difficulty of accepting this conclusion has gone hand in hand with the difficulty of casting both a theory of vision and a theory of mental imagery in
terms other than some form of pictorial or iconic representation—but more
on this later.)

What has led so many people to succumb to the "picture" story depicted
in figure 4.3? What has gone wrong is that we have been attributing the
content of the experience to certain intrinsic properties of a representation
(or, more precisely, of the structure or medium in which the scene is represented). But this makes two untenable assumptions. First, it assumes that
the content of experience reflects the content of some mental representation that plays a role in the process of perception and imagination. Second,
it assumes that the content of thoughts or imaginings reveals the structure
and properties of the format or medium in the brain in which the mental
representations are expressed. I have been discussing the first assumption,

which gives conscious content a special status over other sources of evidence that I have argued it does not merit. The second assumption is the result of the well-known intentional fallacy, the fallacy of attributing properties of what is being represented to the representation itself (as if our representation of a red square were itself red and square). Yet so long as we assume that the form of some mental representation must account for the content of the perceptual experience we are inevitably led to postulate a picture-like representation to match the picture-like experience. Should we, then, discount the experience and start afresh from psychophysical data alone? I will return to this topic below, as well as in the next chapter where I consider what a theory of spatial cognition needs to explain—and where I will in fact appeal to some phenomenology to motivate the conditions that need to be met.

4.4.1 Nonconceptual Representation in Visual Perception

As we have seen in previous chapters, a theory of perception and cognition needs an ultimate link of some sort with the perceived world in order to ground perception-based mental representations. Furthermore, this link must ultimately be causal on pain of infinite regress. Or, more precisely, the link must not be conceptual and must not rely solely on the semantic relation of satisfaction. In the previous chapter I offered a proposal for a particular mechanism of selection and reference based on FINST indexing, which we have seen works very much like demonstrative identification. I ended that discussion with the open question of what happens to the rest of the information in a scene—the information about objects and properties that are not indexed. I hinted that we may have to live with the uncomfortable idea that it is unavailable to the mind, at least at that instant. Such a conclusion seems particularly implausible with respect to visual perception, and in particular with respect to the visual perception of space, because it is here that our phenomenal experience most strongly insists that we have a grasp on space in some sort of bulk manner that is very different from the punctate index-based account I have been offering. This intuition is that we have what people have called a *nonconceptual representation of space*. The experience of space has been the subject of extensive analysis by philosophers, psychologists, and neuroscientists because it offers so much scope for exploring the idea of a different kind of nonconceptual representation—one that departs from the sort of format that seems appropriate for representing propositional attitudes (see, e.g., the essays in Eilan, McCarthy, and Brewer 1993; Gunther 2003; Luce, D'Zmura, Hoffman, Iverson, and Romney 1995; Paillard 1991). The question of how we cognize and represent space will be dealt with in the next chapter. For now my concern is with perception more generally.

As I mentioned above, characterizing the experience of visual perception is a deep and interesting problem on its own. For example, the purely phenomenal content of experience may be relevant to understanding certain distinctions we experience, such as the qualitative difference between vision and mental imagery (Dalla Barba, Rosenthal, and Visetti 2002) or perhaps that between clear perceptions that fail to be convincingly real and vague perceptions that seem very real (a distinction that is orthogonal to perceptual content, as Gestalt psychologists recognized). Beyond such qualitative observations, it is not clear how cognitive science can build on these ideas, because it is not clear how the detailed phenomenological experience of vision or imagery captures the distinctions and the mental structures required by a causal/functional theory.

Perhaps there is a parallel here to the relation between generative theories of grammar and theories of language learning and parsing. Even though it is clear that the rules of grammar characterize what a speaker implicitly knows, the form of the rules required for characterizing the grammar do not appear to be suited for direct application to parsing or language learning (for more on this issue as it pertains to language, see Pylyshyn 1973a). In fact it is plausible that the rules (expressed in some generative formalism such as rewrite rules and transformations) are not themselves explicitly represented (Pylyshyn 1991). Similarly it is not clear that any description of the experience of perception or imagery can be taken as constituting a form of (nonconceptual) representation that is functional in perception.

Even if our perceptual experience were correctly characterized (e.g., in terms of something like Peacocke's *scenario content* discussed in Peacocke 1992), it need not correspond to some representation that figures in an explanation of how perception or thought works in an information-processing account. We have seen many examples of this sort of disconnect between phenomenal experience and functional states in the previous section. But there are even more problems with misinterpretations of experience in discussions of mental imagery. Even when the descriptions of the phenomenology are correct, their functional significance is at best problematic and often simply irrelevant. An example is the explanation offered by a numerical "savant" of how he multiplies two four-digit numbers. According to a story originally reported by Terry Moran and Lenny Bourin on "World News Tonight," June 5, 2005, and reported again in the *Guardian* (Feb. 12, 2005), the savant Daniel Tammett explains how he multiplies two four-digit numbers as follows: "When I multiply numbers together, I see two shapes. The image starts to change and evolve, and a third shape emerges. That's the answer. It's mental imagery." The claim that he "reads off" the answer from the resulting shape is not very different from explaining why it takes longer to report details in a "small" image than in a "large" image by saying that the details are harder to see in the smaller image so one has to "zoom in" to see them (Kosslyn 1980). These examples of appealing to the contents of one's image to provide an explanation illustrate the seduction of the intentional fallacy.

Philosophers have another reason to appeal to conscious experience in characterizing perception; conscious experience is thought to provide a justification for our perceptual beliefs. The idea is that you are justified in believing $F(x)$ if you can see that x is F just by looking, where "see" is taken to mean "consciously experience." This may be what is behind John Campbell's claim (mentioned earlier) that without consciousness we would not know what our demonstrative reference refers to (see section 3.5). But there are many ways to justify a belief (even to justify the belief to ourselves), and, given the examples reviewed earlier, our conscious experience may not be the most reliable. As Jerry Fodor (2007) remarks in a footnote:

The doctrine [that one's justification of a perceptual claim that P, is typically its seeming to one that P], though venerable, strikes me as confused; in particular, as confusing offering a justification for a perceptual claim with offering a justification for making that claim. Compare: My sincerely believing that P generally justifies my claiming that P; but it's not a reason to believe P is true (or, anyhow, it's not much of one. Surely it can't be *my* reason for believing that P is true). Why suppose that the epistemology of perception differs, in this respect, from the epistemology of other sorts of belief fixation.

Discussion of the content of perceptual experience brings us to the question of the nature of mental imagery, which I raise in the next section. In the final chapter I will revisit the question of spatial representation, which many people believe is at the heart of what is special about mental imagery, and offer a suggestion for how spatial "representation" might arise without any internalizing of spatial properties—without an "inner space" of any kind. But for now I will focus on the way that theories of mental imagery are informed (or I should say, misinformed) by phenomenal experience. The pull of subjective experience is so powerful and has so thoroughly misled the majority of cognitive scientists (and cognitive neuroscientists) that even patently obvious fallacies often go unnoticed.

4.5   The Phenomenal Experience of Mental Imagery

If we are tempted by the model of visual perception shown in figure 4.3 above, then we will be equally, if not more, tempted by the view that in the absence of input from the eyes, the inner display in that figure can also be filled from memory or from reasoning (since according to that view there is top-down involvement in painting the inner picture, even in vision). According to that view of visual perception, we have a display surface with the nonconceptual content corresponding to our experience; so it would be logical that we might use that display to imagine as well as to see. This is indeed the received view in much of cognitive psychology (Kosslyn 1980, 1994), neuroscience (see the commentaries appearing with my article in *Behavioral and Brain Sciences*, Pylyshyn 2002a), and even a fair amount of philosophy (see, e.g., the essays reprinted in Block 1981; Tye 1991). Although it is not generally acknowledged (in fact it tends to be vehemently denied), the driving force behind this sort of theorizing is the desire to account for the experience we have when we entertain mental images. The writings on mental imagery typically begin with the assumption that because the experience of having a mental image is very much like the experience of seeing something, entertaining an image must also involve seeing something. And if imagining is seeing something, then there must be *something* that one is seeing—there must be something in the head that plays a role analogous to that played by an actually perceived scene (and of course there must be something playing the role of the eye, though that is less often mentioned).

Why a picture and not something else? The only other possibility is that there is a replica of the world to be perceived. As Nelson Goodman (1968, p. 3) said about art (quoting from an unnamed source), "Art is not a copy of the real world ... one of the damned things is enough." This is even truer when applied to mental representations. If it seems unreasonable that there is a replica of a *world* in the head, perhaps it is possible that there may be at least a *picture* of the world instead.[6] When I am imagining a visual scene it certainly *feels* like I am looking at something and the thing

6. An actual 3-D replica of the world is no more egregious than a picture of the world, given that there is nothing 2-D about the experienced image. In fact our images are distinctly 3-D rather than 2-D, both in their phenomenology and in their psychophysical properties, as I will point out later when I discuss the experiments. For some reason it seems less fantastic to ask for a 2-D replica even though all the problems with 3-D replicas appear with 2-D pictures.

I am looking at looks like something in the world. A picture also looks like something in the world; so maybe what we have is a picture. That brings us to the assumption that what we have in our heads (or brains) is something that shares the essential properties of a picture, namely, it is a structure that is *depictive* (where the latter is defined in the quotation below).

But it is not enough that we have some structure that looks to be depictive when pictured on paper. The structure itself must be implemented in neural tissue in such a way as to impose constraints like those we find in the world, or at least in a picture, such as requiring that when you scan your eye (or your attention) from place A to place B you must pass through the intermediate (possibly empty) places. Many other properties that we discover in mental imagery experiments must also be determined by the structures that underlie the depictive representation. Since most of the constraints that the medium is alleged to impose concern properties of space, I will leave those for the next chapter where I consider the larger question of how we represent space. What I will not do in the present section is revisit aspects of the imagery debate. That debate goes back a long way (at least since Berkeley and Locke quarreled over it) and in its modern form is now nearly thirty-five years old (if we date it from the first salvo in Pylyshyn 1973b). It has changed in emphasis during that time (and has incorporated neural image data), but the basic disagreements remain essentially the same. The debate relevant here is fundamentally about whether postulating certain kinds of mental/cortical constructs that are consonant with our conscious experience constrains the hypothesized mechanisms in any way. If it does not, then these assumptions simply appease our intuitions, derived from our conscious experience, without serving any explanatory purpose. This, I claim, is indeed the case for "picture theories" (or "depictive" theories) of mental imagery.

Images are said to be depictive. This is a well-chosen word because it suggests that the relation between mental images and the world is not a semantic one—as understood in linguistics and logic—but one closer to what one might call "resemblance." Resemblance has a long history in philosophy of mind. It served for Hume as one of the three fundamental principles of association (along with contiguity and causation). But it failed in the end for reasons that are well known—thoughts can use symbols that do not resemble their referents (e.g., words), and if there is a resemblance the resemblance itself cannot be what determines the reference or meaning (this is not the place to rehearse these ideas; see Fodor 1965, 2003; Pylyshyn 1984).

One of the people who has tried to be explicit about what it means for a mental image to be depictive is Stephen Kosslyn, as expressed in the following quotation (Kosslyn 1994, p. 5):

A depictive representation is a type of picture, which specifies the locations and values of configurations of points in a space. For example, a drawing of a ball on a box would be a depictive representation.... The space in which the points appear need not be physical, such as on this page, but can be like an array in a computer, which specifies spatial relations purely functionally. That is, the physical locations in the computer of each point in an array are not themselves arranged in an array; it is only by virtue of how this information is "read" and processed that it comes to function as if it were arranged into an array (with some points being close, some far, some falling along a diagonal, and so on).... In a depictive representation, each part of an object is represented by a pattern of points, and the spatial relations among these patterns in the functional space correspond to the spatial relations among the parts themselves. Depictive representations convey meaning via their resemblance to an object, with parts of the representation corresponding to parts of the object.... When a depictive representation is used, not only is the shape of the represented parts immediately available to appropriate processes, but so is the shape of the empty space.... Moreover, one cannot represent a shape in a depictive representation without also specifying a size and orientation....

I don't know whether this view is universally received (or even whether it is still Kosslyn's view—see chap. 5, note 5, page 156), but it will serve as a basis for my comments because it has the merit of being explicit. What it defines are the constraints that are assumed to hold by virtue of something's being an image rather than, say, a representation in a compositional system of symbols—that is, a *language of thought*. Notice right off that what it describes is unabashedly a picture—a 2-D object laid out in space. True, it says that the space need not be physical; it might be only functional. We will see in the next chapter that this idea is a ruse: there is no such thing as a functional space that is capable of explaining the apparent spatial properties of mental images—it is a blank check that can be used to explain any property one wishes. The idea of depiction does, however, come close to corresponding with one's phenomenal experience of looking at a picture, which, I suppose, is why we call such experiences "images."

But explanatory adequacy requires that one specify *why* the depictive structure has the properties it has. In particular, there are two very different possible reasons why the representation has such properties. One is that this is the nature of the mind–brain—it is part of the relatively fixed architecture of mind or of an encapsulated vision/image module. If the space mentioned in the quotation above were real space such an account would be explanatory: real space has certain properties, including the properties described by the metrical axioms and possibly also the Euclidean axioms that constrain the things that can be represented and the types of transformations or processes that can take place (e.g., moving attention through real space requires that attention "pass over" all the empty places along the way). The second possible reason why the properties described in the quotation hold is that people (i.e., subjects in the experiments) have certain beliefs about what things look like, how they change (e.g., how they move), and how events happen in space and time, and they can use these beliefs to predict or to mimic what would happen in a real situation (e.g., it would take longer to move a greater distance; it would be harder—and so take longer—to see small features than large ones). If the phenomenon holds because a person believes that this is how things would unfold in the world (because of a folk theory or because of recollecting something similar happening in the past) then the phenomenon reveals not a property of the mind–brain but only a property of the person's beliefs or knowledge (often tacit) of how things work in the world. The distinction between a regularity attributed to the nature of the architecture of mind and one that is attributed to tacit beliefs or knowledge is about as fundamental a distinction as there is in this field. If the phenomenon is attributed not to some property of the architecture, but to tacit beliefs or knowledge, then it is in principle changeable by rational means (being told, being shown, etc., any appropriate rationally connected belief-changing information). The notion of *tacit knowledge* is one of the fundamental ideas in cognitive science (Fodor 1968; Pylyshyn 1981).

4.5.1 Phenomenal Experience and Explanation: The Role of Tacit Knowledge

One major problem with relying on introspective evidence (even if one is not aware that one is doing so) is that, as in the case of illusions of will and other types of confabulation discussed in section 4.3, conscious experience is powerless to tell us *why* something happens. And to the extent that it matters why, we cannot get the requisite answers from our conscious experience. Here are a few examples, intended solely to clarify the difference between an architecturally based property and one based on tacit knowledge.

Imagine that you are watching Galileo's (apocryphal, as it turns out) experiment atop the leaning tower of Pisa. A large, heavy cannonball is released at the same time as a tennis ball. You watch what happens to the two objects as they fall *in your image*. You must press one button when the heavier ball hits the ground and another button when the light ball hits the ground. What do you think will happen? In all likelihood, unless you have studied physics, you will press the button for the heavier ball before that for the light ball.[7] But the critical question is: *Why* did you press the buttons when you did? Does it matter whether it was because of properties of the mind–brain, or properties that you learned in school or believed for other reasons (e.g., watching balls fall in various field games)?

Now imagine a person on a bicycle traveling down a hill and then turning around and pedaling back up the hill. Which took longer in your imagining, the downhill portion or the uphill portion? Again, the important question is: Why did those time intervals appear in your imaginings? It should not be hard to think up numerous such imaginings involving time, in which you are likely to agree that the reason one event takes longer than another is not because of how your mind–brain is constituted, but because of what you know, even if you did not know that you knew it (i.e., even if you would give a different answer when asked on a written questionnaire). The use of reaction time in psychological experiments has been a major boon to information-processing theories because it has enabled us to compare the computational complexity (typically interpreted as an indication of the number of operations performed) of processes under different inputs. And yet in this case it seems that it tells us little about the process and its underlying architecture, except that that architecture is capable of storing beliefs and drawing inferences from those beliefs and that it is capable of generating time intervals based on independently computed estimates.

Now try another task using mental imagery. Imagine a beam of blue light and beam of yellow light producing two patches of light on a white surface side by side. Move the patches closer together until they overlap. What

---

7. As it happens, this is also what was found in Pisa, not by Galileo but by opponents of the Galilean theory (see Kuhn 1957). Incidentally in this experiment you are also likely to press the buttons after a delay that is a linear function of the distance fallen, which means a constant velocity and not the Newtonian constant acceleration. The dynamics of your mental image have not, it seems, incorporated Galilean physics but remain stuck in the Aristotelian/medieval worldview (McCloskey and Kargon 1988; McCloskey, Washburn, and Felch 1983). On the other hand, modern sophisticated observers appear to be stuck in Galilean idealizations and have erroneous expectations about motion in air (Oberle, McBeath, Madigan, and Sugar 2005). Thus what you will imagine in the present example will very much depend on factors that are not related to the architecture of the imagery system (even if there were such a thing).

color do you see in your image at the overlap? People who have vivid imagery have no problem providing a quick answer.[8] Once again the question of interest is: *why do they answer as they do?* Here's another example. Imagine two identical glasses, one half full of sugar and another nearly full of water. Imagine slowly pouring the water from the water glass into the glass containing the sugar. Does the water in the sugar-glass overflow in your image? The right thing to say in this case is probably, "How should I know?" That answer captures not only one's state of mind, but also acknowledges that what happens in your image depends on what you think would happen. In this case the correct answer depends on some sophisticated knowledge about what happens to a solid in solution in a liquid so the correct answer (under the right conditions it does not overflow) would depend on such knowledge or on recollections or on informal folk theory. But whatever answer you give surely depends not on properties of your mind–brain, but on what you believe. Now the reader may well ask how I can be sure that in the above examples the outcome depends on what you believe? The answer is easy: Because you could easily make the outcome different by willing it! It is your image, so you can make it do whatever you like. If you don't believe me try the above examples making the outcome something quite different: you can make the balls dropped from the leaning tower of Pisa fly away, or the fluid miss the container and pour on the floor, or the colored light beams mix to form chartreuse or no color at all, if you wished.

I present these examples to illustrate the difference between the two types of causes of imagery processes. Although these are not published experiments, very similar experiments have been published and discussed in the literature on mental imagery.[9] For example, there is a notion of *rep-*

8. The chances are good that you gave the wrong answer because few people know the difference between additive and subtractive color mixing. The example here involves light, which results in additive color mixing, so combining a blue light with yellow light should result in a white patch. But if you were looking though two filters, one blue and the other yellow, you would see a patch of green. For more on this complex but well-studied phenomena see Rossotti 1983.

9. Kosslyn (1981) discusses the color-mixing example and actually cites empirical data to show that many people give different answers when asked to imagine than when they are merely asked to provide a verbal response. It's not clear what this is supposed to show, over and above my present claim that people can make their image have whatever properties they wish. I suspect one can get different answers if one asks the question in different settings or in different ways (in a lab vs. a paint studio, inside vs. outside, in a timed task vs. an untimed condition, in a purported IQ

resentational momentum, hypothesized to account for why in tracking a moving object one generally makes errors in indicating its final position, where it disappears. The idea is that the imagined motion has momentum the way a real moving object does, and like a real object, it does not stop suddenly but continues to move after it disappears. Other such examples are discussed in Pylyshyn 2002a.

Having described the two different sorts of causes involved in imagined processes, we can now look at examples of imagery that have been discussed in the literature. These generally do not depend on knowledge of physical principles, but on geometrical-optical properties, which seem more likely to be built in to the visual system. Consider, for example, experiments involving image size (Kosslyn 1975). In these experiments, subjects are asked to imagine, say, a mouse under two size conditions: (1) imagined next to an elephant so that both are present and fill the entire "mental screen" (in which case the mouse has to be visualized as small— i.e. it has to occupy a small visual angle in the "mental display"), and (2) imagined by itself in your hand and close up, so it occupies a large visual angle in the mental display. Subjects are asked to report details in the image of the mouse (e.g., does it have whiskers?) under these two conditions. It was found that it takes longer to report such details when the image is small than when it is large. Subjects feel that with the small image they can't "see" the details and have to "zoom in" to see them (and the picture theory actually postulates a "zoom" operation). So the question is: Is the increased time attributable to a property of the architecture or to subjects' beliefs of what it is like to see a small mouse? The pictorialists claim it is the former. The argument given (Kosslyn, Thompson, and Ganis 2006, p. 148) is that "the inhibitory connections in topographically organized areas are typically short, and thus when a lot of spatial variation is packed into a small region strong input is required to overcome the inhibition." In other words, the visual cortex is limited in its resolving power so you can't get all the information in if the image is small. But a "larger" phenomenal image is not larger on the cortex. The cortical activity that shows up in PET scans shows at most that a mental image experienced as being larger may be accompanied by activity that is anterior of activity accompanying images experienced as small (though even that is not without some question).

---

test vs. a children's game): Answers—especially when people do not know the correct answer—can be quickly confabulated (as we saw earlier). They can be offered after giving it some thought, carelessly by free association, or by trying to remember what one might have seen in the past.

Thus it may be located in areas where larger retinal images would project from the retina. But even if the locus of cortical activity is shifted when the image size changes, the area of activity for small mental images is not smaller in visual cortex, and so an explanation based on limited cortical resolution is irrelevant. Cortical resolution applies only to the resolution of information originating on the retina, not to information originating internally (from memory) and projected onto the surface of the cortex. For more on the futility of appealing to the neural properties of visual cortex to explain imagery phenomena, see section 4.5.2 below.

But once again I am willing to give the pictorialists all their claims, even though the actual data are problematic in ways discussed in Pylyshyn 2002a, 2003, because the problems here are conceptual. What does it mean to make one's image small or large? Can one distinguish between an image being small and imagining something as being small? What do you know about seeing details on a small or a large object? If the size is what makes it easier or harder to see, consider what would happen if we kept the size fixed and manipulated the amount of detail. Imagine a medium-sized mouse viewed through a pair of steamed or scratched glasses so it is fuzzy. Now imagine the same mouse viewed clearly (you can substitute low-definition and high-definition TV if you like). In which version is it harder to "see" the whiskers? Do we even need to do the experiment? What if we did the experiment and it took more time to see the whiskers on the high-definition image? Would we conclude that the architecture of the visual system has these strange properties? I doubt it. We are more likely to conclude that the subject misunderstood the instructions because what it *means* to be fuzzy is that you can't see the details, and what it means to do the reaction time test is that one is supposed to re-create as closely as possible the phenomena that would occur if one were looking at and seeing the large/small mouse. The details of the neurology of V1 are interesting on their own—for example, that inhibitory processes may explain the limited resolution of vision—but they do not clarify the problem of the resolution of mental images. That problem arises because one is attempting to match the experience of having a mental image with properties of the architecture of vision when the facts at hand have nothing to do with that architecture, but have everything to do with what it means to have a small (or large) image.

The same can be said for the widely cited study of the "visual angle of the mind's eye" (Kosslyn 1978). If you ask people to stand close enough to various objects so that the objects fill their field of view, you can compute the visual angle of the eye. If you then ask people to use their imagination and tell you how close they should stand to a car, a horse, a toaster, and so on, so that it fills their field of view, they also give reliable answers, which establishes that the visual angle subtended by images is similar to that subtended by vision, allegedly showing that the two share a common display. But of course it might also show that subjects *know* how close they should stand to a car, a horse, a toaster, so that it fills their field of view. The fact that they can't tell you those distances if you ask the direct question is irrelevant here as it is in all the other such cases: One thing that psychologists have learned is that how you ask is critical in determining the answer you get. In this case, if you use a different way of measuring the visual angle subtended by images—one that does not invite subjects to imagine that they are getting closer to some object until it overflows their visual field— you get quite different answers. If, for example, you simply provide a task that requires subjects to recall where things are by using their mental image of a room, you find that the visual angle is 360°—what Fred Attneave, whose sympathies have tended toward the picture theory, called a *cyclo-ramic* display (Attneave and Farrar 1977). The pattern is clear: If you ask subjects to pretend that they are looking at some particular display, or if you present them with a display that they memorize, then you tend to get parallels between seeing and imagining, but generally not otherwise. The tacit knowledge explanation should be treated as the default explanation, barring evidence to the contrary, since that is the way we pretheoretically understand what imagining something means: by default it is an invitation to put yourself in the position of watching something unfold before your eyes.

Here is another example, to which I will return in the last chapter. One of the most widely quoted and replicated results cited in support of the depictive nature of mental images is mental scanning. The finding so impressed the pictorialists that they refer to it as a "window on the mind" (Denis and Kosslyn 1999). The typical experiment goes like this. Subjects are asked to memorize a display—usually a map of some fictitious island— until they can reproduce it to within some margin of error. They are then asked to imagine the map and to focus their attention on a particular (named) place on it. Next they are asked to move their attention to another named place. This is done in different ways. In the early experiments subjects were asked to imagine a spot moving from the initial focus to the second named place. In subsequent experiments they were asked to switch their attention or to simply look for the second named place, and in some cases they were asked to report on parts of the map that were off the to side of the imagined region (beyond the visual angle of the mind's eye). What was found is that the time it took to arrive at the second place was a linear function of the distance between the two places on the map. So the question this raises is Why? The pictorialist has a ready answer the image is actually laid out in real space in visual cortex so attention (or gaze) travels across it just as it does across real external space, and therefore the relation *time = distance ÷ velocity* holds. The account for the case where the item being scanned to is off the edge of the image ought to be an embarrassment but it is not viewed that way: there is a story there too (it involves an "image transformation" process—though it's not clear why that should yield a linear reaction time effect; see Kosslyn, Thompson, and Ganis 2006). Now if you imagine a spot moving across your image of your favorite scene you will notice that it takes more time to go further. But you might also notice that you can make the spot speed up, slow down, back up, hop around, disappear from the scene and do any sort of trick you like. Not only is it your image but it is *your spot* to do with as you choose—the motion of the spot is not constrained in any way by properties of your imagery system. So why do you choose to make it take longer when the distance is greater? Surely it is because that's what it would do if there was no reason for it to do anything else—*because moving in a straight line at a fixed velocity is what physical things do in real space.*

But wait, you say, the increase in time with distance occurs under many other conditions. It occurs if the subjects are not told to scan, but only to look for or to notice the other named place. But isn't that the same as asking them to pretend that they are looking at a map? And who would fail to know (or remember) that noticing something further away takes more time—because it takes time to move your line of sight or your attention? But why do I claim that subjects know that? If you ask subjects what would happen in such an experiment, for example, they often say they don't know. And that's the right answer—they don't know what would happen in an experiment. They might even not know what they themselves would do. But that's just the perennial finding that asking subjects an outright question—especially one about what would happen in an experiment—is the worst way to find out what they believe (witness all the cases covered in section 4.3 above). You need to see whether different beliefs would yield different results. And you don't do that by trying to induce strange expectancies by telling unrealistic stories about object movements (such as telling subjects that scanning times would be long for short distances because of some sort of crowding effect or that it would be different for different colored items; see Jolicoeur and Kosslyn 1985).

Another pictorialist defense is to cite an experiment reported by Finke and Pinker (1982), in which no scanning instructions were given. Subjects were shown a display of points on a screen. The points disappeared and an arrow appeared. Subjects simply had to extrapolate the arrow to see whether the line would intersect with one of the points that had been there before. Here too, time increased with distance. I leave it to the reader to explain why this does not entail a "picture-in-the-head" view (just put yourself in the position of a subject and ask what you would do and why). They may not have been given instructions to imagine, but they were given a visual memory task which is much the same thing. It should be clear where this sort of altercation is headed.

Interestingly, pictorialists do not cite the mental scanning experiments we carried out (part of a Ph.D. dissertation by Liam Bannon at the University of Western Ontario) and which I reported in Pylyshyn 1981. In one experiment (which was scarcely worth doing since the outcome is pretty obvious given a moment's thought) we showed subjects a board with a map mounted on it that contained lights and switches. When the appropriate switch was toggled the light that was currently on went off and another went on immediately. Subjects played with this board for a while then were asked to imagine the board and, as in the scanning experiments, to press a button when they *saw*, in their mind's eye, the light come on at the second named place. As you might have guessed, there was no time increase with increasing distance. Why? Because there was none in the situation they were imagining. Notwithstanding such findings, the claim was made (Kosslyn 1994, p. 11) that research "showed that imagery is highly constrained. Subjects can control some aspects of processing, such as the speed of scanning, but not others; in particular they could not eliminate the effects of distance on time to shift attention across an imagined object." Yet so far nobody has shown any phenomena that are constrained by the depictive nature of the display and which are not better explained by appeal to tacit knowledge.

It's also interesting that the scanning effect can be made to disappear simply by playing down the importance of the task of moving one's attention over the image. For example, we asked subjects to use their imagined map to do the following. Start by focusing attention on some specified place. Then when a second place is named, they were to say what direction the first place would be from that second place (using a clock face as the way of specifying direction). This is a task which really does require that one focus on the second place in order to use it as the reference point in giving the direction to the first place. But no movement is mentioned. And in that case we found no distance effect on reaction time (Pylyshyn 1981).

But even if you accept the tacit knowledge view, namely that the scanning effect is the result of subjects' recreating an imagined state of affairs where attention or gaze is scanned over a scene, there is still one remaining question. How does this simulation create the appropriate observed time delays? Surely it is not the case that a subject simply counts the seconds until the right amount of time has gone by! Why do you get an approximately linear time when (and, I assume, only when) subjects imagine the scanning taking place and not, for example, when they are asked to wait a certain amount of time and then press the button? The answer depends on one's theory of what goes on in the interval. My assumption has been that what goes on is that people imagine the spot or focus of attention being *here* and then *here* and so on until it gets to the target. But does this not require some place for the demonstratives *here* to refer? And does this not require a depictive display? As far as I know this question has not been asked, and yet it deserves an answer. Precisely this question will be the focus of the next chapter (although the allusion to demonstratives should give the reader a hint that FINSTs are going to play a role in the story).

4.5.2   Does the Architecture of Visual Cortex Matter to Explanations of Imagery?

I said that the use of tacit knowledge (to simulate what would happen if the event were actually witnessed) is the first line of explanation, but it is not always the last, for there may be other factors involved—some architectural properties often reveal themselves, though not necessarily the architectural properties of the display that are postulated in the pictorialist's canonical story. This sometimes arises in imagery experiments where the task done with imagery is compared with the same task performed with actual vision. Such experiments tend to introduce architectural properties into the picture. I consider one such example because it nicely illustrates three important points: (a) Not all imagery phenomena can be subsumed under the tacit knowledge explanation—many are a mixture of tacit knowledge interacting with some architectural constraint not obviously related to the task; (b) here, as elsewhere, the details matter and we have to look at the postulated mechanisms to see what explanatory work they do; and (c) it illustrates how deeply committed some people are to the literal picture theory, so much so that they are willing to ignore obvious problems in their account in order to salvage the picture theory of mental imagery.

The example I have in mind concerns a low-level psychophysical property known as the *oblique effect*.

The original oblique effect finding in vision is that it is easier to resolve closely packed lines when the lines are vertical or horizontal than when they are oblique (i.e., at 45° from horizontal). This general phenomenon has also been found to be true when the stripes are *imagined* at various orientations (or, rather, when memorized bars of different orientations are used in an image recall task such as mentally comparing pairs of such memorized bars for properties like width and spacing; see Kosslyn, Sukel, and Bly 1999). The explanation given for why performance on such imagery tasks is worse when the stripes are oblique is that the imagined stripes are displayed on the visual cortex, and it is known that there are more cells with horizontally and vertically tuned receptive fields than oblique ones in visual area V1. Now, I agree that this does not sound on first hearing like a phenomenon traceable to tacit knowledge being used to mimic perception, but we have already seen examples where the exact wording of the question or of the task made a major difference in the results obtained. The major problem with the tacit knowledge account in this case is that very few people know about the oblique effect even in some informal guise. Of course the fact that people don't explicitly know about the oblique effect does not mean that they cannot *recognize* cases of it—it does not mean that there is no familiarity with how things look when they are oblique, especially since oblique contours are far less common in our world than are vertical or horizontal ones (Hansen and Essock 2004). We also need to keep in mind that there is a lot we don't know about the oblique effect in general and the (probably many) reasons for it. Notice, however, that the oblique effect is found in the haptic modality as well as in vision (Gentaz and Hatwell 1998; Kappers and Koenderink 1999); there are many cases where oblique lines are perceived better than horizontal or vertical ones (e.g., when the spacing is variable and broadband or when the measure is adaptation rather than discrimination, Essock et al. 2003; Heeley, Buchanan-Smith, Cromwell, and Wright 1997; McMahon and MacLeod 2003; Wilson, Loffler, Wilkinson, and Thistlethwaite 2001); and it seems that the frame of reference for classifying orientation depends on gravity, and so on—all in all not a strong argument for connecting the visual and imaginal oblique effect via properties of a common display in cortical area V1.

What explanation does the pictorialist offer for this effect? Here is their most recent explanation (Kosslyn, Thompson, and Ganis 2006, p. 69):

if the result emerges from the neurophysiology of the visual buffer, it is easily explained.... neurons in topographically organized areas are known to have orientation-tuning ... and to be less sensitive to distinctions along the diagonal. In addition, at least in area V1 in the cat brain, so called simple cells (which fire when the animal sees edges and not to complex combinations of features) not only fire more vigorously when horizontal and vertical lines are shown, but also have sharper tuning for horizontal and vertical lines.... These results underscore the fact that the oblique effect reflects properties of the neurons that populate the early visual cortex.

So there is the story. There are more finely tuned receptors for vertical and horizontal lines in V1, where mental images are projected as a pattern of activity, and so imagining horizontal and vertical bars get preference in imaginal tasks. But there is a critical assumption in this story which reveals how the seductive picture theory can blind us to assumptions that are essential to the explanation but remain unstated and unquestioned. The assumption is that a pattern of activity projected onto the surface of V1 by higher cognitive functions, as assumed by the picture theory, is equivalent to the same pattern of activity applied at the retina. But cells that are sensitive to orientation are *sensitive to the orientation of patterns on the retina*—as picked up by photoreceptors—not to patterns imposed on the cells themselves (i.e., patterns *depicted* on the surface of V1). The orientation sensitivity of cells in V1 is the result of the arrangement of photosensitive cells on the retina and how they are connected to the simple cells in visual cortex. The exact form of this arrangement is uncertain—it could be a simple template, as postulated by the organization of simple and complex cells reported by Hubel and Weisel (1968), or it could be a more complex arrangement such as the wiring of a perceptron-like mechanism—but whatever it is, it is clear that activating an oriented pattern of cells in V1 will not selectively activate orientation-tuned cells. If a pattern of activation, such as a grid of parallel stripes, were imposed ("depicted") on the surface of V1 it would activate all sorts of cells in its path and would not favor different orientation-specific cells depending on the orientation of those parallel stripes. Although parallel stripes on the retina might create parallel stripes of activity on V1 (assuming the retinotopic mapping is accurate), the converse does not hold: activating stripes on the surface of V1 does not produce striped activity on the retina or anywhere that serves as input to orientation-tuned cells.

I have belabored this point because it is a recurring theme in recent picture-theory writings (including the recent overview in Kosslyn, Thompson, and Ganis 2006). When certain phenomena of mental imagery, such as the apparent lower resolution of imagery relative to vision reported in

Kosslyn, Sukel, and Bly 1999, or the longer time it takes to report fine details from a small image, or the "visual angle of the mind's eye" result reported in Kosslyn 1978, the explanation always alludes to properties of cells in V1, in order to support the view that images are projected onto V1. But the properties of cells in V1 could not account for such patterns since these properties arise from the way those cells are activated from the retinal photoreceptors; the alleged top-down activation from memory or imaging instructions would not produce the same effect as activation from photoreceptors. The only way this sort of explanation would work is if when we imagine something, images were projected onto the retina, which so far nobody has had the audacity to propose.

4.5.3 Problems in Accounting for Phenomenal Space by Appealing to Brain-Space

In addition to the problems raised by attributing properties of imagery to properties of cells in V1, there are even more serious problems with the basic premise behind the evidence cited in favor of the picture-in-V1 view of imagery, namely the assumption that the phenomenal experience of looking at a picture arises from the activation of a pattern on the corresponding display in the brain (specifically on the surface of visual cortex). Many of these reasons are discussed in Pylyshyn 2002a, 2003. Here is a quick listing.

(1) Displays in visual cortex (V1) are retinotopic Fibers run from the receptors on the retina to cells in the early visual cortex and map spatial patterns in a fairly direct manner (as shown by the activity on monkey cortex when it was made to stare at a flashing pattern—see the photographs in figure 4.4). This photograph shows that there is a continuous mapping from activity on (half of) the retina to activity on (half of) the occipital cortex of the macaque monkey.

Being retinotopic means that, as is the case with patterns on the retina, the patterns move with eye movements and have a small area of high resolution. If patterns were projected onto the visual cortex in the course of mental imagery and there were eye movements, the interpretation of the patterns would be garbled (and there generally are spontaneous eye movements during imagery; see Brandt and Stark 1997). Moreover, the mental image is fixed in allocentric space (see section 5.5.1)—its natural inclination is to remain fixed in extrapersonal space when you turn your head or your body and even when you walk around it. Also as noted earlier, one of the purposes of the depictive image display is to provide a place where the

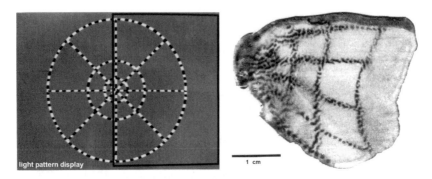

Figure 4.4
Developed "image" on monkey cortex of a pattern of flashing lights shown on the left. The right half of this pattern of flashing lights produced the pattern on the surface of the monkey's occipital cortex that was made visible in this photograph using chemical tracers. (From Tootell et al. 1982. Copyright 1982, American Association for the Advancement of Science, used with permission.)

experienced information could be depicted as a panorama with gaps filled in, and where mental scanning might take place (since it seems that "mental scanning" can occur even off the central "foveal" region of the mental image and can cross the middle of the image, thus requiring it to switch cortical hemispheres!

(2) Displays in visual cortex (V1) are two-dimensional Mental images are three-dimensional, not only in their phenomenology, but also because all objective mental imagery phenomena involving distances or angles produce the same results if they are done in depth as in the plane.[10] To suggest that the display in cortex depicts depth the way we might depict it in a drawing (by using an isometric or perspectival convention) is to miss the basic fact that the depictive image is supposed to be the *interpretation* as ex-

10. Oddly enough, the dimensionality of the display has even been used to support the pictorial view. It has been suggested that the display is able to represent 3-D shapes in some unspecified way (orthographic or isometric projection?), but that it is incapable of representing 4-D shapes and that this is an inherent constraint of the display itself, which accounts for our inability to imagine 4-D objects (Kosslyn 1981). This ignores the simple fact that we do not know what a 4-D object would *look like*, which by itself is all we need to explain why we can't imagine 4-D objects. Some physicists think that objects in fact are 4-D (or 6-D or higher according to string theory)—in which case there is no problem imagining them, since they look like the ordinary things we see around us!

perienced, not a figure from which such an interpretation is to be derived. If it were not, then we would require yet another form of representation for the interpreted mental image. Since mental scanning and rotation experiments can be done in three dimensions, this new form of representation would have to be depictive as well, so the 3-D problem would still be with us.

(3) The same cortical display cannot be used by vision and imagery If the same V1 display area were used for vision and imagery then it should be possible to superimpose visual and imagined images to get a composite. There have been a few claims of this sort, though none of them withstands scrutiny (see Pylyshyn 2003, section 6.5). If images and percepts both involved patterns on V1 they would be indistinguishable, or at least interpretable in similar ways. But images painted on the retina (e.g., afterimages) work very differently from images created by mental imagery. For example, Emmert's law holds of afterimages but not of mental images. Emmert's law says that the apparent size of a pattern projected onto the retina depends on how far away the background is. For a given retinal image, if you look far into the distance the image will appear very large, but if you look at a surface close by it will look small. Although pictorialists are always quick to deny the literal interpretation of a picture displayed in V1, Emmert's law constitutes a serious challenge to any homeomorphic mapping of retinal onto cortical topography. As long as the image preserves relative size of objects (which has been the explicit assumption of image-scanning experiments), then it should be equivalent to a retinal image of a certain retinal size and Emmert's law ought to hold. It's puzzling why pictorialists ignore this particular problem.

(4) Images are not (re)perceived by early vision If images are projected onto V1, then perceiving information from an image should not be very different from reading it from a display. But images cannot be scanned freely; they cannot be freely reinterpreted visually; they do not show signature properties of vision (ambiguity, bistability, visual illusions, apparent motion). Most important (and probably the main reason behind all the above problems) is that images are *intentional objects*—they are conceptual interpretations, not raw sensory signals. If an image of a line drawing of an ambiguous figure is imagined, it does not switch between interpretations, because it already *is* an interpretation—it is a representation of a 3-D object and it does not change as you look at it (at least it does not change for the same reason that corresponding visual displays change—i.e., because the visual system is reinterpreting it). If I ask you to imagine two identical parallelograms, one directly above the other, and to connect each vertex of one with the corresponding vertex of the other by a vertical line, no amount of gazing at this in your mind's eye will enable you to see what you would automatically see if you drew it.[11] In addition it seems clear that although you can carry out certain kinds of reinterpretations of geo- metrical patterns in your image (e.g., you can tell that if you rotate an upper-case D by $90°$ counterclockwise and attach it to a J the result will look somewhat like an umbrella), you cannot perform a visual reinterpreta- tion (reperception), as Peter Slezak has shown (Slezak 1992, 1995; for fur- ther discussion of this issue and other related experiments, see Pylyshyn 2002a).

There is also evidence (some of it described in chapter 1 of Pylyshyn 2003) that images retrieved from memory or created from descriptions do not function the way displays on the fovea do. Even with visual patterns that are too large to be accommodated in one fixation (e.g., if they exceed the visual angle of the fovea—just under $2°$, or about the angle covered by your thumb at arms' length) the part that is off-fovea shows signs of being already interpreted. For example, if you see a reversing figure such as a Necker cube or an impossible drawing (e.g., the "devil's pitchfork") that is elongated so that some of it is off-fovea, the spontaneous reversals are not observed nor is the conflict caused by the mismatch of two local views that occurs with "impossible figures." Similarly, the famous eye-of-the-needle or anorthoscope presentation, in which a slit is moved back and forth in front of a figure (or a figure is moved back and forth behind a stationary slit), does not yield a true percept with the signature properties of visual percep- tion. Moreover, the ability to recognize the shape in the anorthoscope is sensitive to the way the figure can be decomposed. If the figure is one that requires a larger number of line labels to be held in memory during the tra- verse of the slit then it will not be readily seen (see figure 4.5). In fact quite a few phenomena suggest that off-retinal figures are treated differently than those on the retina—they show more general-memory properties (e.g., they depend on the number of items held in memory) that are the hallmarks of constructed and interpreted figures.

11. What this describes is a Necker cube such as the one in the left panel of figure 4.1. Even if you guessed that it was a Necker cube it would not automatically turn into a 3-D object and involuntarily switch between its two perceptual interpre- tations (although if you knew about Necker cubes you could switch interpretations voluntarily).

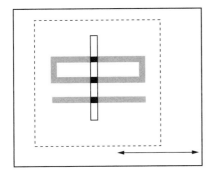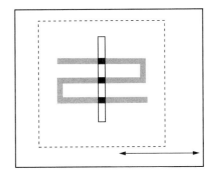

Figure 4.5
A pattern is viewed through an anorthoscope in which a slit moves back and forth (or a pattern moving back and forth is viewed through a stationary slit). How many distinct line segments are there? These two displays are identical in terms of their inventory of features, so distinguishing which has one line and which has two requires keeping track of which currently visible segment was connected to which in an earlier part of the viewing sequence. If the figure is rotated 90 degrees the number of line labels that need to be retained is reduced and the alternatives are easier to distinguish. (From Pylyshyn 2003; example due to Ian Howard.)

4.6   Does Phenomenal Appearance Correspond to a Level of Representation?

As the examples listed earlier show, what is typically referred to as the "appearance" of the perceived world includes not only the operation of the perceptual system, but also of our beliefs and expectations and folk theories, and it incorporates these to a much more profound degree than generally believed. Our perceptual experience is the experience of seeing familiar people and things, not of seeing surfaces, textures, shapes, and colors. Our experience of our own actions reflects what we believe about the agency (or authorship) of the actions, and so on. In other words, experiences are generally experiences of interpreted sensory information.[12] A dramatic illustration of this is what happens under hypnosis, during which it seems that even the experience of pain (or at least one's involuntary

12. There are also intransitive conscious experiences that are not experiences of something or other, but merely floating experiences, such as sadness, dizziness, or free-floating anxiety. Since I am here concerned with the use of the content of experiences in developing theories of perception I confine myself to transitive experiences (experiences as of some sensory input).

reactions to it) can be altered. Thus we have every reason to be skeptical about what our subjective experience reveals about the information that is functional in the perceptual process. An even more serious problem with the use of conscious contents for inferring the processes underlying perception is that there is no room in phenomenology-based theories for the growing evidence of vision-without-awareness mentioned in section 4.2.1, including change blindness, inattentional blindness, visuomotor control without conscious awareness, blindsight, visual agnosia, and disorders of visual-motor coordination, as well as other sources of behavioral and neuroscience data.

I am not suggesting that the perception itself is contaminated by expectations and beliefs—as proposed by many writers in the past, including those of the "New Look" movement that dominated perceptual theorizing in the 1960s and later (Bruner 1957), and by linguist Benjamin Lee Whorf (Whorf 1958) and his latter-day followers (Gumperz and Levinson 1996) who claimed that language and culture determine how we perceive the world (the Sapir-Whorf Hypothesis). Quite the contrary, I have argued repeatedly that a major part of what we call visual perception is cognitively impenetrable (Pylyshyn 1999, 2003). The claim I am making now is that the content of one's *conscious experience* is the result of these manifold influences, which is a very different claim. Of course if you think that one's phenomenal experience in seeing the world is constitutive of visual perception, then this does mean that seeing is cognitively penetrable to the extent that the content of one's visual experience is penetrable. The widespread assumption that what we see is given by *how things look*, or that how we perceptually experience the world *defines* what we mean by perception, may explain why the recent evidence of unconscious perception or of inconsistencies between how things look and what information is made available to other aspects of cognition (such as motor control) has attracted so much attention. I am not suggesting that we ignore perceptual experience (as behaviorists advocated). Not only would this be impossible, given that our conscious experiences of seeing, hearing, touching, smelling, and so on present deep scientific puzzles themselves; perceptual experience is also (and will continue to be) one of the main sources of evidence about perception. The alternative, rather, is to take conscious experience as one of many fallible sources of evidence concerning perception, which may in fact indicate not only what perception yields, but also the process by which we interpret incoming information. This also suggests that we may need to develop methodologies to take cognizance of the multifaceted origins of perceptual experience, the way that signal detection theory provides a methodology for separating sensitivity and response bias in certain decision-making situations (Swets 1964).

Although there are some differences between consciously held beliefs and perceptions and those that are not conscious, these differences appear to be contingent rather than principled, in the sense that most of the unconscious ones could have been conscious and in any case function in similar ways in perceptual information processing. The failure to find a specifically distinct role for the content of conscious experiences, as opposed to the information content of unconscious or unreported experiences in information-processing theories of perception, raises the question of whether the experienced content corresponds to a level or to a type of representation. Representations play a central role in explaining how cognitive processes work, and why they lead to the behaviors they do. If there were a type of representation that had a different role, that did not contribute to capturing systematic features of behavior, the question would naturally arise what role it does play in our theories. It may be that conscious contents do not constitute a distinct level of representation because they are a mixture of levels.

Consider, for example, that the inverted retinal image is not part of our experience (at least not *as an inverted image*), although inversion produced by special glasses is. The proximal (retinal) size of a tree, before it is adjusted for the perceived distance away, the whiteness or color of a surface before it is adjusted for the perceived ambient light (see Gilchrist 1977), and other preconstancy properties are not part of our experience, but they nevertheless function in information processing the same way as features that we are conscious of (in fact they would continue to function the same way if you did notice them and they became conscious, as happens when one is taught to draw). It is also possible that preconstancy unconscious states such as those just alluded to are not representations at all, or if they are representations they may be conceptual but subpersonal, in that they involve concepts that do not enter into general reasoning because they remain inside encapsulated modules (see section 3.2.2). It seems that what we experience is a mixture of sensory information, subpersonal representations, and some high-level cognitive recognitions (i.e., familiar people, places, things, and events), so it is likely that experiential content draws on many types and levels of representation.

Although conscious perceptual experience cannot be discounted in the study of perception, neither can one assume that the experience itself is to be taken at face value as an indicator of the nature of a functional mental state—a state that plays a role in the explanation of how perception works.

The question of how to interpret a particular observation can be resolved only as we build more successful theories. The situation here is very similar to that which linguists faced some sixty years ago. Intuitions of grammatical structure, which play a central role in linguistics, similar to the role played by conscious contents in perception, resulted in many disagreements early on. Take Chomsky's famous sentence "Colorless green ideas sleep furiously," which was meant to illustrate the distinction between grammaticality and acceptability judgments. The question of whether this sentence was grammatical led to arguments in which people provided interpretations of the sentence (you can always interpret a sentence, no matter how bizarre it is). This and other such linguistic intuitions were debated because what constitutes grammaticality, as opposed to acceptability, is not given by intuition alone but must await the development of the theory itself. As generative linguistics became able to capture a wider range of generalizations, it found itself relying just as much on linguistic intuitions. What changed is that the use of the intuitions was now under the control the evolving theories. Even such general questions as whether a particular intuitive judgment was relevant to linguistics became conditioned by the theory itself.[13] So, as theories of vision formulate general principles, the theories themselves will direct us to the interpretation of evidence from conscious experience.

13. For example, it was once suggested that grammaticality may not be effectively computable because the judgment of which of the two sentences "I am having trouble choosing among/between P" is grammatical is undecidable (since for a general number-theoretic predicate P it is undecidable which numbers satisfy it). One answer to this apparent conundrum was that this just shows that although the choice between "among" and "between" may be taught in grammar classes, it is not a syntactic distinction after all.

5   How We Represent Space: Internal versus External Constraints

This chapter reviews a wide spectrum of research and makes a particular proposal for how we achieve a sense of space without the postulation of an inner space. Because the empirical evidence relevant to this thesis covers several strands it might be helpful to offer a road map for this chapter. I begin with a brief review of the problem of representing space and describe two influential theories (known as *natural constraints* and *psychophysical complementarity*) that propose that general constraints rather than space itself, are internalized. Then I discuss the extremely tempting view that spatial relations are internalized by being mapped onto actual cortical space. I provide a summary of why this view is attractive but ultimately untenable. I then turn to a discussion of an option that has frequently been cited, sometimes referred to as *functional space*, which appears to provide some of the benefits of the literal-space model without succombing to its problems. I argue that these alternatives either fail to explain the spatial properties, or they reduce to a slightly disguised version of the literal cortical-space proposal.

I then list a number of conditions required of a theory of spatial representation. These are not conditions for spatial perception in general, but only for the representations involved in active episodes of spatial reasoning (what many people characterize as *spatial mental imagery*, although the conditions apply more generally where there is no conscious experience and where the sense of space is not specifically visual). I refer to this type of case as involving *Active SPAtial Representations*, or ASPARs. At the end of this section I also include a discussion of the much more complicated case of spatial information involved in navigation (often referred to as a *maplike* representation) and suggest that although part of this problem (planning a route) seems to make it relevant to ASPARs, a great deal more goes on in navigation that is beyond the scope of this chapter.

Finally, in sections 5.5 and 5.6 I turn to the proposal of how ASPARs get their spatial properties (i.e., the sample of six conditions of spatial representation laid out in section 5.4.1). It is an externalist proposal, which claims that the spatial properties of what ASPARs represent are inherited from the spatial properties of the concurrently perceived world (I call this idea the *index projection hypothesis*). The objects of thought in ASPARs are associated with particular things in the concurrently perceived world by the mechanism of FINST indexes, and by this means the spatial layout of these things becomes available to perception. Thus such properties as the apparent analog representation of distances and the configurational properties of sets of objects can be accessed perceptually since they are now out in the world rather than in the head. I provide an example of the way this hypothesis works in vision.

The next step is to suggest how the index projection hypothesis works in other modalities—how one indexes and binds things in nonvisual modalities. To arrive at that point I make several detours to introduce findings from perception and neuropsychology. These include a number of experiments showing that concurrent stimulus input plays a role in spatial reasoning and that, because of temporal lags, this influence endures slightly beyond the duration of the stimulus itself; that deficits such as unilateral spatial neglect can be modified through concurrent stimulus inputs; and that the ubiquitous presence of mechanisms of coordinate transformation in the brain makes it unnecessary to represent spatial properties in a single allocentric frame of reference, and makes it possible for proprioception and motor control to operate as though they can access places specified in an allocentric frame of reference, including places of intended (but not executed) actions. In the end I suggest that although this proposal is somewhat speculative, the evidence I have marshaled is compatible with the thesis that the spatial character of representations of space derives from the concurrent perception, through many modalities, of objects laid out in space around us, to which we can bind the objects of thought and then inspect perceptually.

5.1 What Does It Mean to Represent Space?

Any analysis of the mind–world connection will sooner or later have to face the problem of how a mind is able to cognize space. Indeed, the problem of spatial representation is one of the deepest problems in cognitive science (see, e.g., Eilan, McCarthy, and Brewer 1993; Paillard 1991). The problem of understanding how mental imagery functions is to a large extent the problem of how we represent and cognize space. One of the difficulties in understanding our commerce with space is the fact that it is so extremely intuitive to us that it is unclear what we mean when we ask how we cognize space, how we deal with spatial properties that we obtain from our sense perceptions. It seems simply obvious that space is that unique three-dimensional receptacle in which objects reside, and that spatial relations are there for us to see and experience without needing to make any inferences.

In addition, our conscious experience of space is all pervasive and fine grained; we experience ourselves as being totally immersed in the space around us which remains fixed as we and other objects move through it. Our spatial abilities are remarkable and have resisted a causal explanation despite the efforts of some of the best minds over the past two centuries. We can orient ourselves in space rapidly and effortlessly and can perceive spatial layouts based on extremely partial and ambiguous cues. We can judge depth through extremely subtle cues, either retinal disparity or parallax based on extremely small movements. We can recall spatial relations and re-create spatial properties in our imagination. We can move through space rapidly while avoiding obstacles. Animals and insects low on the phylogenetic scale, who may not have concepts inasmuch as they arguably do not have the power to reason about things that are absent from their immediate perception, nevertheless exhibit amazing powers of navigation, revealing that they have *quantitative* representations (or at least registrations—see section 3.2.2) of space and that they update these representations continually as they move through the space or interact with it in various sensorimotor modes. Although perception science is arguably the most developed of the cognitive sciences, there are many areas where it is far from clear that we have even posed the problems correctly; and the problem of spatial cognition strikes me as an extremely likely candidate for one of those problems.

To our modern sensibilities it also seems that space consists of a dense array of points that can be connected by straight lines. But these notions, which have been enshrined in our view of space at least since Euclid, may not be the right notions in terms of which to describe how we perceive space and especially how we represent space in our mind when we think about it or imagine events taking place in it. But what does it mean to say that this is not the way we cognize space? How can it be that the way we register space does not give a privileged place to points and lines?

I begin by trying to outline the nature of the problem that faces us. What does it mean to see the world as being laid out in space? What must the architecture of a mind be like that can do this? Given the patterns of energy that impinge on our sense organs, what must the mind do to create the particular understanding of space that we have, and the special skills that we have for reasoning about it, perceiving it, and moving through it? Many of our greatest thinkers have sought to answer such questions, from the early Greek thinkers like Euclid through those of the Enlightenment, such as Kepler and Descartes, and later Poincaré and Kant. The problem fascinated thinkers like Johannes Kepler, who (as we saw in chapter 1) was one of the first to recognize what we now take for granted, namely that (a) the retinal image plays an important role in the causal chain by which we come to know about space, and (b) the gap between the retinal image and the apprehension of space does not succumb to the same style of geometrical analysis that worked so well in explaining the connection between the light, the objects, and the image on the retina (Lindberg 1976). René Descartes's arithmetization of geometry was one of the seminal accomplishments in understanding that the problem had a formal structure that was amenable to rigorous study. Then, in the twentieth century, several great French natural philosophers were struck by the problem. Henri Poincaré (see Poincaré 1913/1963) was one of the most important of these and I will return to his views below. The problem of developing a sensory-based Euclidean geometry was raised again by Jean Nicod, who in the 1930s wrote a dissertation entitled "Geometry and the Sensory World" which laid the groundwork for a very different way of looking at this question (see Nicod 1970) and which influenced the thinking that led to the FINST theory.

For Nicod the problem was that the basic building blocks of the Euclidean (and Cartesian) view are *points* and *lines*, together with a way of constructing figures from them and the relation of *congruity*, none of which seemed to Nicod like the sorts of things that perceptual systems are equipped to detect and to use—they are complex *types* that collapse collections of sensory experiences into categories that make the statement of geometrical principles simple at the cost of making their connection with sensory data opaque.[1] Nicod pointed out that since there are many models of the Euclidean axioms (the Cartesian mapping of points in space onto tri-

---

1. In talking about Nicod's views, Bertrand Russell put it this way: "the formation and growth of physics are dominated completely by the pursuit of simple laws or, better, by the simple expression of laws. This expression can in fact only be obtained by marking complex things by simple names. For nature is constituted in such a way that it is not the simple things that enjoy simple laws, and so, in order to simplify the laws, we must complicate the meaning of terms" (Nicod 1970, introduction by Bertrand Russell). Nicod attempted to find simple things in geometry at the cost of complicating the statement of the geometrical principles.

ples of real numbers being the best known) we should seek the one that captures Euclidean spatial properties in terms of primitives best suited for creatures with sensory systems like ours. After considering a variety of such possible primitives, he developed several "sensible geometries" based on the geometry of volumes and volume-inclusion (what he called *spatiotemporal interiority*) and argued that this basis is closer to our sensory capacities than one based on points and lines (one reason being that volume inclusion is invariant with viewpoint, so it can be sensed as we move through space). With the addition of a few other novel ideas (such as *succession* and *global resemblance*), Nicod set out a new direction for understanding what space might consist in for a sentient organism. In the end he did not succeed in developing a complete formalization of geometry based on these sensory primitives, but he did point the way to the possibility of understanding sense-based space in a way radically different from the Euclidean, Cartesian, and Kantian approaches that seem so natural to us.

If Nicod had been able to carry out his program (he died at the age of 33 shortly after writing the thesis on sensory geometry) he might have provided a set of tools for viewing space that would have been more useful to us than the view that is thoroughly embedded in our way of thinking. But he did at least show us that thinking in terms of points and lines may not be the only way, and indeed may not be the most perspicuous way, for cognitive science to proceed in studying the psychology of space. This theme is one with which the present book has some sympathy, insofar as it begins not with points in space nor with lines and shapes, but with the notion of an object (or proto-object).

5.2 Internalizing General Spatial Constraints

Since Watson's identification of thought with subvocal speech there has been a strong mistrust of accounts of mental phenomena that appeal to direct internalizations of external properties.[2] I share this mistrust and continue to believe that cognitive theories that exhibit this sort of interiorizing of externals betray our latent behaviorist instincts, our tendency to focus on observables even if they are hidden just below the skin. But not all internalizations are misleading; in fact, our being intentional organisms entails that *in some sense* we have internalized (i.e., represented or registered)

---

2. Those acquainted with epistemology will find this use of the terms "internalize" and "externalize" somewhat deviant, for I am not concerned with epistemological questions of justification (Goldman 1986). Nonetheless the terms seem appropriately descriptive for present purposes.

aspects of the outside world and thus that our behavior is not continuously under the control of stimulus features, as assumed by Skinner (for a devastating critique of the behaviorist project as applied to language, see Chomsky 1959). In earlier chapters I argued that in addition to representations that are related to what they represent by the semantic relation of *satisfaction*, we need a more direct or causally based relation. I suggested that other sorts of internalizations besides conceptual ones play a role and therefore that we should take a second look at the general issue of internalization. In what follows I briefly sketch two approaches to the question of internal constraints on spatial representation that, unlike the internal display or picture theory, provide useful ways of looking at aspects of the problem.

5.2.1 Marr's Principle of Natural Constraints

Computational vision, perhaps more than any other approach to understanding visual perception, has faced squarely the problem of the poverty of stimulus information in relation to the richness of our perceptions. As is well known, the mapping from a distal scene to the retinal image(s) is not invertible—an unlimited number of distal patterns is mapped onto the same proximal pattern, so the proximal pattern does not univocally determine the distal pattern. Yet the visual system computes a univocal inversion: we almost always see a unique spatial layout despite the ambiguity of the incoming information. How we do this has been the subject of speculation for many years, with the prevailing view in the second half of the twentieth century being that visual interpretation depends on our knowledge of how things are likely to be in the world, and in particular on our knowledge and expectations of the particular scene in question. James Gibson questioned this assumption, insisting that the information was all there in the ambient light if we only looked for it in the right way. But it was David Marr (and others working on human and machine vision, such as Horn 1986; Koenderink 1990; Rosenfeld, Hummel, and Zucker 1976) who made the case convincingly that vision does not need (and indeed, is *unable* to use) information from our general store of knowledge in interpreting a scene (the argument is also made at some length in Pylyshyn 1999, where the reader can also find counterarguments and discussion). Rather, the reason that vision comes to a unique interpretation of spatial layouts is that it is unable to entertain the many alternative hypotheses compatible with the sensory evidence. And the reason for that is the existence of what Marr called "natural constraints," very general constraints on interpretation and representation that were compiled into the visual system through evolution and that reflect the nature of the sort of world we inhabit. It's not that the visual system knows that the scene before it consists of rigid objects, but rather that the visual system is so constituted that (to a first approximation) only interpretations consistent with the rigidity of most objects are available to it. If you knew that the objects were not rigid it would make no difference to the interpretation that vision would provide.

This idea, though not entirely unprecedented, was revolutionary when combined with a program of research in computational vision. The task then became to uncover the various natural constraints that are built into vision and to show how a system that respects these constraints could see spatial layouts the way humans do. This led to a series of projects typically entitled "structure from X" where the Xs are such sources of information as motion, shading, stereo, contour shape, and so on. This is a sense of internalizing of constraints that is both theoretically plausible and empirically validated, at least in many cases. The approach is closely related to a similar one in linguistics, where both language learning and sentence comprehension are underdetermined: The data on the basis of which languages are learned and on the basis of which sentences are parsed are similarly impoverished. Indeed there is a mathematical proof that in general you could not univocally infer a grammar based on samples of sentences alone (Gold 1967), and there are also proofs that some particular principles of, say, English arise because without those principles certain aspects of the grammar of the language could not be learned (Wexler and Cullicover 1980). What is assumed to enable the learning of a natural language in the face of the indeterminacy of grammatical rules are the innate brain structures described by Universal Grammar which prevent the infinite number of logically possible but humanly inaccessible languages from being learned or the similar infinite range of sentence parsings from being considered. Similarly, the interpretation of visual signals is constrained by internalized natural constraints.[3]

3. Even though the existence of such constraints in both perception and language is well accepted, there is some disagreement as to whether these reflect properties of our sort of world or whether they should be attributed to some sort of very general innate optimization (or "regularization") process in the brain (see, e.g., Poggio, Torre, and Koch 1990). For our purposes it does not matter—in either case there are constraints that prevent all logically possible analyses from being actual candidates, and it is the existence of these constraints that allows otherwise indeterminate problems to be resolved uniquely (in vision it is the analysis of a 2-D signal as originating from a 3-D world and in language it is the acquisition of a grammar from an impoverished set of exemplars).

The question of whether these constraints allow the representation of spatial information without conceptualization is an interesting one. If the representation of space as we experience it were achieved without our first carrying out inferences (which would require conceptualization), it would be a good candidate for a nonconceptual form of representation. This is very close to what the idea of natural constraints proposes. It claims that the representation of space is achieved without inference and therefore without necessarily conceptualizing the sensory information. A major question this story raises is whether such natural constraints also apply to representations constructed in thought as mental images.

In general, it is not clear how our ability to imagine certain spatial layouts (e.g., four-dimensional ones) can be explained by general constraints of the sort that are postulated in vision. Thinking is, by definition, carried out with conceptualized representations; yet there is no principled reason why a nonconceptual representation could not play a role if the cognitive architecture made this possible. We can, after all, make use of external representations such as diagrams and drawings, so why couldn't such things be constructed in thought? As we saw earlier, one of the problems with such a proposal is that imagination is creative in ways whose boundaries are unknown. While we may not be able to imagine a four-dimensional space, we can readily imagine objects moving in very nearly any way at all, with or without maintaining rigidity, with or without obeying the laws of physics or the axioms of geometry. And this plasticity of thought is a major problem for any internalization theory, as we will see.

5.2.2 Shepard's Psychophysical Complementarity

Roger Shepard (see Shepard 2001) has taken the idea of internalized properties and principles even further. Citing the example of the circadian rhythm which internalizes the earth's daily light–dark cycle, he argues that many reliable generalizations of human behavior can be traced to our internalizing universal properties of the world. His argument is based on the evolutionary advantage of our being constructed in the way that we are—a sort of Leibnizian "preestablished harmony" between world and mind. Such an argument should lead us to expect that universal physical properties would be internalized, for what is more important than correctly anticipating where and when a rock will fall on you? Yet this is not the case; physical principles do not seem to have been internalized the way geometry has in either vision or in thought, and especially not in infant cognition despite infants' ability to recover many abstract categories such as causality and agency (Leslie 1988). What appears to be internalized, according to

Shepard, are "principles of kinematic geometry" or of transformations of objects through space. Because of these internalized principles we tend to perceive objects as traveling through the simplest geodesics in a six-dimensional space (three dimensions of translation and three of rotation). Shepard presents some interesting examples of this principle, involving apparent motion of asymmetrical 2-D forms that tend to be seen as traveling in 3-D according to a screw transformation, as predicted by the "simple geodesic" story.

These are interesting and suggestive ideas, and if there is anything to the internalization principle these are certainly good candidates. But neither Marr's natural constraints nor Shepard's geodesics constitute internalizations of space in the strong sense that has been assumed by many psychologists (see section 5.3); rather, they are principles of abduction that determine which hypotheses the organism is able to entertain. In that respect these constraints are like Universal Grammar. The alternative to such constraints is the conceptual story: rather than internalizing properties, we learn about them (by induction) and then we draw inferences from them. In the end this cannot be the case for all spatial properties, for reasons that I have discussed (mainly that our beliefs must eventually make contact with the world), so the initial step must be causal and therefore the only open question is how this happens. Internalizing is a way of incorporating *principles* or *constraints* in a nonconceptual way. It is thus not surprising that the only candidates for this sort of internalization are constraints that apply to modular parts of the perceptual systems where general reasoning does not occur because the processes there are encapsulated from the rest of cognition.

Although the Shepard type of constraint does not entail a particular format or medium of spatial representation, some people have taken the proposal as evidence that the properties of Euclidean space are somehow internalized as an inner space (e.g., a space defined by states of assemblies of neurons—as proposed by some of the commentators on Shepard's paper, such as Edelman 2001). If they are, then there is little evidence of their operating in thought—particularly in mental imagery. We can easily imagine objects flouting kinematic principles, traveling along nongeodesic paths—in fact, violating just about any principle or constraint we can think of.[4] And this, as I remarked earlier, is what eventually leads most

4. As noted in the previous chapter, a major factor controlling how we imagine things is the implicit requirement of the imagery task, namely that it is about recreating how things would look if they were seen. Thus one apparent constraint on mental images is that they are viewed from a single point in space, as opposed to

inquiries into the cognitive architecture to the view that the mind is much more like a Turing machine than any multidimensional space or connectionist network (Fodor and Pylyshyn 1988).

5.3 Internalizing Spatial Properties by Mapping Them Onto an Inner Space

Before proceeding with this survey of approaches to the representation of space I need to mention two proposals that arise primarily in the context of the mental imagery debate. Both involve strong forms of internalization in that they propose that we cognize perceived or imagined space by mapping it onto an internal space. The strongest form of this proposal locates the mental representation of spatial properties in the literal space of the surface of the unfolded visual cortex. The weaker form, which most supporters cite when pushed on the question of whether there is a literal space-in-the-head, is the idea of a *functional space*. The former proposal (brain space) runs into both conceptual and empirical problems, and the latter proposal (functional space) is either a confusion about the explanatory value of such a "space," or it reduces to the proposal that spatial properties of the representation arise from the nature of the architecture of the mind–brain—which is a disguised form of the brain space proposal. Because these proposals illustrate several points about the explanatory role of representations, I will take a few pages to discuss them before proceeding to the present externalist proposal.

5.3.1 Brain Space

If perceived or imagined space were mapped onto a literal space—a neural layout in the brain—then we could have an account that explained many of the spatial properties of represented patterns.[5] In particular, it could pro-

---

several places at once (like the subject of a Picasso painting) or from no perspective at all. This is surely because we do not know what it would *look like* if viewed in any other way. To imagine that the world is some other way (e.g., 4-D) may in fact be possible if we put aside the requirement that we imagine *seeing* it that way. It is not inconceivable that one could learn to solve problems in 4-D space (perhaps with some *virtual reality* training). Some people claim to be able to *reason about* such objects, if not visualize them (Hinton 1906).

5. A puzzling turn in this discussion is Kosslyn's recent claim that the depictive display need not be literally spatial in the way described earlier (page 127). He now says (Kosslyn, Thompson, and Ganis 2006, p. 131): "The fact that topographically

vide an explanation of many of the apparent metrical properties of mentally represented space. For example:

(1) If we represent the fact that A is further from C than from B (AC > AB), then there would be a greater quantity of represented space (as distinct from a representation of more space, which makes no commitment about "amount of represented space") between A and C than between A and B. In other words, distance is represented in some form (perhaps in an analog form) so that each point in empty space is somehow explicitly represented.

(2) If we represent A, B, and C as being ordered and collinear, then there would be an explicit representation of B as being *between* A and C (where by an "explicit representation" I mean that the relation "between" need not be inferred, but can be "read off" by some noninferential means such as by pattern matching).

(3) If we represent three objects A, B, and C, then it would always be the case that the distance from A to B plus the distance from B to C would never be less than the distance from A to C (i.e., the *triangle inequality* of measure theory would hold so that $AB + BC \geq AC$).

(4) If we represent three objects A, B, and C so that AB is orthogonal to BC, then for short distances AB, BC, and CD it would be the case that $AC^2 = AB^2 + BC^2$ (i.e., distances would be locally Euclidean so that the Pythagorean theorem would hold for short distances).

---

organized areas are physically depictive is irrelevant for present purposes. The neurons in these areas could be interconnected arbitrarily, but as long as *fixed* connections to areas further downstream 'unscramble' the activity in earlier areas appropriately, the earlier areas will function to depict." You can certainly get such spatial behavior as the scanning effect from a display that does not *look* spatial, as long as the relevant spatial properties can be recovered by a mechanism that in effect remaps them back to the literal spatial form. Indeed, you can get it from a verbal representation so long as you can use that description to reconstruct a spatial display. Notice that unless the downstream connections do in fact unscramble the information back into a depictive display, this version of the "depiction" story no longer sits well with either the phenomenology or the psychophysical properties that made the picture theory attractive, e.g., the assumption that mental images have metrical properties including distance, visual angle, and certain patterns of resolution. Being able to recover these properties is not the same as having them, and it's the latter that make the pictorialists' claims principled (it's the existence of real distance and not some simulacrum that give a principled explanation of such empirical relations as *time = distance ÷ velocity*). I will return to this question in section 5.3.2(2).

(5) If A is represented as being above B, and C is represented as being below B, then there would also be an explicit representation of A above C (so three-term series problems could be solved by "spatial paralogic"; De Soto, London, and Handel 1965).

(6) If object D is added "far enough away" from the representation of A, B, and C, it would not affect the spatial relations among A, B, and C (so "irrelevant properties and relations do not change existing spatial relations").

The last property, (6), is the sort of requirement that in its most general form raises what people in artificial intelligence call the *frame problem* (Pylyshyn 1987): In planning a series of actions one must infer all the possible consequences in the entire represented universe for each possible action, including which relations remain invariant, because there is no *a priori* way to catalog everything that is relevant to a particular action—in principle anything can be relevant to any inference, because inferences are holistic (which is why this is sometimes also called the *relevance problem*). Having a physical spatial layout of the represented situation might solve the frame problem for the properties that were mapped onto the model. Otherwise property (6) requires an inference and may entail "frame axioms" that state what won't change for various actions.[6]

In addition to these geometrical questions, which can be dealt with in a straightforward way if there were a real space in the brain onto which the represented space is mapped, there are dynamic properties that could be addressed with the addition of other assumptions. For example, we know that it takes longer to imagine traveling a longer imagined distance than a shorter imagined distance (the so-called *image-scanning phenomenon*). If a "longer distance" were mapped by a monotonic (or at least locally affine) projection onto longer brain distances, then the equation *time = distance ÷ speed* would apply and would therefore provide an expla-

6. Notice that even in this simple example I had to add the qualifying phrase "far enough away from" for the point to go through. Otherwise, if A bore the relation "resting on" to B, and D were added "between" A and B, assumption (6) would fail since A would no longer be "resting on" B. What makes the frame problem so difficult in general is that there is no limit to the relations that objects can enter into and so there is no limit to what might change when a new relation is added to the representation. Consider, for example, the effect on the representation of adding the relations: "Turns_Green_If_within_2mm (x, y)," or "Connected_by_string(x, y)." Adding the first relation to a representation, requires checking every pair of objects, of which there might be very many, and recomputing colors after any location is changed, including location changes that are inferred from the second relation.

nation of this regularity whereas other forms of representation would not (i.e., there is no principle of the form *actual time = represented distance ÷ represented speed*). Problems such as these (and others as well) do not arise if space is mapped onto real space in the brain.

But is there any reason to think that imagined space is represented by cortical space in this way? Is there any reason to think that when we imagine or think about things laid out in space we create what I called (in chapter 3) a *neural layout* in the brain? I postpone that question until later, since this is one of the questions addressed by the proposal I will offer.

5.3.2 Functional Space and Principled Constraints

(1) Virtual space? Suppose, despite its *prima facie* attraction, we find no support for the assumption that perceived space is mapped onto real space in the brain. Can we still reap the explanatory benefits with something less that literal space? Can we, in other words, get some of the benefit of real space with some sort of "virtual" or "functional" space? This option is very frequently raised (see, e.g., the Kosslyn quotation in section 4.5 on page 127). Consider the phenomena you would like the representational system to explain. You would like it to account for the sorts of geometrical regularities mentioned by way of examples in the six points listed above (e.g., it should allow noninferential recognition of such things as the relation "between" that holds of the second item when three ordered items are arranged collinearly; that for three imagined items A, B, and C, the distance AB plus the distance BC is never less that the distance AC, and so on). Also, you would like the sorts of properties that Shepard discussed (under the title "kinematic principles") to hold. In addition, if it is a Euclidean space (which it should be, at least locally, if it is to be veridical) the Pythagorean theorem should hold. Simple physical laws such as the relation between time, distance, and speed should also hold. This requires a homeomorphic mapping (a continuous neighborhood-preserving mapping) of space onto a set of properties that bear the same relations to one another as do the properties of space itself. Why couldn't this be done computationally, using a symbolic data structure such as a matrix (as mentioned in the quotation)? This is the most widely cited option in the literature on spatial mental images (Denis and Kosslyn 1999).

There is a simple reason why a data structure such as a matrix will not do: A matrix is a formalism that *embodies no processing constraints whatever*. It can have whatever properties one stipulates it to have. It can represent empty places, or not (sparse matrices in a computer generally conserve space by not keeping empty cells but generating them as needed, much as list processing languages deal with the addition and deletion of cells); it can be traversed by moving through intermediate cells, or not (and even the property of being "intermediate" has to be stipulated for each relevant pair of cells); it can be used to exhibit the rotation of an object by retaining its shape rigidly, or not; it can take more time to move through more cells, representing greater separations, or not. The mere fact of its being a matrix does not ensure any constraints at all. But then why does a matrix appear to be more natural than other representations such as a set of sentences in the language of thought? There is only one reason why operations such as moving a focus of attention or translating or rotating a rigid shape appear to be more natural in a matrix representation: Since we think of a matrix as two-dimensional, it is natural for us to think of it as a simulation of locations in real space. But if that is true, then it is the real space that has the properties in a "natural" way—in which case it is the real space, not the matrix, that provides the principled constraints. Certain constraints, such as the requirement that one move through intermediate cells, are natural only if the matrix is a simulation of space. The matrix itself appears to be a two-dimensional object only because it is convenient to use pairs of names to characterize individual cells. In fact in the computer the cells are accessed by a single atomic name, a fusion of the two individual names that we consider to be "dimensions." As for the apparent naturalness of moving through adjacent cells in a computer implementation, this relies on the convention of viewing names as numerals and on the existence of the addition/subtraction operations (and possibly also matrix multiplication) in most computer architectures—none of which is likely to apply to the architecture of the brain.

What is relevant for our purpose in explaining the metrical nature of spatial representation is that a data structure such as a matrix either imposes constraints on possible operations or it doesn't. If it doesn't, it is of no interest in this discussion because it does not explain anything. If it does, there still remains the question of whether it does so because of an implicit assumption that it is simulating real space (which derives its explanatory force from real space, thus making this strategy equivalent to the "brain space" option) or because one merely stipulates that this is how it should behave in order to match the data at hand. None of the relevant spacelike properties is an inherent property of the matrix format; they are merely collateral stipulations. But in that case the matrix—or any other "functional space" proposal—is no different from any other form of representation, notwithstanding its intuitive appeal. It is important to see this problem in terms of the question of what constrains the model to have certain properties. If the constraints must be stated as additional assumptions then the format does no work in explaining how the spatial character comes about, since such additional assumptions can be added to any form of representation.

Here is another way to look at this issue. In appealing to functional space to explain many of the spatial properties of what we think and imagine we need to ask whether properties we appeal to are fixed properties of the functional space, or are stipulated simply to match the data at hand. This can be viewed as an issue of degrees of freedom: if we postulate ad hoc property P to account for some particular phenomenon, then P serves as a free empirical parameter. We always need *some* such parameters, since we are building a theory in part to account for data at hand. But the more such free empirical parameters there are the weaker the explanatory power of the theory. The goal is to account for the greatest range of phenomena with the fewest such free parameters. How can we reduce the number of free parameters? One way to eliminate free parameters is to determine which parameters are due to the relatively fixed properties of the format or the medium of representation—in this case, the architecture or brain structures—thus decreasing the options available for fitting the given data, thereby increasing the explanatory power of the resulting theory. This is the strategy of attributing as many empirical phenomena as possible to the fixed architecture of the visual (or imaginal) system—a policy that I have strongly advocated (Pylyshyn 1991, 1996; see also chapter 3, section 3.2.2, of the present volume). What, then, if we were to assume that the spatial properties arise from fixed brain properties other than the spatial layout of topographically arranged neurons?

(2) Space as a property of the architecture There is some understandable uneasiness with the view that to account for the spatial properties of mental imagery we must postulate a spatial screen or neural layout. Consequently, alternatives have occasionally been proposed that appear to provide the same functions but without having to assume a literal spatial layout in the brain. Consider the following thought experiment in which we start off with a real quantized[7] spatial display in the brain—the sort of

7. The assumption that the display is quantized into a finite number of cells would appear to be unimportant since the cells can be made arbitrarily small. But in fact a quantized display leads to problems if taken literally since distances measured in terms of cells vary with direction, so such a space is not isotropic (and distances do not obey Euclidean axioms).

"depictive" neural layout postulated in the earlier Kosslyn quotation (p. 127), together with associated neural connections appropriate for the next stage in the neural pathway (e.g., some pattern-detection function). Now imagine that the neural fibers are long enough to allow us to move the cells in the early layer (V1) around—to scramble the physical locations of these cells while keeping the connections the same. The result no longer appears to be a real spatial display, yet the function of the network remains the same since the connections have not been altered. This is a case in which the spatial character of the representation appears to derive from the fixed neural wiring and is independent of the geometry of the physical arrangement of cells. Does such a set of cells genuinely implement a functional space, or does it merely derive its properties from real space? The answer, depends on whether the prescrambled locations are part of the explanation of the system's function.

This example is an instance of a class of spatial representations in which the spatial functions arise from the fixed properties of the perceptual or the cognitive system—from its architecture. For purposes of the present discussion I do not distinguish between various ways that the architecture itself might constrain the behavior. These might include proposals in which spatial properties are imposed by an analog mechanism of some sort, or any fixed mapping of space onto properties of the cognitive architecture, so long as the right relations among spatial properties are maintained. One example is suggested by Kosslyn, Thompson, and Ganis (2006; see also footnote 5 above) in which the "depictive" array is actually realized by some complex but fixed network of neurons that treats certain pairs of neurons as representing adjacent places even though the neurons themselves may in fact be located far from one another in the brain. This option uses what might be called an encrypted version of literal space. The question is: Does this mechanism use a literal space or a functional space, according to the present taxonomy?

To count as literal space, as I understand the term, the essential requirement is that the system must get its explanatory force from real spatial properties, that is, the sample of properties listed at the beginning of section 5.3.1 must hold. The system of representations counts as using literal space if it meets two requirements: (1) The properties derive from a fixed architecture and therefore are cognitively impenetrable; and (2) One must appeal to real spatial properties in providing explanations of why certain behaviors hold. For this to be true of the encrypted space option, the real spatial layout must not only be recoverable (decryptable) but must be cited in providing explanations because it is the source of the principles that determine the behavior of the neural circuits. In other words, the circuits have the properties they have not by mere ad hoc stipulation (they are not free parameters), but rather because they really derive from spatial locations and it's these locations that explain their geometrical properties.

For example, some pairs of cells are treated as being adjacent to each other while other pairs of cells are treated as being far from one another. Which pairs count as close together and which count as far apart cannot be determined without the decryption function. Without the recoverability of a spatial display there would be no independent motivation for the spatial properties that the representation exhibits. Thus the answer to a question such as, "Why does it take longer to shift attention over a greater represented distance?" will refer to the literal meaning of "distance" in the decrypted display, not to properties of architectural network onto which distance is mapped. That's because the equation *time = distance ÷ speed* has the explanatory force of a nomological principle, whereas any other ad hoc arrangement of neurons that happens to yield this same pattern would be unable to answer the question, Why that time function rather than some other? It is no accident that talk about the nature of spatial representations makes essential use of spatial terms (e.g., patterns in representations are said to be bigger, above, inside, in relation to other patterns). The frequently cited notion of an analog architecture is a special case of a fixed architecture, though perhaps with some added requirements, depending on how we understand what constitutes an analog representation.[8]

What, then, do we say about the encrypted-space option, or any option that attributes spatial properties to the architecture of the visual (or imaginal) system? Such architecture-based explanations do not circumvent the most serious criticisms raised in chapter 4 in connection with the literal brain-space proposal.

(a) Architecture-based explanations for how spatial properties arise are not consistent with relevant empirical data. By definition, properties of the

8. Despite the existence of clear and easily understood cases of analog processes, and despite the frequent references made to this notion, it remains poorly understood. In particular it has turned out to be extremely difficult to give an acceptable set of conditions for something being an analog. I have used the term to refer to any case where behavior is attributable to a fixed architecture (e.g., Pylyshyn 1984, chap. 7). Others have reserved the term for processes or representations involving continuous properties (see, e.g., Goodman 1968; Lewis 1971). Fodor (2007) has recently argued that what makes something an analog representation is that it has no canonical decomposition into semantically interpreted constituents.

architecture do not change in ways attributable to changes in beliefs—they are cognitively impenetrable. Thus empirical phenomena ought to be insensitive to beliefs (e.g., about the task or about how events would unfold in the world). But the data do not support this assumption. Consider any empirical phenomena described in terms of size or distance, such as we observe with different mental sizes or different distances in, for example, mental scanning experiments. These phenomena are cognitively penetrable (see section 4.5.1). So far as I am aware all examples described in terms of spatial features of mental representations are either penetrable or their robustness is due to their task demands—that is, subjects take the task to require that they simulate what they would see if they were to witness the relevant event. As I pointed out in footnote 4, if we require that the task be accompanied by the specified conscious content (e.g., "imagine that the mouse occupies a small part of your field of view," or "find the named place on your image of the map"), this requires further that you re-create the experience of seeing the event unfold and that, in turn, depends on your knowing what things would look like, how long they would take, and so on, which adds another constraint to the resulting observed behavior. The way things *would look* is the way you believe they *would be*, hence the conformity of the data to the theory that postulates a spatial display.

(b) Architecture-based explanations that do not appeal to literal space (e.g., encryptic space or analogs) are not compatible with the natural and intuitively satisfying story told by those who appeal to a literal-spatial display about why, for instance, it takes more time to scan greater imagined distances or why it takes longer to detect small features in a small image. Recall that the story for the mental scanning experiments, which agrees with the phenomenology that motivates the literal display account, is that it takes longer to scan attention between imagined places that are further apart on the original scene, *because* the *distance on the representation* is greater (and you have to scan over empty spaces in the representation). Without that story, which refers explicitly to the image's distance, the attraction and motivation behind the display view are lost. Similarly in the image-size phenomenon, it takes longer to report details of a smaller image *because* fine details are harder to see and so one has to "zoom in" on the image first. In each case a literal spatial property (in these examples, distance and size) is invoked. If we attribute the time function to the architecture without mentioning any spatial properties, the claim becomes that, in effect, it takes longer because that's just the way it is given the kind of brain we have; and that claim has to be stated without mentioning the distance on or size of the representation. There is nothing left of "distance on the image,'' which is the reason for the interest in the mental scanning experiments (and is why they have served as a ''window on the mind''; see Denis and Kosslyn 1999). Consequently we are left with no principled *explanation* of the scanning results or the image-size results, only a restating of the finding.

To summarize, the issue here is simply that an explanation of how spatial properties are represented needs to appeal to principled, as opposed to ad hoc, properties (or post hoc stipulations). A ''functional space'' may or may not be principled. It would be principled if it was viewed as a *simulation* of real brain space since in that case it's the real space (in the brain) that provides the explanatory principle, and the matrix is simply a convenient way to implement it in a conventional computer (otherwise you would need a computer with a display and a visual system to examine it, etc.). Of course, though, this version is simply the picture-in-the-head alternative which has so many other problems (see section 4.5.3). The architecture-based account could also be principled if it is the result of independently motivated properties of the architecture; but in the case of the spatial examples, such as the distance and size phenomena, the independent motivation must be based on properties of space, so literal spatial properties ultimately are not avoided.

5.3.3   Internalizing by Incorporating Visual-motor Experience: Poincaré's Insights

There is another way to understand our sense of space that approaches an internalist view, but only insofar as it emphasizes an internal link with the motor system. In what follows I will develop this general idea and show that rather than internalizing space, it actually does the converse: On this view, the mind actually externalizes space by projecting spatial relations onto visual-motor and proprioception-based sensory information. The basic idea for this direction can be traced to the work of Henri Poincaré early in the twentieth century. Below I sketch this idea, which requires a brief detour from my narrative in order to link the view I am presenting to the work of Poincaré.

In a series of essays written almost a century ago, Poincaré analyzes the nature of space. In one of these essays he describes how a three-dimensional sense of space might arise in a sentient organism confronted with information in various forms and modalities and in many (not just three) sensory dimensions (Poincaré 1913/1963). A central idea in Poincaré's account is that the organism has to be able to distinguish between experiences that correspond to changes in position and those that do not.[9] According to Poincaré, the key to being able to recognize the difference depends on being able to distinguish between changes brought about by our own actions and changes that are externally caused. Here Poincaré makes use of the notion of the reversibility of certain sensory states—what he calls a *correction*—whereby we can undo an externally caused change by a complementary voluntary change that brings back the original sensory state. Suppose, for example, that you are touching some object with the index finger of your right hand and receiving the tactile signal T while at the same time you sense the object visually, yielding the visual signal V. According to Poincaré, if the object is moved by external causes, you will perceive the visual signal change from V to V' and the tactile signal will disappear. But you may be able to bring back the original tactile signal T and visual signal V by an action, represented by a series of muscular movements accompanied by a sequence of proprioceptive sensory signals $S_i = (S', S'' \ldots)$. This action in effect undoes the movement of the object in space by a compensatory voluntary movement. Moreover, this same "renewal" of the tactile signal can be accomplished equally by any member of an equivalence class of sequences $\{S_1, S_2, S_3, \ldots\}$. What the members of this equivalence class have in common is that they can be described as "moving your finger from a common starting position to a common final position." According to Poincaré, what you, or your evolutionary ancestors, have internalized is the principle that if you are touching an object and your visual signal changes from V to V', you can once again touch the object by carrying out a motor sequence in which the proprioceptive signal follows a sequence corresponding to one of the members of the equivalence class. Thus the basis for your knowledge of spatial locations is this skill of moving in such a way as to bring back a tactile or visual signals (as noted in footnote 3 of chap. 1, my use of the terms "sensation" or "sensory signal" refers to sensory information and does not assume that such signals are conscious).

Poincaré used the notion of an equivalence class of sequences of sensory signals that correspond to moving a finger from a particular initial position to a particular final position as a way to define a common location across the several fingers and hands. The classes of movements define "spaces"

9. Interestingly, Clark (2000) makes a similar point when he discusses why sensations that correspond to different locations are fundamentally of a different kind from sensations that correspond to qualitative properties such as color, size, shape, and so on.

and the spaces marked out by each finger are then merged by the recognition that when two fingers touch one another they define the notion of "same place" and so lead to the convergence of the initially distinct spaces. Poincaré then goes on to argue that we represent space as having three dimensions, rather than two or four, because of the adaptive conditions on the equivalence classes; two sequences of sensations are deemed to be equivalent if and only if they take us to the same final position (where the tactile sensation is renewed). It is this boundary condition that yields the three-dimensionality of space. The reason I have belabored this point is that apart from providing an elegant account of the basis of the dimensionality of space, Poincaré's analysis touches on several issues that will be relevant to our present discussion.[10]

The details of this analysis don't carry much conviction these days, and indeed the condition of the reversibility of sensation was criticized by Jean Nicod, but many of the ideas remain sound. For example, the first point of contact between Poincaré's analysis and the ones I will propose concerns the recognition of two distinct kinds of changes in sensory states: those that signal a difference in location and those that signal a difference in some sensory quality, say, color or texture. Whether or not you like Poincaré's way of making the distinction in terms of the capacity to "correct" or revert to an earlier location-marking sensory state,[11] the distinction does play an important role in recent discussions of sentience, and it is especially central in the work of Austen Clark (2000), though for different reasons. The second point of contact concerns the emphasis on sequences of muscular actions and sensory inputs and equivalence classes of such sequences. This a remarkably modern idea, although it is not expressed in this way in current writings. What Poincaré's analysis shares with contemporary analyses of what I called the "sense of space" is the idea that the

10. Poincaré's examples use fingers and the capacity to sense the locations of fingers. His essay was on my mind at the time I was formulating the FINST index theory and may be the reason for the appearance of the term "finger" in FINST.

11. This use of reversibility of sensory states as the signature of voluntary movement plays a central role in a recent model of how properties of space can be inferred from minimal information about the dependencies between actions and sensory inputs (Philipona, O'Regan, and Nadal 2003). There is in fact a great deal in common between the present analysis and the ideas on the importance of sensorimotor factors in visual perception proposed by the Kevin O'Regan and his colleagues (spelled out in O'Regan and Noë 2002), although the claims made in the latter publication on the nature of conscious perception seem to me unconvincing (for reasons I allude to in my commentary on the O'Regan and Noë paper, in Pylyshyn 2002b).

nonvisual apprehension of space may be a construct based on mechanisms that compute the equivalences among otherwise very different sequences of muscular gestures. How we manage to compute the relations among registrations of positions of limbs, sensors, and other movable parts of the body is arguably one of most ubiquitous and best understood functions of the brain—functions carried out primarily in the posterior parietal cortex, but also in the superior colliculus, and in the motor and premotor cortical areas.

Computing a position-representation given a position-representation in a different frame of reference is commonly referred to as *coordinate transformation* (CT; for a review of the biological basis of this function, see Gallistel 1999). One way to view CTs is as a function from the representation of an articulated part of the body (e.g., the eye in its orbit) in one orientation to the representation of that part (or a different part) in a different orientation or relative to a different frame of reference. It also applies to computing a representation of a location within the reference frame of one modality to a corresponding representation in the reference frame of another modality. The relevant representations of limbs in these cases are typically expressed within a framework that is local to the parts in question—such as the states of the muscles that control the movements, or the joint angles that characterize their relative positions, or to endpoint locations relative to the body. The relevant representations of sensory inputs may similarly be in proximal coordinates (e.g., locations on the retina or on the basilar membrane) or other local coordinates.

The importance of these ideas in the present context relates directly to the theme of nonconceptual contact between mind and the world. In particular, since I have argued (in chapter 3) that this contact does not begin with the selection of spatiotemporal regions I need to say how places in space are represented—and indeed whether they are represented *as such*. What I will do in the last part of this chapter is consider another approach to the question of what it means for the nonconceptual visual system to index or pick out a place or region in space. We have already discussed the problems with the traditional view that the first, nonconceptual (or sentient) contact with the world occurs through the detection of features-at-locations (the idea developed by Peter Strawson as part of his analysis of the representation of particulars, and adopted recently by Austen Clark in his theory of sentience). What I want to do now is suggest another way in which what appears at first glance to be spatial selection might be achieved without the selection of places, specified in terms of a unitary

frame of reference. But first I will see if any general conditions on this problem can be set out.

5.4 What Is Special about Representing Space?

5.4.1 Conditions on a Theory of Active Spatial Representation (ASPAR)
The impression that spatial representation is different from other kinds of
representation is usually associated with examples from perception and
spatial reasoning (or mental imagery). In other words the evidence comes
from phenomena that involve active working memory, as opposed to
more permanent long-term memory. There is reason to think that the representation of space under these conditions, which I will refer to as *active
spatial representation* or ASPAR, is special in a number of ways.[12] Although
many of the characteristics of ASPARs are also shared by other nonspatial
representations, representing space appears to involve all the following
characteristics in essential ways.

**(1) ASPARs must be able to represent magnitudes in a continuous man-
ner** Psychophysical evidence shows that we have encodings of relative
magnitudes and that the magnitudes that are encoded have a particular,
systematic effect in reasoning. Examples of such systematic effects include
scalar variability, in which error variance is proportional to the mean (so
that the coefficient of variation, $Variance(T)/T$, remains constant); *Fechner's
law* (or the *Weber-Fechner law*), in which the discriminability of the magnitude of two property values varies in proportion to the mean magnitude of
the properties (i.e., $\Delta T/T$ is constant); and the *symbolic distance effect*, in
which the time required to compare two magnitudes, including nonsen-
sory ones like cost, increases in proportion to the ratio of the magnitude
of the difference to the mean magnitude, as in Fechner's law. Although
the inference from psychophysical regularities to conclusions about the
format of representations is by no means free of problems, since it requires
some (unspecified) assumptions about the nature of the mechanisms that

12. Although I am loath to propose yet another acronym, the closest constructs in
general use, "visual short-term memory" and "visual workspace," both have the
wrong connotations since what I am trying to capture is not a type of memory, visual or otherwise, or a storage place, but rather the representation one constructs
when reasoning about spatial properties and relations. I make no claims about
whether this is located in a distinct place in the brain, whether it is part of a more
general amodal memory, and whether it is conscious.

interpret the representations, as well as a theory of how errors arise, it has led many people to conclude that at least some magnitudes may be represented in analog form, where both the content and the vehicle of the representation are continuous (see note 7, this chapter).

(2) ASPARs must represent stable spatial configurations Spatial configurations involve relations over multiple objects; in that sense they are holistic and require simultaneous access to multiple represented objects. Access to such configurational information may allow some spatial consequences to be arrived at by pattern match or by table lookup, without inferences based on independent geometrical axioms. Take, for example, the well-known three-term series problems which are assumed to involve spatial mental images (Huttenlocher 1968). These are problems involving ordering syllogisms such as: "John is taller than Mary; John is shorter than Fred; who is tallest (or shortest)?" The explanation of many of the observed effects is that the subject forms a spatial image, using an imagined spatial relation such as "above" to map "taller," and then is able to "read off" the correct answer from the resulting spatial array apparently without using the axiom of transitivity or any similar rule of syllogistic logic (of course such a rule is implicit from the very start since it determines which spatial property in the representation is of the same logical type as the relation in the problem being represented; the relation "above" could not be used to map an intransitive symmetrical relation such as "is married to"). Such "reading off" the properties of a spatial display requires that configurational or pattern information among all relevant objects be available at once, or at least that they remain in place as the objects are examined.

(3) ASPARs must represent spatial relations in three dimensions Relations in depth must be in the same format as the encoding of relations in the plane since the two must work together seamlessly. Experimental evidence from such phenomena as mental rotation and mental scanning show identical functions in depth as in the plane.[13] As we saw in the

13. The mental scanning experiment was briefly sketched in section 4.5.1 and illustrated in fig. 5.2. These results are the same when "scanning" in depth. The mental rotation experiments are not described (but see Pylyshyn 1979, 2003). The latter showed that when asked whether two oriented shapes are congruent or mirror images (enantiomorphs) of one another, the time it takes to respond is proportional to the angle between them—in either two or three dimensions (the original 3-D finding is reported in Shepard and Metzler 1971).

previous chapter, this 3-D requirement is one of the decisive reasons why a mental image cannot be identified with a topographical display in visual cortex.

(4) ASPARS represent spatial properties acquired through different modalities   It seems that at least some spatial representations may be amodal, or multimodal across the auditory, tactile, and proprioceptive modalities (Spence and Driver 2004). Patterns and locations perceived initially in one modality are often remapped onto other modalities. For example, Jon Driver and Charles Spence carried out a number of ingenious experiments that involved presenting cues in one modality and observing the effect on discrimination tasks at the same general location in another modality (described in Driver and Spence 1998, 2004). They found a high degree of cross-over, so that a cue on the left side of a visual display improved elevation discrimination ("which of two stimuli is higher?") of both auditory and tactile stimuli on the cued side. Interestingly, with tactile stimuli the same result is observed even if the hands are crossed, showing that it is the location of the tactile stimuli in extrapersonal space rather than their location relative to the body that matters. Similarly, when subjects expect a sound on one side, both auditory discrimination and visual judgments on that side are improved—even if visual events are twice as likely to appear on the other side. Perhaps even more surprising, in an experiment in which subjects had to judge relevant tactile stimuli on one hand while ignoring concurrent tactile distractors on the other, the distractors interfered less when the two hands were held further apart—so again it seems that it is the location of tactile stimuli in external space that matters even when the task is to discriminate relative location on the skin. But spatial location information is not entirely shared across modalities. There have been some reports that we cannot easily recognize shapes if some of the location information is presented visually and other information is presented in the tactile or auditory modality. The question of whether one can transfer shape information across modalities without learning is called *Molyneux's problem*; it appears that very young infants are able to transfer at least simple shapes (Meltzoff 1993), so cross-modal shape representation may be at least partly an innate capacity.

   The unitary first-person experience of space, together with demonstrations of cross-modal spatial attention, has promoted the assumption that we have a *single global representation* of space in an allocentric frame of reference. I will suggest shortly that this assumption is not warranted if it is interpreted to mean there is a single representation of space *in a single frame of reference* that cuts across perceptual modalities as well as thought and imagination.

(5) ASPARs must be able to engage the motor system   One of the characteristics of spatial representations is that they allow us to "point to" represented things (e.g., in our mental image). When you imagine your office you can think (and even making corresponding pointing gestures while having the thoughts) "my computer screen is *here* and my keyboard is *there*." Eye movements when examining a mental image exhibit similar patterns to those observed in vision (Brandt and Stark 1997). In fact, one of the things that makes mental images seem literally spatial is our ability to orient ourselves to and refer to parts of the image in a demonstrative manner (using the terms "here" and "there").

But there are also significant differences in detail between motor reactions to mental objects and to actually perceived ones. Though we may gesture toward imagined objects, they do not engage the visual-motor system the way perceived objects do. Detailed analyses of gestures such as reaching and grasping show that these actions differ in detail when the object of the reaching is remembered or imagined from when it is seen. Actions toward remembered objects have the characteristics of pantomimed movements rather than movements that are under the control of vision (Goodale, Jacobson, and Keillor 1994). This suggests that visual and imagined or recalled objects may engage different perceptual-motor systems (Goodale and Milner 2004).

(6) ASPARs must capture the continuity and connectedness of space The continuity and connectedness of space is an important ingredient of spatial representation even though it is not clear exactly what it entails. In particular it leaves open questions such as the following (the proposal I will be making later provides tentative answers to these questions):

• Are empty places explicitly represented *as such* (as opposed to there being some indirect way of answering the question, "is there something at location *x*")?
• Does the system of representation (or the architecture) itself ensure that distances meet *metrical axioms* (e.g., the triangle inequality $AB + BC \geq AC$) or that they are *Euclidean* (e.g., follow the Pythagorean theorem)? Or is that the result of subjects' tacit knowledge of geometry?
• Are representations of the movements of objects (or the movement of representations of objects) constrained so that in getting from A to B they

must pass through "intermediate" locations? And must they take longer if the distance from A to B is represented as greater?

• Are primitive non–conceptually mediated perceptions of such properties as causality the result of properties of the ASPAR mechanisms, or do they have their origins elsewhere? For example, is the perception of causality in the Michotte tunnel effect or in the launch effect (where a moving object collides with a stationary one, which then begins to move and is perceived as having been launched) a result of the same mechanism in the ASPAR that enforces the metrical properties of space? Insofar as such effects may be nonconceptual and originate within the architecture of the visual system, an argument could be made that they are part of what an ASPAR provides noninferentially. A similar argument has in fact been made by John Campbell who takes the position that the connectedness of space is a matter of the causal structures of space.[14]

These six properties constitute strong constraints on any theory of the representation of space in active memory. They clearly are not met—at least not without significant additional assumptions—by a system that represents spatial properties in terms of Cartesian coordinates. They are also not met by the proposal that spatial properties are represented by locations in a functional space, since that begs the question of why the functional space has the assumed properties; and they are not met by the proposal that spatial locations are mapped onto locations on the surface of the visual cortex—though in that case it fails for a number of purely empirical reasons. Before I present a proposal that offers a provisional answer to these questions I will briefly touch on one special type of spatial representation and ask whether it might use the same form of representation as used in ASPARs. This is the spatial representation involved in navigation (e.g., an internal map).

5.4.2   Maps and Maplike Navigation Behavior

I have been focusing exclusively on spatial representations constructed in perception (primarily vision) and thought, which I refer to as active spatial

14. Campbell (1993, p. 69) writes, "It is only its figuring in an 'intuitive physics' of one's environment, through regularities connecting spatial properties with other physical properties, that makes it reasoning that is not purely mathematical, but rather, reasoning about the space in which one lives." Peacocke (1993) also takes the position that there is an intimate relation between spatial reasoning and what he calls "intuitive mechanics," but his primary concern is with what is needed for one to have a conception of the material world, not what is entailed by one's sense of space.

representations (ASPARs). Although this remains my focus in this chapter, largely because it provides an interesting application of the ideas introduced in earlier chapters, I should at least mention one other context that involves rich spatial information, that of navigation. Because navigational planning is itself a task that involves reasoning about spatial layouts, it is plausible that navigation may involve a form of representation similar to ASPARs. In the context of navigation, the notion of a maplike representation or of maplike behavior (see, e.g., Menzel et al. 2005) has been widely invoked since Tolman's introduction of the idea of a cognitive map in the 1920s (see, the summary in Tolman 1948). When engaged in finding their way from a starting location to a goal, or between geographical landmarks, people often navigate by using a two-dimensional display (the usual sort of printed terrestrial, marine, or road map) which represents the relative locations, the types of various visible landmarks, and the nature of the terrain through which the person will travel (together with a scale so that real distances can be measured on the map). Similarly, when navigating from memory, one's experience is often that of examining a map with one's "mind's eye," which suggests the picture-in-the-head view that I have been discussing here and in the previous chapter. Partly for this reason, the notion of cognitive map has frequently been associated with a two-dimensional display similar to what many people have assumed constitutes an ASPAR.

The salient empirical fact is that for many animals, as well as for birds and insects, the spatial information available for navigation appears to be not only quantitative and remarkably precise but also allows the animals to engage in behavior that looks very much like the product of goal-directed planning. The complexity of this behavior leads to the assumption that these animals (including ants and bees) have an internal "map" of some kind. The problem is, as it is in the case of reasoning with the aid of a mental image, to specify not only the content of maplike representation, but also the constraints imposed by the map format. Here the research with rats, birds, and insects may be extremely useful; these organisms have very well developed navigational skills, yet presumably have limited resources and limited capacity to reason from general knowledge, so their behavior may more directly exhibit the content and the constraints of such maplike representations.

Whether ASPARs and navigational maps use the same form of representation is an open question. On the face of it there are some clear differences. Navigation is an interactive process in which perception of the environment plays an essential role as the organism moves through it. Moreover, the way in which spatial information comes to be in the "map" is different from the way it comes to be in the ASPAR. In the examples discussed earlier involving ASPARs, the information either comes from perception or it is constructed from cognitive descriptions. By contrast, spatial information in a navigational map is the result of precise measurements of time, distance, and direction that are the result of having traveled through the terrain. Insects use a sophisticated method for establishing how far and in what direction they have traveled. The method, called *path integration*, requires integrating the vector speed with respect to time, a process that yields a continual record of distance and direction from starting point (Collett and Collett 2000). To measure speed, bees use motion over the retinal image (visual flow fields), whereas ants use a measure based on motor output, and other animals may use some other measure or combination of measures (Collett and Collett 2002). Birds and bees also spend some time doing what might be called reconnoitering the territory through which future travel will take place, and in some cases (e.g., in the case of bees) it involves communicating the relevant information (e.g., to other members of the hive). How this information is assimilated from the exploration is largely unknown, but the ability to integrate new measurements during trips with related information stored in memory looks very much like an application of vector algebra: computing the distance and direction between two places that have been visited when the path between them itself has never been traveled requires taking vector differences. Similarly, finding a shortcut through unfamiliar territory, or finding a way around a barrier or a dead-end path, suggests that the animals can coordinate representations at several scales. It is thus plausible that the maplike information that is stored in long-term memory and controls goal-directed movement uses a different mechanism and form of representation, at least some of the time, from that used in reasoning about spatial layouts.

A representation used in navigation may also differ in many ways from the usual sort of canonical map. Local features of landmarks may or may not be represented and may be encoded in a context-dependent way (e.g., so that landmarks would be recognized only when traveling toward the same goal as when the landmark was first encoded; see Collett and Collett 2002). Also some landmarks may be selected temporarily during travel without an encoding of their properties. Given the story I have been unfolding in this book, it should come as no surprise to find that when an animal sees a layout of objects it is moving through, it might keep

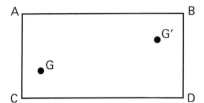

Figure 5.1
Mirror image indeterminacy in the navigation module (Cheng 1986; Gallistel 1990).

FINST-like pointers on the salient landmarks without encoding their properties or locations, and it might even use its perceptual-motor skills to set a course in relation to these FINSTed target landmarks.[15]

The assumption that properties of selected landmarks may not always be encoded is in fact supported by data from rats and other animals (including human infants). For example, Cheng (1986) and Gallistel (1990) showed that a "map" representation may not contain any identifying information of the individual landmarks—only their geometrical relation to other landmarks (and to the larger room space). Consequently, if the information takes the form of a map, it would in this case be a map without labels and legends. This entails that certain systematic ambiguities in locating objects necessarily result from the representation. For example, if a particular goal landmark is located as in figure 5.1, the animal would show no preference between the actual location of the goal G and the mirror-image location G′

15. I don't want to overstate how much of the planning and course-setting can be done "online" while traveling a route and tracking landmarks using indexes since Gallistel and Cramer (1996) showed that a vervet monkey can plan a minimum distance route that involves looking ahead at least 3 landmarks. It is not known exactly what information the monkey has stored and what its plan takes into account in advance of initiating its travels, but these findings do suggest that the monkey does better than a nearest-neighbor search together with an orientation toward the goal. But it is also clear that in executing a plan the monkey must select and keep track of some of the individual target landmarks and final goal at some point in the course of its travel. There are reports that monkeys can track at least 2 moving targets among 4 objects in a MOT paradigm (tracking in the macaque has been demonstrated by Mitchell, Sundberg, and Reynolds 2006, but these investigators did not explore the limits of how many could be tracked), so it is at least possible that the plan may refer to individual visible landmarks indexed at the time of initial observation of the landmarks being baited, which are then tracked with indexes when the monkey executes the initial segment of the plan.

which bears the same local geometry to landmarks A, B, C, and D. This is exactly what Ken Cheng found. In fact he found that not only does an animal not represent features of the landmarks, it is unable to take into account the relevant (disambiguating) intrinsic properties (including color, texture, size, shape, odor) of the landmarks (or of the walls AB, BD, DC, CA when these were distinctively marked). In an animal that has been disoriented by being rotated a few times, local distinctive features don't seem to be used in navigating to the goal—perhaps local cues have not even been entered into memory and associated with corresponding landmarks (just as we found that properties of objects in MOT were not encoded and used in tracking). These properties can, however, be discriminated and used for other purposes, such as choosing between two targets located side by side. This appears to be a quite general phenomenon and is found in human infants as well (see Hermer and Spelke 1996). Infants, it seems, also do not use local cues in navigating, just as in the experiment by Tremoulet, Leslie, and Hall (2000) described in section 2.5, in which infants were able to use color cues to determine that there were several distinct objects but were not able to use color to recognize whether particular colored items placed behind a screen had changed.

There are other ways in which animal navigation departs from the ideal that would be expected if the animal were using a canonical map. For example, Wehner et al. (2006) showed that while the desert ant (which has exceptional navigation skills) uses information about some familiar landmarks in navigating to and from its nest (in addition to its principal method of relying on dead reckoning based on path integration), the recognition of these landmarks depends on whether the ant is on its way from or back to the nest. On the way out it freely uses landmarks acquired on its previous outward journeys but ignores familiar landmarks acquired during previous inbound journeys, and the converse happens when traveling on the inward journey. This was shown by observing the ants' behavior when an inbound ant is captured and displaced to a point on its habitual outbound path. Under that condition the ant ignores the landmarks and engages in systematic search, repeatedly passing outbound landmarks without recognizing them until it finds an inbound landmark which then allows it to get back to its nest. So the ants' "map" appears to have some feature-based labels but in a way that applies to only one direction of travel.

It would be useful to have an analysis of the behavioral capacities underlying the use of what is generally referred to as ideal "maplike behavior." For Tolman, being able to take novel short-cuts to the goal was the most important criterion of map use (this includes detouring around new obstacles and ignoring local cues in favor of more global direction in making route choices). This is probably still the most widely accepted criterion. Some investigators have listed additional criteria. For example, Menzel et al. (2005) cite as symptomatic of maplike behavior the ability to make different choices about where to go next in the course of the travel, even when the animal has been transported by the experimenter to an unfamiliar location. But however impressive these behaviors may be, and even when they reveal something about the content of the representation (what information must have been encoded), they reveal little about the form of the representation involved that makes it maplike.

These and other issues concerning the representation of maplike information for navigation leave open many questions about the form and content of these representations as well as the way in which they are used in planning a course.[16] In this book I do not address most of these questions because I confine myself to the problem of how (and whether) we construct an internal representation of space in the course of thinking about spatial problems (i.e., spatial imagery, whether or not it is conscious) and also to some extent during perception (insofar as I address the picture-in-the-head assumption illustrated earlier in figure 4.3, which sometimes makes its way into perception as well as mental imagery).

In what follows, then, I will sketch an alternative way to look at the problem of how space is represented in an ASPAR (if it is represented at all) so as to satisfy the desiderata sketched so far. It is a strong form of what philosophers will recognize as an externalist position—though it is not concerned with justification of beliefs, which is where externalism most often appears in epistemology. The view is just this: In imagining a spatial layout, we use visual indexes (FINSTs) to pick out concurrently perceived objects that are roughly in the same relative locations as objects in the scene we are imagining. Each indexed object is associated with a unique label of a recalled or imagined object. These labels allow the system to keep the individual indexed objects distinctive, and also allow the visual system to treat the indexed objects as though they were marked—the visual system can thus detect patterns among indexed objects. The spatial

16. The study of automatic plan generation in AI has come a long way from the early systems that generated complete plans in advance and has moved to more "reactive" plans that make allowances for what will be discovered in the initial steps of executing a plan (see the discussion of reactive planning in Kabanza, Barbeau, and St-Denis 1997). The question of just how reactive animals' navigational plans are is an interesting open problem.

properties that concern the mental objects (i.e. the conditions listed earlier) result from actual perception of the spatial relations among these indexed objects. This simple idea, called the *index projection hypothesis*, is developed in the next section.

5.5   Externalizing Spatial Properties: The Index Projection Hypothesis

5.5.1   Where Is Our Spatial Representation?

The standard view about spatial representations is that they consist in some sort of picture or map laid out in the head; most often they are thought to be in the topographic (even retinotopic) areas of the visual system, notably the earliest parts of the visual cortex (area V1). Clearly *something* is in the head when you imagine a spatial layout. But it does not follow that the spatial properties (especially the metrical and geometrical properties) that are available to you derive from whatever is in your head. Neither does it follow that your representation is in a retinocentric or corticocentric frame of reference. The notion that spatial properties are in your head is not consistent with either the phenomenology or the psychophysical data. When we imagine, say, a simple geometrical pattern, the figure may feel like a picture, but it is also clear that it is imagined as being *out there*, and not in the head. When you move your eyes, turn your head or turn your body, the image does not move but tends to remain fixed in extrapersonal space, in what is called the allocentric frame of reference. As a result it must move in the retinotopic frame of reference and it takes extra effort to imagine it as fixed on your retina as you turn or move your eyes. But you are typically unaware of making eye movements while you imagine, and so it would be odd if you experienced the image as moving with your saccades (just as it feels odd to experience an afterimage because that *does* move with eye movements).

In fact, Brandt and Stark (1997) have shown that we explore our mental images using eye movements that are very like the ones we use when we examine an actually scene, which provides even more reason to think that we locate the image in extrapersonal space. Even if we walk toward or around the object we are imagining, it remains fixed in space. If you are not convinced, do the following experiment. Close your eyes and point to some places in the room you are in. You will find that you can do so with a fair degree of accuracy. Now imagine yourself standing in a different part of the room—say, on the opposite side of the room—and repeat the exercise by pointing as though you were at this imagined location. You will find that your accuracy in pointing to the same places drops considerably. Now if instead of imagining yourself on the other side of the room, you close your eyes and walk (or are led, blindfolded) to the spot on the opposite side of the room, you will once again find that you can point to places with nearly the same accuracy as when you were in the initial position. And, as you might expect, you are now very bad at pointing to where things would be if you were still at your starting position, or if you imagine that the things in the room had moved with you as you walked (these findings have been demonstrated by a number of investigators; see, e.g., Farrell and Thomson 1998, 1999). Real movement interacts with imagined objects in a very natural way and such movements treat the imagined objects as fixed in space (so that, for example, your relation to your mental image undergoes the automatic updating of your frame of reference with your movement that is characteristic of moving in a real environment). These are among the reasons for saying that images are in an allocentric frame of reference and not in a cortico-centric frame of reference. What exactly this means and how it is possible for the spatial properties of your spatial representation to be outside your head is the subject of this chapter.

The claim that the spatial properties we represent with our mental images derive from properties that are located in extrapersonal space does raise some problems. To get a feel for the sorts of problems it raises, imagine a simple shape, say, a rectangle. Pick out some part of it, say, the left vertical side. There is nothing problematic about being able to focus your attention on *that* part, or on any part. Now think about some arbitrary place inside the rectangle, for example *there*. There is something odd about that. Although the imagined figure is experienced as being out in the world, where is the *there* to which you just referred? Since the particular rectangle does not actually exist, where are the places in it located? It is common to think of a representation of a rectangle as a type of description—some set of proposition-like descriptors, or some network such as those used in artificial intelligence systems (see, e.g., Pylyshyn, 1973b). That sort of a representation does contain parts that can be attentionally selected. But unlike parts of the imagined rectangle, locations (especially empty locations) are not parts of a description; there is no sense in which a description *contains* locations. The trouble is, as Gertrude Stein is said to have quipped about her childhood town of Oakland, There is no *there* there! Notwithstanding our phenomenology, there is no actual place that is picked out by the locative "there" when we refer to a place in our mental representation. Saying that it is the place in the representation is no help, since we are trying to understand where the place you select with the locative *here* is represented as being. The place it is represented as being is not in some representation.

One obvious way to understand this apparent puzzle is to treat the representation as a mere fiction; Dorothy might have said "correctly" that the Yellow Brick Road was *there*, in Kansas, even though Oz and everything in it are fictitious. The problem with this option is that it does not easily explain why certain geometrical properties are true of the fictitious imagined figure. For example, when you slice the rectangle that you imagined earlier through one diagonal you can readily see that it yields two identical (congruent) right-angled triangles oriented 180 degrees from each other and located in two different places; one is *here* and the other *there* (the reader may want to check whether that is true in his or her imagination). If the rectangle were a mere fiction then why does slicing it create two fictitious triangles that are distinct but congruent tokens separated in the fictitious space by a rotation of 180 degrees? You might say that the two parts created by the slice have the properties they have because in some real but implicit sense you *know* that this is what happens when you slice a rectangle. Exactly so, but still it is unsatisfactory to say that the two triangles, which you know with some precision are now located *here* and *there*, do not have a location at all except in the way that the Yellow Brick Road has a location—especially since we have already agreed that the figures are *out there* in extrapersonal space, and you can show that they remain *there*, fixed in allocentric space, as you move around them. In fact in this example, you can point to where the two triangles are located. It would be much more satisfying to actually attribute the *thereness* and the spatial relation between the two triangles to real space, even if the rectangle and two triangles are themselves fictions. It is their spatial coherence and their relative locations that are problematic, much more than the metaphysical existence of the figures themselves.

Two main options have been widely considered for how representations manage to exhibit the spatial properties discussed earlier. One option, which seems to have become the received wisdom in much of cognitive science and cognitive neuroscience, is that the spatial character (which includes the six properties listed in section 5.4.1 above) derives from the spatial nature of the surface on which the representation is displayed, which many people think is on the surface of the first topographically organized region in the visual cortex—area V1. The other option is that it derives from the concurrently perceived world by a process that, with some hesitation, I have called *index* (or indexical) *projection*. By "index projection" I refer to the hypothesis that certain real things in one's perceptual field, which happen to be in roughly the same spatial configuration as the objects being imagined or recalled, are selected and indexed by FINSTs.

These selected things act as though they were visually *marked*, or had visible labels assigned to them (an assumption that is common to most of the theories that have talked about visual marking, e.g., Ballard, Hayhoe, Pook, and Rao 1997; Ullman 1984; Watson and Humphreys 1997; Yantis and Johnson 1990; Yantis and Jones 1991). What I *do not* mean is that some sort of picture is projected onto the world; only FINSTs are projected, much as Plastic Man (in figure 1.2) might stretch out his fingers and place them on things that are roughly in the same relative locations as things he is imagining, just as FINSTs might be attached to FINGs (see figure 1.4 or figure 2.2). This process occurs across many different modalities (including the proprioceptive modality, about which I will have more to say later). Below I sketch how such a mechanism allows the spatial properties represented by a mental image to be inherited from the spatial properties of the perceived world.

5.5.2   FINST Indexes Can Anchor Spatial Representations to Real Space

In earlier chapters I described the FINST index theory. It is perhaps illustrated most clearly in multiple object tracking (MOT) studies discussed in chapter 2. In MOT, observers are able to select four or five briefly cued objects (the "targets"), among a number of identical objects (the nontarget foils) and then to keep track of these targets as all objects move with unpredictable interpenetrating paths for some period of time, some ten seconds or more. We have shown that these objects can be tracked without their properties being encoded—indeed, changes in their color or shape are not noticed (Bahrami 2003; Scholl, Pylyshyn, and Franconeri 1999), and making them all different colors does not enhance tracking (Pylyshyn and Dennis, forthcoming). Targets can be tracked without significant decrement in performance even when they disappear by moving behind an opaque occluding surface or when they all disappear entirely for up to one second, as though you had blinked. We have shown that the indexes (or FINSTs) can be assigned automatically by the onset of a new object, or voluntarily under certain conditions (when enough time is available to scan focal attention serially to each of the targets; see Pylyshyn and Annan 2006 for details). We have also shown that indexes can be used to preselect a subset of items to search through (Burkell and Pylyshyn 1997) and that this selection can withstand saccadic eye movement (Currie and Pylyshyn 2003) or movement during multiple object tracking (Alvarez et al. 2005; Cohen and Pylyshyn 2002). Selected items can also be enumerated quickly, accurately, and effortlessly, providing they can be automatically individuated (Trick, Audet, and Dales 2003; Trick and Pylyshyn 1994a). Although tracking seems like an attentionally demanding task, we have reason to believe that there are certain other tasks known to require attention that can be carried out simultaneously with tracking without impairing tracking performance (e.g., monitoring for brief color changes or searching through targets for a specified letter; see Alvarez et al. 2005; Leonard and Pylyshyn 2003). Target-specific priming effects are also observed without the explicit requirement to track the targets (Haladjian and Pylyshyn 2006; Noles, Scholl, and Mitroff 2005). I have described some of these experiments in chapter 1.

Given such a mechanism (illustrated in figure 2.2), which allows stable access to a few individual things in the world and allows information relevant to each object to be associated with that object, we can bind the arguments of predicates and movement-commands to these objects (so that, for example, we can detect patterns such as collinearity among them or switch our attention or gaze to them). This FINST mechanism provides a natural explanation of numerous phenomena that have misled people to postulate an internal spatial medium or display. If we know (from instructions or from memory) the rough relative locations of a number of objects of thought or imagination, we can then associate these mental objects with indexed things in space. Once we are in such a relation to actual things in space, we are in a position to use our perceptual system to detect previously unnoticed patterns among these things or to scan our attention (or our gaze) from one to another indexed thing, or to judge relative distances between pairs of such things, and so on. Of course when vision is not available we must assume that the equivalent object-based perception in, say, the auditory or proprioceptive modalities takes its place. Since some of these nonvisual modalities are importantly different from vision (e.g., their initial frame of reference is not the same), we will need to examine that option with some care. To introduce this topic, however, I begin with the visual case since it is not only easier to understand, but also the most important modality for spatial orientation, as we will see.

Here is an example of an empirical phenomenon that can be accounted for in this way. One experiment mentioned briefly in the last chapter (and which has been frequently cited as providing a "window on the mind"; see Denis and Kosslyn 1999) is that of *mental scanning*—a phenomenon whereby the time to switch attention between imagined objects increases roughly linearly with the imagined distance between them. As I noted in chapter 4, this phenomenon appears only when subjects take their task to require simulating, in whatever manner they can, a situation in which they are examining a real map; the basic finding disappears if they take their task

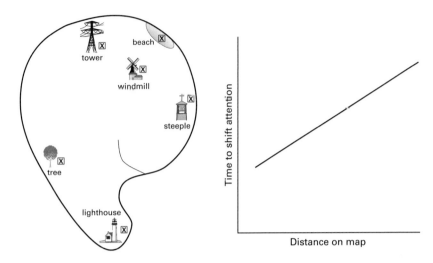

Figure 5.2
The task in this experiment is to learn the above map and then to imagine it while focusing on a specified location. Under appropriate conditions, the time it takes to shift attention to a second named place (and to "see" it in the "mind's eye") is given by the linear function shown on the right (Kosslyn 1973).

to be imagining that they viewing a map in which lights go on and off, or when the attention scanning is downplayed, even in a context where they clearly need to switch their attention between two imagined objects (for details see section 4.5.1). Still, under the appropriate conditions subjects do show this linear relation between distance and time, so the question arises how they can simulate the observed reaction-time function (other than by generating a time interval without imagining any movement, which I don't believe is what happens). Although this linear relation between distance and time has been interpreted as showing that mental images "have" metrical distances, it can also be seen in terms of scanning attention in real space between indexed objects. Here is how it might work.

If, for example, the map on the left of figure 5.2 is imagined and a subject is asked to scan attention from one object (say, the tree) to another object (say, the tower), the time taken is typically found to be proportional to the relative distance between the two imagined places. But suppose an observer is able to attach FINST indexes to a few objects in the room where the experiment is being carried out, with the objects chosen so that their relative locations correspond roughly to memorized locations of objects on the map (we assume that one can memorize such locations in some unspecified

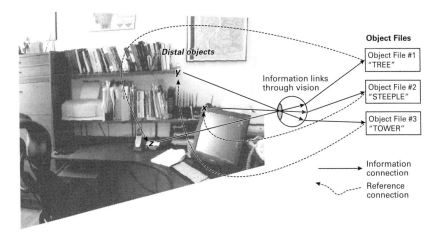

Figure 5.3
Binding indexes to objects in an office scene, thereby associating these objects with
the imagined mental objects (or, more accurately, indexed objects are associated with
labels that indicate which objects are to be thought of as being at those locations).
The indexing mechanism here is the same as the FINST mechanism illustrated in
figure 2.2.

qualitative configurational way that itself does not involve imagery). This
sort of selection of concurrently perceived objects is illustrated in figure
5.3. The subject would then be able to scan attention (or even direction of
gaze) through physical space between the two relevant physical objects in
the room. In that case the equation *time = distance ÷ speed* literally applies
by virtue of physical laws. Thus this real scanning time would be proportional to the actual distance in space.

The view I am proposing is that the spatial properties represented by our
mental representations derive from the spatial properties of selected (i.e.,
FINSTed) concurrently perceived objects that are located in real space. The
spatial properties I have in mind include the six properties listed above (in
section 5.4.1) as well as the many properties that have been cataloged
in connection with studies of mental imagery or spatial representations in
general (such as the mental scanning experiment mentioned above, and
also examples of problem solving that use spatial "mental models"; see,
e.g., Johnson-Laird 2001).[17]

17. But for a critique of the interpretation of these mental model studies, see Bonatti
1994, 1998; Pylyshyn 2003, chap. 8.

This alternative story of how some mental representations get their spatial properties is that they arise from the subject's ability to select and keep track of individual objects in the world and then to visually detect their spatial patterns and also to perform visual operations on them, such as scanning focal attention between them. In chapters 1 and 2, I sketched a number of experiments illustrating nonconceptual selection and I described how FINSTs could provide an account of this process. These FINSTs may be usefully viewed as mechanisms of demonstrative identification. The assumption is that the small number of available FINST indexes can be captured by, or assigned to, salient things in the perceptual field, which then remain attached while either the individuals or the viewer moves. I suggested that this mechanism has widespread use in keeping track of a small selected subset of items of special interest (e.g., in order to search through them for a specified target), evaluating predicates for certain patterns (including such properties as collinearity and the cardinality of small sets of FINSTed objects), and maintaining the identity of individual objects across saccadic eye movements. These reference "pointers" can be assigned automatically by events in the visual world, or, voluntarily, by the viewer's serially scanning the items and thus selectively enabling the index grabbing operation to work on things that are selected by focal attention. Since indexes select individual objects, it is reasonable to assume that these selected objects can be distinguished by the visual system, just as the things one selects with focal attention can have a distinct visual role. Thus, assuming that indexes can provide input to the visual system, indexed objects can in effect be visually distinguished as though they were marked. This would allow the visual system to detect the spatial configuration among indexed objects. In this way, indexes make it possible to use the stable spatial properties of real objects located in real space to determine spatial properties of mentally represented space.

This idea also accounts for a number of findings cited in support of the picture theory of mental imagery. For example, Podgorny and Shepard (1978) showed that there is a consistent pattern in the amount of time required to detect a small spot flashed at different places on a simple displayed pattern (e.g., it is faster when the spot occurs at the vertex or T-junction of a pattern such as the block letter F). They also found that the same reaction-time pattern is observed when the display is no longer visible but merely recalled while viewing the blank grid on which the pattern had been displayed. Such a finding is compatible with the view that columns and rows of the grid that correspond to the projected pattern (e.g., the F) are simply indexed. The visual system treats the imagined F pattern as present during the imagery part of the experiment by indexing the columns and rows that had contained the pattern. In general, findings that involve projecting an image onto a visual scene are compatible with the assumption that certain geometrical features of the imagined pattern are effectively re-created by merely selecting features of the display where the image is supposed to be projected (including texture elements on the surface of the visual display that may not even be consciously noticed).

Another often-cited example is the finding that perceptual-motor adaptation can be induced by imagery rather than vision. In the classical adaptation paradigm, a subject wears prism goggles that shift the location of the perceived world by a fixed amount (say, 23° to the right). After just a few minutes of attempting to reach for some objects on the table, the subject is easily able to correct for this displacement of the visual field. Moreover, this correction becomes automatic, so that when the goggles are removed the subject undershoots by the adapted amount (say, by 23° to the left). Ron Finke repeated this experiment except that subjects could not see their arm (which was hidden under a surface). They were instructed to imagine that their hidden hand was at a particular location (the location chosen is where it would have appeared had they worn the prism goggles). The same adaptation and undershoot were observed in this imagined displacement condition as when prism goggles were worn. Although the experiment (described in Finke 1979) involved other controls, the one feature it could not control for is the fact that the adaptation effect depends entirely on a mismatch between the seen position of a hand and its felt position. All one needs to induce adaptation is some indication of the hand's location (which, as in the visual adaptation case, is different from its felt position). No other visual property of the hand is required. Indeed, Mather and Lackner (1977) found that adaptation can be produced in the dark with subjects viewing a point source of light attached to their hand rather than the hand itself. In addition, it appears that what subjects attend to is important (Canon 1970, 1971); even an immobile hand can produce adaptation providing subjects visually attend to it (Mather and Lackner 1981). Thus the imagery condition in Finke's study provides all that is needed for adaptation, without any assumptions about the nature of imagery. In particular, subjects direct their gaze or their attention toward a particular (erroneous) location where they are in effect told to pretend their hand is located, thus focusing their attention on the discordance between this viewed location and their kinesthetic and proprioceptive sense of the position of their arm. Since the subjects are told to direct their attention to a particular feature in the scene to which a FINST can be attached, the results are easily explained.

Another visual-motor phenomenon that has attracted some interest among pictorialists is the finding that a perceptual-motor compatibility effect (known as *S-R compatibility* or the *Simon effect*) can also be induced by visual imagery. It is well known that, regardless of what the response signifies, responding in the direction of a relevant stimulus feature is faster than responding away from the stimulus feature. For example, suppose that two stimuli are presented and a subject is asked to indicate whether one of them has a certain property (say, the property of being the letter "A") by pressing one of two buttons (one marked YES and the other marked NO), as shown in figure 5.4. If the A is on the left and if the YES

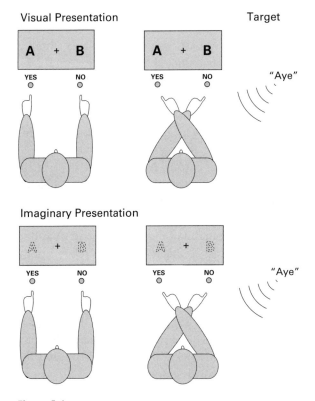

Figure 5.4
The S-R compatibility effect (this version is called the *Simon effect*). Response (with either hand) toward the location of the relevant stimulus is faster than toward the irrelevant stimulus. This is true both for visual presentation (top two) and for an imagined (or recalled) presentation. (This illustration is based loosely on Tlauka and McKenna 1998, although it differs from their design which uses more complex stimuli.)

button is also on the left, the response is faster. If the YES response button had been on the right, or if the A target had been on the right, the response would have been slower. Generally, responding in the direction toward the relevant visual pattern is faster, regardless of the significance of the response. This effect is location specific rather than hand specific since it holds even if the hands are crossed. What Tlauka and McKenna (1998) showed is that the same reaction-time finding is obtained when the patterns (e.g., letters) are recalled after they are no longer visible or if subjects are instructed to imagine them at compatible or incompatible locations. Thus the same pattern of spatial compatibility is observed with mental images as with actual visual perception. This too can be easily accounted for if one assumes that the locations where the letters are imagined are indexed (by some visible feature at that location) and the letter name associated with the appropriate locations. The task then becomes essentially the same as the corresponding visual task.

In many experiments there are no obvious objects located at the relevant locations. Does this mean that, contrary to our earlier assumption, an empty location is indexed? Not necessarily. There are two possibilities as to what determines the allocation of indexes in these cases. One is that there is always some feature near enough to the relevant places where the index is to be placed (keep in mind that the locations might be quite inaccurate since they come from a qualitative recall). If you were to view digitized luminance-levels of a scene (such as illustrated in computer vision texts like Ballard 1982) you would see discontinuities near almost every place in a scene—even in regions of blank walls. Since, by assumption, FINST allocation occurs early on in vision, it would have access to such preconstancy discontinuities—brightness differences that have not been adjusted by whatever processes smooth out and replace the jagged input. Another possibility is that one can select empty locations under certain limited conditions; in particular, we can pick them out relative to indexed objects in special cases. For example, it may be that one can index an empty space if it can be specified as, say, midway between two indexed objects. Although this is speculative there are no principled reasons for excluding the possibility of such special cases.

Another type of evidence that supports the index projection hypothesis comes from clinical cases that suggest that representations constructed from memory work differently when they are accompanied by visual perception than when they are not (e.g., in the dark or with eyes closed). Take, for example, the famous experiments in which Edoardo Bisiach (Bisiach and Luzzatti 1978) showed that patients with unilateral spatial neglect (USN) tend to neglect not only one side of their visual world, but also the same side of their recollected or imagined world. Particularly remarkable is that the patients could recall information from both sides of their visual field, as shown by the fact that if asked to imagine the same scene from a perspective rotated by 180 degrees, these patients accurately reported the formerly missing details. This was interpreted as showing that one side of an internal spatial display might be damaged in patients with USN. However, in a recent interesting twist on this result, Chokron, Colliot, and Bartolomeo (2004) showed that the neglect in mental images occurs only when the patients are simultaneously *viewing* a scene and does not appear when they imagine it with eyes closed. This supports the idea (championed by Bartolomeo and Chokron 2002) that neglect is a deficit in attention control. There is also evidence that certain proprioceptive inputs can alter the axis of the imaginal neglect in USN patients, since neglect can be shifted with a shift in felt body orientation. Karnath, Christ, and Hartje (1993) showed that either turning the body by 15 degrees or decreasing the proprioceptive input by using vibrators applied to the neck muscles on the contralateral side will reduce the neglect. Also, USN patients' tactile exploration in the dark shows that the explored field is shifted in the direction away from the neglected side, but the search pattern remains symmetrically distributed about the shifted direction and voluntary saccades do not show eye-centered directional deficits. Moreover, blocking proprioceptive signals over a series of treatments (using neck muscle vibrations) resulted in long-term reduction of USN symptoms (Schindler et al. 2002). This and other results are consistent with the general thesis that the spatial representation (and its deficit in USN) is sensitive to concurrent spatial inputs (especially visual and proprioceptive inputs).

These results also support the claim that in spatial mental imagery, the spatial properties (including the distinction between left and right sides of the imagined scene) arise from the actual location in the currently perceived scene of objects, with which the imagined objects are associated. There are many demonstrations in nonclinical patient populations showing that both perception and recall of location are sensitive to concurrent spatial information. For example, orienting to auditory stimuli while visually viewing a scene improves one's performance compared with performance in the dark or without visual patterns (Warren 1970). Spatial cues based on ambient auditory stimulation with landmark auditory locations also improve report of the location of auditory stimuli (Dufour, Despres, and Pebayle 2002). Conversely, viewing displays without any structure (as in the structureless display called a Ganzfeld—see Avant 1965) or being immersed in a impoverished sensory environment (e.g., an environment with low gravity; see Watt 1997) results in spatial disorientation.

The data cited above provide further corroboration of the involvement of concurrently perceived spatial information in the process of realizing what might be called the "spatial sense." I should point out that although most of these examples involve concurrent visual patterns, we are able to represent spatial information (and demonstrate the six spatial conditions listed in section 5.4.1 above) without concurrent vision. Later, I will discuss how nonvisual information can serve the required anchoring function.

5.6   Index Projection in Nonvisual Modalities

5.6.1   The Unitary Frame of Reference Assumption
As with other seductive features of conscious contents, the fact that we have a unitary conscious spatial experience makes it tempting to assume that we have a single global representation of space in an allocentric frame of reference. There is also the independent assumption that this frame of reference is amodal, since information from several modalities can be assimilated into a global frame of reference (or, in some cases, it is assumed that vision serves as the single frame of reference, since there is some evidence that auditory localization may be referred to a visual frame of reference; see Warren 1970).

However, there is also a great deal of evidence that we maintain a large number of different representations of spatial locations in different frames of reference (Colby and Goldberg 1999). We know that the gaze-centered frame of reference plays an important role in visual-motor coordination (Crawford, Medendorp, and Marotta 2004; Henriques et al. 1998; Medendorp et al. 2003; Snyder et al. 1998); but even within this frame of reference the actual coordinates are modified extensively online by what are called *gain fields* (Salinas and Thier 2000), which reflect head and body position, and also by not-yet-executed intentions to move the eyes (Andersen 1995b; Duhamel, Colby, and Goldberg 1992). There is also the famous distinction between ventral and dorsal visual systems that use different frames of reference, illustrated most famously by patients such as "DF" reported by Milner and Goodale (1995). These findings show that even within one modality, different functions (e.g., motor control and object recognition) involve different frames of reference—with the ventral system using a relatively local frame of reference (possibly object-centered for ease of object recognition), which represents qualitative rather than metrical spatial relations, as opposed to the dorsal system, which uses many frames of reference but primarily body-centered ones, and represents relatively precise spatial magnitudes (see Bridgeman et al. 1979). These representations (what I called *quasi-representations* in section 3.2.2) are likely laid out as neural layouts of activity. Note that the existence of neural layouts is not in question, only the frequent additional assumption that there is a layout that is global, allocentric, and conscious—a layout that corresponds to the conscious experience of perceived extrapersonal space.

The use of multiple frames of reference is also illustrated by cases of unilateral spatial neglect (USN)—the deficit, discussed above, in which patients with damage in their parietal cortex fail to notice or respond to objects in half of their visual field. Even so clearly a spatial deficit appears to show the many frames of reference that may be involved:

Neglect occurs in all sensory modalities and can be expressed relative to any of several spatial reference frames, including retinocentric, body-centered, and environment-centered. For example, neglect can be specific for stimuli presented at particular distances. Some patients tend to ignore stimuli presented near the body, in peripersonal space, while responding normally to distant stimuli, or vice versa.... Distance-specific neglect may be apparent only when the subject must produce a motor response to the stimulus, and not when spatial perception alone is tested. (Colby and Goldberg 1999, pp. 320–321)

Others have also found that more than one frame of reference may be affected in USN—in fact, neglect may occur simultaneously in several frames of reference. For example, Behrmann and Tipper (1999) reported that a patient showed neglect in both visual and object-centered frames of reference at the same time.

Properties of many of these frames of reference have been investigated, often with surprising results. For example, there appear to be integrated visual-tactile reference frames in peripersonal space, the near space around the body, especially surrounding the hands and face (Graziano and Gross 1995; Làdavas 2002). Visual stimuli presented near the body tend to be processed together with tactile stimuli at those locations, so that when one modality shows deficits, such as extinction (a deficit in processing two stimuli together bilaterally when neither is impaired when tested individually), the other tends to show similar deficits. The visual deficits in these cases are in a frame of reference relative to a body part (e.g., the hand or the face). The visual experience of the region around a body part becomes tied to the somatosensory experience of the body part itself so that it moves with the body part, as in the "phantom limb" experiences of amputees; this has even been shown to occur with tool use (so that the experience of the space of one's limb is extended to include a tool being used to explore space; see Làdavas 2002). There is also evidence for hand-based visual representations or frames of reference[18] as well as gaze-centered and head-centered representations or frames. For example, pointing without the aid of vision is less accurate when the starting position of the hand is not visible, and the undershoot errors along the sagittal plane are larger when the hand begins from a point further from the body (which Chieffi, Allport, and Woodin 1999 interpreted as suggesting that the visual target is encoded in hand coordinates); and, as noted above, auditory localization is poorer without spatial visual stimulation, such as provided by a textured surface, which many writers interpret as indicating that auditory information is encoded in a visual frame of reference (e.g., Warren 1970).[19]

The visual and motor frames of reference are closely linked. For example, the accuracy of pointing to a seen object after the eyes are closed is surprisingly high and persists for more than fifteen seconds after the eyes are closed. More important, as mentioned earlier, the accuracy of pointing from a different imagined location is very poor *unless the subject actually moves to the new location*, even without using vision during the move (Farrell and Thomson 1998). It seems that many coordinate systems are automatically updated when we move. Of course these examples of multiple frames of reference do not show that we don't also have a unitary frame of reference. However, if there is such a global frame of reference, it does not displace the individual ones and in fact would have to exist at the same time as the individual frameworks. Perhaps the main argument against the global frame of reference is that it is not needed given the prevalence of coordinate transformation functions, described in the next section.

5.6.2   The Role of Coordinate Transformations in Externalizing Space
One of the main motivations for the assumption that there is a uniform global frame of reference available to cognition is the fact that we go easily back and forth between perceptual modalities and, more important,

18. In the interest of expository simplicity I sometimes use the common convention of referring to neural layouts as representations, notwithstanding my earlier proposal that these may not be representations in the strong sense. A more neutral term I sometimes use is "neural layout" itself or "registration."

19. Although this is a reasonable hypothesis, others (e.g., Dufour, Despres, and Pebayle 2002) have subsequently shown that an auditory reference point also improves auditory localization, suggesting that it is not the visual frame of reference per se that is responsible for improved auditory localization, but the presence of perceptual anchors in any modality. This is consistent with the present thesis that localizations and other spatial skills rely on concurrent spatially structured perceptual stimulation.

between perception and motor action. Since perception begins with various peripheral frames of reference (e.g., vision starts with a retinal image, audition with an image of pitch on the basilar membrane) and motor control eventually requires a body-centered or world-centered frame of reference, an obvious solution is to convert everything into a common allocentric reference frame. Such a unitary coordinate system could then serve as the *lingua franca* for representing locations accessible to all modalities and effectors. This also comports well with our experience of seeing things in a stable allocentric frame of reference, as required by our unitary sense of first-person consciousness. But there are problems with this view. Motor control is not in an allocentric frame of reference; commands must be issued in many different frames, including joint-angle frames and limb-centered frames (e.g., there is also evidence for coding in a hand-centered frame of reference). There are also many intermediate frames involved. For example, in vision there are not only two retinal frames but also a cyclopean frame (which combines patterns from the two eyes into a 3-D or stereo frame of reference) as well as a full 3-D frame that is relative to a more distant frame of reference (e.g., the room).

There is also evidence that representations in different frames of reference are not deleted after conversion to another frame of reference occurs. Many of these intermediate representations leave their mark on ultimate motor performance, showing that intermediate frames of reference coexist with downstream frames of reference (Baud-Bovy and Viviani 1998). An interesting case occurs when we reach for an object after brief exposure to it. While we are able to reach successfully even when eye movements occur between perceiving the object and reaching, both the retinal location and the motor representations are relevant in determining the outcome, as can be seen from errors in reaching that occur with intervening eye movements. Analysis of reaching errors reveals that "motor error commands cannot be treated independently of their frame of origin or the frame of their destined motor command" (Crawford, Medendorp, and Marotta 2004, p. 10). It seems that the retinal location affects the direction of reach (see also Batista et al. 1999). Many other studies confirm the residual effect of the multiple reference frames involved in the entire process, thus suggesting that a single conversion to a global frame of reference, if it occurs at all, cannot be the whole story.

An alternative to translating the many frames of reference into a uniform global frame is to carry out the translation pair-wise for the relevant frameworks. Although this may sound inefficient, there is reason to think that special mechanisms are able to perform this transformation efficiently. In fact, numerous coordinate-transformation sites have been identified through neurophysiological studies (many of these are described by Gallistel 1999), consistent with coordinate transformations being a basic operation in the central nervous system (see also Andersen 1995a; Bizzi and Mussa-Ivaldi 1995; Gallistel 1999; Ghahramani, Wolpert, and Jordan 1996; Snyder 2000). Such transformations occur not only between modalities, but also between many distinct and constantly changing frames of reference within a modality. Thus, in moving your arm to grasp a perceived object, you not only have to coordinate visual location information with proprioceptive location information, but also a frame of reference in terms of joint angles with a frame of reference in terms of body-centered spatial coordinates, and then move from body-centered coordinates to allocentric coordinates. Since in reaching for something you generally move your eyes, head, and body (thus dynamically changing the body-centered coordinates), the coordination must occur rapidly online. Although one might in principle convert each of these frames of reference to one global (e.g., allocentric) frame of reference, neurophysiological evidence appears to support pair-wise coordinate transformations among closely connected frameworks (e.g., eye- and head-centered frames of reference to a body-centered frame of reference, or a joint-angle frame of reference to a body-centered frame of reference).

There is evidence that the many frames of reference are tied together by a web of coordinate transformation operations. By contrast, there is no known mechanism that operates directly in a global framework;[20] rather,

20. This is notwithstanding the remarkable work of O'Keefe and Nadel (1978) and others, demonstrating the existence of "place cells" in the rat hippocampus that respond selectively to places in an allocentric frame of reference. Place cells fire when the rat is at a particular place (in the primate there are also "spatial view cells" that reportedly fire when the viewer merely looks at the specific place; Rolls 1999). These cells may also respond to a number of other properties (e.g., the direction of the animal's head), but nobody has suggested that they fire when the animal is planning a route. It is not known whether (or how) the hippocampus place cells *could* be used in constructing a plan that would, e.g., need to represent the relative distance and direction of A and B when the animal is situated at some other place C. The ability of some animals to plan multidestination routes is amazing (Gallistel and Cramer 1996), but it is not clear how the hippocampus place cells would play a role in this. Without some idea how an animal could use the hippocampus representations to plan a route, calling that representation a "map" is misleading; it's more a very simple global positioning system that detects when the animal is in the cell's "firing field" but provides no directions or distances between distant waypoints. Without such flexibility the information is referred to as a registration of self-location rather than a representation or map.

there seem to be transformations only among cascades of frameworks beginning with receptor surfaces and ending with relevant effectors. Moreover, there are reasons to think that we do not need a single intermediary representation for coordinating spatial representations across modalities and between perception and action, but that rather such coordination may operate by a series of coordinate transformations that are modulated by attention and intention. In their review of spatial representation in the brain, Colby and Goldberg (1999, p. 319) suggest that a "direct sensory-to-motor coordinate transformation obviates the need for a single representation of space in environmental coordinates."

Coordinate transformations are central in allowing perceptually based frames of reference to coordinate with one another and with action systems in the brain. In the motor system, coordinate transformations implicitly define equivalence classes of gestures from a given starting position to a fixed end point. These are just the classes $\{S_i\}$ that Poincaré postulated. Such equivalence classes accomplish for proprioception what perceived location in space does for vision: they provide unique proprioceptive information for unique places in extrapersonal space. As with vision, however, only a small subset of these—the occupied places—are indexed by a generalization of FINSTs to the proprioceptive modality (which in Pylyshyn 1989 I referred to as *anchors*.)

The concern that such pair-wise transformations are an inefficient way to get from stimuli to responses is ameliorated by the suggestion that only a limited number of objects in different frames of reference are translated or transformed online *as needed*. The plurality of reference frames and the speed with which we generally have to coordinate across such frames of reference make this idea of selective transformation plausible. A great deal of evidence, both behavioral and neurophysiological, suggests that only a small portion of perceptual information is selected and, moreover, very few objects need be converted to a motor frame of reference. The richness of the perceptual input and the complexity of the transformations that would be involved if the entire contents of each reference frame were converted also suggest that such a conversion is not only computationally intractable but unnecessary given the selective nature of the properties that go into the sensorimotor control process.

This conclusion, that only a small portion of information is selected, was also reached in a recent review by Colby and Goldberg (1999), who argued that attention plays an important roll in determining which objects are selected and converted. For similar reasons, Henriques et al. (1998) proposed a *conversion-on-demand principle* in which only objects involved in a particular planned motor action are converted from retinal coordinates. A great deal of the location information is retained in eye-centered coordinates, as modified by eye, head, and body position, until it is needed (Batista et al. 1999; Klier, Wang, and Crawford 2001; Snyder 2000), and this may even be the case for auditory inputs (Stricanne, Andersen, and Mazzoni 1996). The same may well be true of other pairs of reference frames, such as cyclopean, joint-angle, and so on (Colby and Goldberg 1999), where in each case only selected objects are converted. No global allocentric coordinate system need be constructed since one needs nothing more than reference to a few objects as postulated by FINST theory.

5.6.3 Proprioceptive FINSTs? The Index Projection Hypothesis in Nonvisual Modalities

The foregoing sets the scene for a possible answer to the question: How can the index projection hypothesis work in the absence of vision? A simple answer is that we can index objects without vision by simply using acoustical and other sense modalities whose distal causes are also laid out in space. There is no principled reason why the sort of picture illustrated in figure 5.3 could not be realized if there were sound sources as well as sound-reflecting objects that function the way light does in vision. We know that people can use sound to find their way around; certainly blind people are able to localize objects—not only sound sources, but sound-reflecting objects (Ashmead, Davis, and Northington 1995; Voss et al. 2004). Although audition tends to be less accurate than vision, spatial-hearing of auditory landscapes may be sufficient to establish several auditory FINST anchors for purposes of the index projection hypothesis.

More interesting are the various processes grouped under the category of *proprioception* and motor planning or preparatory motor actions (including kinesthetic, tactile, haptic, and other somatosensory modalities, as well as preparatory motor programs). These are involved in spatial representation. For example, it is known that the motor system is involved in thinking about spatial layouts. I have already mentioned experiments demonstrating that in some circumstances motor actions impair our ability to examine spatial layouts. Take, for example, the task of recalling the shape of a pattern by indicating what left or right turns one would have to make in traversing its outer contour. In one study, performance was measured for two types of responses, verbal (saying "left" or "right") and motor (pointing to the correct terms in a column of symbols). Lee Brooks (1968) found that performance was impaired when a motor response was made. Brooks interpreted this result as showing that mental images are spatial; but what it really shows is that spatial gestures, when made concurrently with the examination of a spatial pattern, impair performance—as would be expected given the index projection hypothesis as applied to the combination of visual and motor involvement in the pointing response. The work on unilateral spatial neglect mentioned earlier shows that the representation of space (more precisely, the exercise of attentional control) is also sensitive to the availability of concurrent vision (Chokron, Colliot, and Bartolomeo 2004) and to concurrent motor actions (Robertson, Nico, and Hood 1995). There are also data showing that certain spatial operations on represented space (e.g., mental rotation) are affected by concomitant motor actions (Wexler, Kosslyn, and Berthoz 1998).

Thus there have been many demonstrations that engaging the visual system or the proprioceptive and motor system has an impact on active spatial representations (ASPARs). But we need more than that: We need to show that the proprioceptive and motor systems can serve as the source of anchoring of represented space to actual perceived space. Also, since people do not have to make overt movements in order to think about spatial properties, we need to show that there is stable location information corresponding to the target of *potential* or *intended* motor actions as well as the right kind of potential proprioceptive information.

5.6.4 Motor Control, Proprioception, and Intention—Define Places in Allocentric Space

I begin by characterizing what has sometimes been called the spatial sense, a competence that is essential for proprioception to operate in allocentric coordinates, and therefore to provide the anchors assumed by the index projection hypothesis when vision is not available. People are able to orient themselves very well in space even if they are deprived of sight and sound, although the mechanisms that make this possible are not well known (apart from the fact that it involves the proprioceptive and kinesthetic and to some extent the vestibular system). For the purposes of the index projection hypothesis, what is required is the capacity to identify particular places in extrapersonal space using proprioception, and to issue motor commands to move to places in extrapersonal space. These basic capacities, the explanation of which was a major concern for Poincaré, depend heavily on coordinate transformation operations. It is these transformations that compute the equivalence of proprioceptive information and/or motor actions with a common allocentric end point. The extrapersonal locus is required because we are interested in how it is possible to bind FINST indexes (or *anchors*) to stable places in extrapersonal space, using the proprioceptive modality, so they can provide stable references from which the spatial character of mental space can be derived perceptually (as suggested in the visual examples discussed earlier, and illustrated in figure 5.3).

For example, if you are incrementally constructing a representation of a geometrical figure, each part of the representation must remain in place as other parts are added. And they must remain fixed despite movements of the eyes, head, or body that occur during the process of indexing various perceived objects. It is the coordinate transformation operations that make it possible for proprioception to operate in a stable extrapersonal frame of reference. For instance, these operations are what make it possible to use your right-hand index finger to point to places that had been occupied by the index finger of your left hand shortly before. This capacity was demonstrated by Baud-Bovy and Viviani (1998), who showed that although there are constant errors in pointing to proprioceptively marked places, the pattern of errors is the same whether the initial "locating" or marking hand is the same or different from the pointing hand. To put this a less technical way: Our ability to sense or reach toward fixed points in space, independent of the position of our eyes, head, hands, or body, gives us potential access to points in allocentric space.[21] Of these potentially accessible places, we need only access a small number—the indexed subset.

There is a great deal of evidence that the preparation for making a gesture is a separate stage in the process of undertaking an action. This is a stage that has been well studied, both in psychophysics (Hannus et al. 2005; Libet et al. 1983; Musseler and Prinz 1996) and in neuroscience (Andersen and Buneo 2002; Buneo et al. 2002; Ghahramani, Wolpert, and Jordan 1996; Gnadt, Bracewell, and Andersen 1991; Henriques et al. 1998; Karnath 1997; Stricanne, Andersen, and Mazzoni 1996). In psychophysics studies there are measures of the time it takes to prepare a response-sequence as distinct from the time it takes to execute it.[22] One of the reasons that

21. At a recent conference entitled "Frames of Reference in Spatial Cognition" held in Paris (Nov. 17–19, 2005), Yves Rossetti presented a talk ("Questioning reference frames for sensorimotor transformations: Driving the hand to eye-centered locations in space") in which he warned against the assumption that motor control and proprioception occur in an egocentric frame of reference and provided reasons why they are more correctly viewed as being in an extrapersonal frame of reference, a conclusion that agrees with the present thesis.

22. The earliest theorizing about such a preparatory stage is by Broadbent (1958) and Sperling (1967) gives the demonstration of this stage by chronometric analysis, postulating a special buffer (the R-buffer) to hold information in a form that is intermediate between an "iconic memory" and an articulated verbal "rehearsal memory."

researchers postulated the existence of a "program of motor commands," as distinct from movement itself, is the simple fact that a series of movements can be carried out without any kinesthetic feedback to keep track of where the person is in the sequence at any given time (Fleishman and Rich 1963; Gandevia and Burke 1992). (The most dramatic example of the ability to carry out action sequences without any proprioceptive information is provided by deafferented patients, such as the one described in Cole 1995, who have developed the ability to preplan a sequence and monitor its execution visually or in some cases without any feedback.) For that to be the case, the sequence would have to be specified in advance and simply run off when needed. All so-called ballistic movements are of this sort, as are rapid serial sequences like playing familiar overlearned runs on the piano or sequences on a computer keyboard.

The idea that the intention to perform an action is carried out separately from the execution of the intention is now well accepted in neuroscience. A classical study by Jean-René Duhamel and colleagues (Duhamel, Colby, and Goldberg 1992) showed that in the monkey, just before eye movement, a cell in the part of parietal cortex called the lateral interparietal area (LIP), whose receptive field would include its signature feature after the saccade, becomes active (i.e., responds readily to a signal in that part of the visual field) before the saccade is actually completed. Thus the shift in the location of the receptive field of the neuron precedes the actual saccade. This suggests that this cell, which normally fires when the feature to which it is responsive occurs in its receptive field, actually anticipates the location that its receptive field will occupy after the eye movement is completed—it becomes sensitized in advance! Many have interpreted this to mean that the entire visual field is remapped (as was assumed in earlier theories that claimed that eye movements produced an "efference copy" that shifted retinotopic information; see von Holst and Mittelstaedt 1971/ 1950). But there is no need to make this assumption. In the cases studied by Duhamel and his colleagues, only certain of the salient features in the

---

This buffer was found to be necessary in modeling the process of reading a display of briefly presented letters in order to match the different speeds of information intake by the iconic and rehearsal buffers. By using a masking pattern Sperling was able to show that letters could be encoded in some form in a very short time (at a rate of about 10 ms/letter) but could not yet be recoded into subvocal speech (which takes about 200 ms/letter). That leaves the need for some sort of storage, which Sperling suggests has the form of a "program of motor instructions" for pronouncing the letters, which is subsequently executed during the "rehearsal" and "response" stages.

visual field need to be remapped[23] just as Henriques and colleagues (1998) claimed in their "conversion on demand" principle. It seems, then, that a sparse representation of the motor/proprioceptive scene is available that contains the "intended" but as yet unexecuted move. There are now many known examples of brain activity (usually in parietal cortex—particularly in area LIP) associated with the intention to act (see, e.g., Gnadt and Andersen 1988; Shadlen and Newsome 1996). Can this map of intentional preparation-for-action serve part of the function required by the index projection hypothesis?

5.6.5   Summary of Evidence in Support of the Index Projection Hypothesis

I have reviewed a range of evidence relevant to the psychophysical capacity to pick out sensory objects (including intentional ones) in proprioceptive and motor space. This evidence, together with the general finding that concurrent spatial stimulation appears to be necessary to our sense of space, provides support for the index projection hypothesis even when no visual input is available. This discussion has ranged over a variety of topics, so it is appropriate now that we pause to examine the inventory of findings that support the index projection hypothesis.

(1)   Concurrent spatial stimulation may be necessary for our sense of space   There is reason to believe that without sensory information from the world around us we would lose not only our orientation but also our sense of space. If looking at a scene free of visual features, the subject's visual-motor coordination is lost after only a short time. These so-called ganzfeld condition (in which subjects see only a uniform featureless expanse) results in disorientation and seriously impaired form perception after only 90 seconds. The observer finds it difficult to locate a small object

---

23. Jean-René Duhamel has suggested to me in conversation that this implication may have arisen from the fact that the publication reporting this phenomenon (Duhamel, Colby, and Goldberg 1992) showed a drawing of the monkey's view, which may have suggested that *all* the features in that view were remapped. This was not intended and is unlikely to be true. The retina does indeed contain a different (shifted) image after the saccade, but there is no reason to believe that all receptive fields of neurons in LIP are remapped to accommodate this shift. In fact it was argued in a slightly different context by Henriques et al. 1998 that only a few task-relevant objects are remapped, and the selection depends on attention (see also Colby and Goldberg, 1999).

in the ganzfeld because "The observer not only does not know where he is looking, he also does not know where he has been looking previously" (Avant 1965, p. 252). The same is true in total darkness where we get the so-called autokinetic illusion, in which a stationary point of light appears to move and one's orientation is disrupted (see Levy 1972). There are also the recent interesting findings that one's orientation to sound is better when there are visual and/or auditory landmarks, and that unilateral spatial neglect with respect to mental images does not occur when the patient describes the scene with eyes closed (Chokron, Colliot, and Bartolomeo 2004).

(2) Reasoning with eyes closed may still rely on visual persistence of objects in space   There is evidence of short-term persistence of detailed visual-spatial information, and there may also be persistence in other modalities (including audition and proprioception). Estimates of the duration of such storage varies from a few hundred milliseconds to a few minutes. One of the earliest reports of visual persistence was by George Sperling (1960), who used the method of partial report to show that information sufficient to report letters is available for about 250 ms after the disappearance of the information from a screen. More recently, Krekelberg (2001) reported that position (though not color or shape) is available for 180 ms after the stimulus is extinguished in moving displays. There are various forms of visual memory that persist even longer and appear to be connected even more intimately with the motor system. For example, Tyrrell et al. (1993) have shown that visual information sufficient for guiding motor movement (placing a luminous dot at the right place in three dimensions) persists for more than 15 seconds. David Ingle has recently reported what he calls "central visual persistences" that last for up to 15 seconds (Ingle 2005). These visual persistences are reminiscent of eidetic images but are not as detailed or long lasting. They are, however, clearly situated in extrapersonal space and are closely connected with the motor system (e.g., it seems that the images can be moved manually by moving the hand). At the other extreme of duration, Ishai and Sagi (1995) found that accurate spatial information about flanking visual masks—capable of enhancing detection thresholds—is available for up to 5 minutes. Such examples, most of which involve sensory persistence of locations in extrapersonal space, suggest that observations with eyes closed may not really be observations without visual input. None of the experiments that I am aware of, involving spatial images, required the observer to wait a few minutes in the dark (or with eyes closed) before being tested; so long-term

visual persistence may still be a factor in anchoring images to a visually perceived scene (as suggested in figure 5.3).

**(3) Locations of targets of intended movement are registered, even if no
movement occurs**   There is evidence that the motor system activates locations in the visual cortex that are the targets of intended actions, even
when no movement occurs. Recall the single-cell study by Duhamel,
Colby, and Goldberg (1992) mentioned earlier, which shows that a cell
with a receptive field that is about to cover a feature to which it is sensitive
begins to respond before the eye movement is completed. It has also been
shown that visual search is influenced by intended actions on the target
objects even if no actual actions occur (Bekkering and Neggers 2002). Such
findings show that the loci of intended actions have measurable consequences even when the actions are not executed. There is converging evidence for the representation, in posterior parietal cortex, of the location of
targets of intended actions, in an extrapersonal frame of reference (Andersen and Buneo 2002; Snyder, Batista, and Andersen 2000). This shows that
coordinate transformation operations on visual inputs occur even without
the actual execution of motor actions. Thus, imagining potential actions
toward the recalled location of objects in space may create a frame of reference in the space of potential motor commands (or in the space of intended actions). Such a sparse registration, involving only the loci of
intended actions, might also serve the function of anchoring the index projection of individual objects, as required by the index projection hypothesis. These findings are also consistent with the hypothesis that when
making saccades, observers encode only the target of the saccade (this
saccade-target theory is described in Currie, McConkie, and Carlson-
Radvansky 2000).

**(4) Acoustical and proprioceptive signals provide anchors the same way
that vision does**   There are many relevant properties in common between
vision, audition, and proprioception, which suggests that the earlier discussion about how objects can be indexed in vision (section 5.5.2) applies
equally to other modalities. Vision and audition both present a vast array
of information about the sensory properties of the spatial layout before us.
Even though only a very small subset of the potential information is
encoded, the information is there as a possibility; it is what James Gibson
referred to as the *ambient array*. There is evidence (surveyed above) that audition has some of the same object-locating capacities as does vision. I have
suggested that proprioception and intended motor actions also present

something like an ambient sensory array because, thanks to coordinate transformation operations, they can register a small number of individuals in what is effectively an allocentric frame of reference. If we think of the salient information that is selected (and indexed) from this proprioceptive array as "objects," then these objects also provide the capacity to anchor thoughts in stable allocentric space.

Given all these considerations, it is not too far-fetched to assume that when we imagine a spatial layout in the dark, it is meaningful for us to use demonstrative and locative thoughts, such as *this* or *that*, as we do with vision, where the demonstratives pick out filled places in the proprioceptive landscape or the potential (intentional) motor landscape. The evidence I have quickly surveyed makes such a premise plausible. In fact it is quite intuitive to think of places in an imagined scene as being in the space in front of the observer, guided not by a retinotopic *internal* mental image but by externally sensed proprioceptive inputs, or even signals for intended (but not executed) actions.

Conclusions

The research and theoretical ideas described in this book take as their fundamental premise that the mind is tuned to the world in certain ways, ways that no doubt come down to us through eons of evolution. Elsewhere I have discussed some of the ways this tuning manifests itself in what David Marr and others have called natural constraints. The principle also appears in many other domains, where it shows up as the capacity to compute certain functions that would be logically impossible as described were it not for certain innate structures that allow a special sort of approximation to the ideal function. The approximation is more than a rough guess or heuristic: It is a function that *in our sort of world* will be very near the ideal function. The standard example in vision is the process of reversing the mapping from the 3-D distal world to 2-D proximal images so as to permit the recovery of 3-D shape. In that case not only does the visual system use additional cues based on contour, shading, motion, and so on to compute the inverse mapping from proximal to distal layout, but the process that computes this mapping is inherently constrained so that an unlimited number of logically possible constructions are not available. The constructions that result are typically unique in our kind of world (and in our ecological niche). A simple example is the interpretation of line drawings as 3-D shapes (e.g., figure 4.1). The label-consistency constraint I spoke of in section 4.2 ensures that a unique labeling is given to the figure in cases where we actually have a unique percept. Similarly, in the case of grammar, an (approximately) unique set of grammatical rules is induced even though the sparse input available for language learning is compatible with an unlimited number of grammars. What ensures the uniqueness of the induced grammar is the innate constraint on humanly possible grammars embodied in Universal Grammar. UG prevents language-users from considering all logically possible candidate grammars, forcing them to converge on one.

In the present context the mechanism in question is one that helps to solve the problem of concept grounding as well as the problem of how we capture the numerical identity of enduring individual things. I do not claim that I have a solution to these problems, or even a serious candidate. What I present is a set of ideas, based on empirical research in my laboratory and elsewhere, that suggests how these problems might be approached in the spirit of the natural constraints idea. The proposal is that there is, in the early visual system, a primitive mechanism which accomplishes two tasks: It individuates things in the visual scene, and it provides direct reference to a small number of them. In this statement, "individuates" means that the visual system parses the visual world and segregates things in space and time so they can be treated as enduring individuals. This entails not only carrying out a figure-ground segregation (which is segregation in space), but also solving the correspondence problem (which is segregation in time). By "direct reference" I mean essentially a demonstrative reference or a pointer or index (a FINST) that allows epistemic access to a small number of the spatially and temporally segregated individuals without specifying any of their properties. It is crucial to this theory that neither of these functions involves appeal to concepts—that is, individuating is done prior to the encoding of any properties as falling under concepts. I have been careful to point out that a property's not being encoded is not the same as its not being causally involved in the process: There are specific properties that cause a FINST index to be assigned and that enable it to keep track of the indexed individuals—but these properties are not encoded, and a representation of these properties is not used in carrying out those functions.

I have devoted a significant part of this book to explicating the notion of FINST indexes and demonstrating the need for such a mechanism in accounting for many diverse empirical phenomena. I have argued that the idea arises naturally from the well-accepted notion of focal attention, although it does constitute an extension of this notion both in the assumption that there are several indexes (whereas there is typically only one locus of attention) and in the assumption that properties of indexed things are not involved in the indexing process: such properties need not be encoded in the course of individuation, nor are they used to support the process of tracking. The major use of indexes is that of binding the indexed individuals to the arguments of mental predicates or motor commands (including the command to move focal attention to a particular individual). Once attention (which I treat primarily as the focus of visual processing) is allocated to indexed individuals, their properties can be encoded and stored (in object files) in association with those individuals.

Because only predicates whose arguments are bound to individuals can be evaluated, only properties of indexed individuals can be conceptualized. This leads to a strong claim about conceptual and nonconceptual representations (and registrations): The only nonconceptual contents there are in perception are demonstratives or FINST indexes. Nonconceptual content consists solely in the demonstrative reference to a small number of objects. There are no rich nonconceptual representations of the sort postulated by most philosophers who speak of nonconceptual representation.

But what about the major philosophical motivation for postulating non-conceptual representations, namely to account for the discrepancy between the rich fine-grained content of perceptual experience and the much more restricted content of conceptual representations? Several answers are offered to this conundrum. First, much of the content of conscious experience is problematic, if not irrelevant, to explanations of how vision works. There are many reasons to take this view. The main one is that the content of conscious experience is a fallible source of evidence, like any other form of observation, and thus can be overridden by other evidence—and very often must be overruled because it is subject to many forces, from bias effects to unconscious confabulation even in the presence of what ought to be clear experiences. If the claim is correct that only properties of indexed individuals are represented (except for very short times during which the inertia of sensors may provide a rich registration of information), it raises the question of how to account for the large quantity of information required by the encapsulated processes in vision, language, action planning and executing, and other domains. In my view it remains a real possibility that this sort of information may have to be treated as a subspecies of concepts—the subpersonal concepts, which have many of the characteristics of concepts (e.g., they appear to be symbolically encoded and take part in a form of unconscious reasoning, such as that involved in parsing natural language or in early vision), yet may be different in kind from the usual *personal* concepts—for example, we are not aware of them and they do not take part in general reasoning, that is, they are not "inferentially promiscuous" (to use Steve Stich's term; see Stich 1978).

To illustrate how the use of conscious contents as a privileged source of evidence is both tempting and misleading, I have sketched a number of places in cognitive psychology where it has been a serious problem, and I then focused on two closely related cases in more detail. These cases not only make the point that accepting conscious contents as necessarily corresponding to the contents of some mental representation is a mistake; they also help to develop the connection between FINST indexes and nonconceptual content. The first case illustrates the way that conscious content has led us astray in developing theories of the representations underlying mental images used in reasoning. The second case, which is closely related to but in many ways deeper than the first, is the question of how we "represent" and use spatial properties. I have put "represent" in scare quotes here because the proposal I make in the last chapter is that we do not need to represent most spatial properties in reasoning, beyond the way we represent any subject matter in long-term conceptual memory. Nonetheless, we do need to account for the special spatial properties that appear when we actively use spatial relations in reasoning spatially, as we do when we think about problems in geometry, when we examine images for previously unnoticed geometrical properties, and when we try to account for some remarkable parallels between visual imagery and visual perception.

The proposal I make in the last chapter is an externalist one. I propose that all we need to account for the apparently spatial properties exhibited (as opposed to represented) by mental representations is a rough qualitative schema specifying spatial relations among a few salient landmark objects that we can use to pick out individuals in the concurrently perceived spatial surround using FINST indexes (or what, for nonvisual modalities, I call anchors). With this capability we can do what is rather similar to "projecting" an image onto the perceived world, with indexed objects being treated as labeled individuals. This then allows us to scan attention or shift our gaze from one indexed individual to another, to judge the pattern that they form, estimate their relative distances, and so on. The point is that these judgments are all done by the visual system, because the pattern that is being examined is now *out there* in the perceived scene. This idea, though simple, raises many problems, such as how such judgments can be made without vision (e.g., in the dark), which in turn raises the question of how the proprioceptive system is able to make such judgments without actually reaching out and touching things in the world. All these complications reduce to empirical questions, such as the frame of reference in which proprioception and motor control operate. The major idea at this junction turns out to be the mechanism, well known in neuroscience, for transforming representations (registrations) in one frame of reference into another frame of reference. This function is known as the coordinate transformation operation and has been studied extensively by neuroscientists. I argue (based on a proposal by Henriques et al. 1998, called "transformation on demand") that only a few selected individuals need to be considered when superimposing memory representations onto proprioceptive signals. To explain how the latter can indicate locations fixed in allocentric coordinates we appeal to the ubiquitous coordinate transformation operations.

This brings the analysis full circle, to where FINSTs and various types of representation are seen to be interrelated and support the classical picture of a representation-governed system, such as I advocated in Pylyshyn 1984, augmented by direct causal links in the tradition of Dretske (1991, 1981) and Fodor (1990). The analysis brings together a number of long-standing puzzles. Although it does not provide a definitive solution, it at least points a possible way to resolving a number of long-standing problems in cognitive science.

References

Aglioti, S., DeSouza, J. F. X., and Goodale, M. A. (1995). Size-contrast illusions deceive the eye but not the hand. *Current Biology*, *5*(6), 679–685.

Allen, R., McGeorge, P., Pearson, D., and Milne, A. B. (2004). Attention and expertise in multiple target tracking. *Applied Cognitive Psychology*, *18*, 337–347.

Alvarez, G. A., Arsenio, H. C., Horowitz, T. S., and Wolfe, J. M. (2005). Are multielement visual tracking and visual search mutually exclusive? *Journal of Experimental Psychology: Human Perception and Performance*, *31*(4), 643–667.

Alvarez, G. A., and Cavanagh, P. (2005). Independent attention resources for the left and right visual hemifields. *Psychological Science*, *16*(8), 637–643.

Alvarez, G. A., and Scholl, B. J. (2005). How does attention select and track spatially extended objects? New effects of attentional concentration and amplification. *Journal of Experimental Psychology: General*, *134*(4), 461–476.

Andersen, R. A. (1995a). Coordinate transformations and motor planning in posterior parietal cortex. In *The Cognitive Neurosciences*, ed. Michael S. Gazzaniga, pp. 519–532. Cambridge, Mass.: MIT Press.

Andersen, R. A. (1995b). Encoding of intention and spatial location in the posterior parietal cortex. *Cerebral Cortex*, *5*(5), 457–469.

Andersen, R. A., and Buneo, C. A. (2002). Intentional maps in posterior parietal cortex. *Annual Review of Neuroscience*, *25*, 189–220.

Ashmead, D. H., Davis, D. L., and Northington, A. (1995). Contribution of listeners' approaching motion to auditory distance perception. *Journal of Experimental Psychology: Human Perception and Performance*, *21*(2), 239–256.

Attneave, F. (1959). *Applications of Information Theory to Psychology: A Summary of Basic Concepts, Methods, and Results*. New York: Holt.

Attneave, F., and Block, G. (1973). Apparent movement in tridimensional space. *Perception and Psychophysics*, *13*(2), 301–307.

Attneave, F., and Farrar, P. (1977). The visual world behind the head. *American Journal of Psychology*, *90*(4), 549–563.

Avant, L. L. (1965). Vision in the ganzfeld. *Psychological Bulletin, 64*, 246–258.

Ayers, M. (1997). Is physical object a sortal concept? A reply to Xu. *Mind and Language, 12*(3–4), 393–405.

Bachmann, T. (1989). Microgenesis as traced by the transient paired-forms paradigm. *Acta Psychologica, 70*, 3–17.

Bahrami, B. (2003). Object property encoding and change blindness in multiple object tracking. *Visual Cognition, 10*(8), 949–963.

Baillargeon, R., and DeVos, J. (1991). Object permanence in 3.5- and 4.5-month-old infants: further evidence. *Child Development, 62*, 1227–1246.

Ballard, D. H., and Brown, C. M. (1982). *Computer Vision.* Englewood Cliffs, N.J.: Prentice-Hall.

Ballard, D. H., Hayhoe, M. M., Pook, P. K., and Rao, R. P. N. (1997). Deictic codes for the embodiment of cognition. *Behavioral and Brain Sciences, 20*(4), 723–767.

Bartlett, F. C. (1932). *Remembering: A Study in Experimental and Social Psychology.* Cambridge: Cambridge University Press.

Bartolomeo, P., and Chokron, S. (2002). Orienting of attention in left unilateral neglect. *Neuroscience and Biobehavioral Reviews, 26*(2), 217–234.

Batista, A. P., Buneo, C. A., Snyder, L. H., and Andersen, R. A. (1999). Reach plans in eye-centered coordinates. *Science, 285*(5425), 257–260.

Baud-Bovy, G., and Viviani, P. (1998). Pointing to kinesthetic targets in space. *Journal of Neuroscience, 18*(4), 1528–1545.

Baylis, G. C. (1994). Visual attention and objects: Two-object cost with equal convexity. *Journal of Experimental Psychology: Human Perception and Performance, 20*, 208–212.

Baylis, G. C., and Driver, J. (1993). Visual attention and objects: Evidence for hierarchical coding of location. *Journal of Experimental Psychology: Human Percepton and Performance, 19*, 451–470.

Behrmann, M., and Tipper, S. (1999). Attention accesses multiple reference frames: Evidence from unilateral neglect. *Journal of Experimental Psychology: Human Perception and Performance, 25*, 83–101.

Bekkering, H., and Neggers, S. F. (2002). Visual search is modulated by action intentions. *Psychological Science, 13*(4), 370–374.

Berlin, B., and Kay, P. (1969). *Basic Color Terms: Their Universality and Evolution.* Berkeley: University of California Press.

Best, C. T., Studdard-Kennedy, M., Manuel, S., and Rubin-Spitz, J. (1989). Discovering acoustic coherence in acoustic patterns. *Perception and Psychophysics, 45*(3), 237–250.

Biederman, I. (1987). Recognition-by-components: A theory of human image interpretation. *Psychological Review, 94*, 115–148.

Bisiach, E., and Luzzatti, C. (1978). Unilateral neglect of representational space. *Cortex, 14*(1), 129–133.

Bizzi, E., and Mussa-Ivaldi, F. A. (1995). Toward a neurobiology of coordinate transformations. In *The Cognitive Neurosciences*, ed. Michael S. Gazzaniga, pp. 495–506.

Black, A., and Pylyshyn, Z. W. (2004). Developmental differences in multiple object tracking. *Journal of Vision, 4*(8), 371a.

Blaser, E., Pylyshyn, Z. W., and Domini, F. (1999). Measuring attention during 3D multielement tracking. *Investigative Ophthalmology and Visual Science, 40*(4), 552 (abstract).

Blaser, E., Pylyshyn, Z. W., and Holcombe, A. O. (2000). Tracking an object through feature-space. *Nature, 408* (Nov. 9), 196–199.

Block, N. (ed.). (1981). *Imagery*. Cambridge, Mass.: MIT Press.

Block, N. (1995). On a confusion about a function of consciousness. *Behavioral and Brain Sciences, 18*, 227–247.

Block, N. (2005). Two neural correlates of consciousness. *Trends in Cognitive Sciences, 9*(2), 46–52.

Bonatti, L. (1994). Propositional reasoning by model? *Psychological Review, 101*(4), 725–733.

Bonatti, L. (1998). What the mental logic-mental models controversy is not about. In *Mental Logic*, ed. Martin D. S. Braine and David P. O'Brien, pp. 435–445. vii, 481 pp. Mahwah, N.J.: Lawrence Erlbaum.

Bonatti, L., Frot, E., Zangl, R., and Mehler, J. (2002). The human first hypothesis: Identification of conspecifics and individuation of objects in the young infant. *Cognitive Psychology, 44*, 388–426.

Bornstein, R., and Pittman, T. (1992). *Perception without Awareness*. New York: Guilford Press.

Brandt, S. A., and Stark, L. W. (1997). Spontaneous eye movements during visual imagery reflect the content of the visual scene. *Journal of Cognitive Neuroscience, 9*(1), 27–38.

Brentano, F. (1874/1995). *Psychology from an Empirical Standpoint*. New York: Routledge.

Bridgeman, B. (1992). Conscious versus unconcious processes: The case of vision. *Theoretical Psychology, 2*, 73–88.

Bridgeman, B., Lewis, S., Heit, G., and Nagle, M. (1979). Relation between cognitive and motor-oriented systems of visual position perception. *Journal of Eperimental Pyschology: Human Perception and Performance, 5*, 692–700.

Broadbent, D. E. (1958). *Perception and Communication*. London: Pergamon Press.

Brooks, L. R. (1968). Spatial and verbal components of the act of recall. *Canadian Journal of Psychology, 22*(5), 349–368.

Bruner, J. S. (1957). On perceptual readiness. *Psychological Review, 64*, 123–152.

Buneo, C. A., Jarvis, M. R., Batista, A. P., and Andersen, R. A. (2002). Direct visuomotor transformations for reaching. *Nature, 416*(6881), 632–636.

Burkell, J., and Pylyshyn, Z. W. (1997). Searching through subsets: A test of the visual indexing hypothesis. *Spatial Vision, 11*(2), 225–258.

Calis, G. J., Sterenborg, J., and Maarse, F. (1984). Initial microgenetic steps in single-glance face recognition. *Acta Psychologica, 55*(3), 215–230.

Campbell, J. (1993). The role of physical objects in spatial thinking. In *Spatial Representation: Problems in Philosophy and Psychology*, ed. N. Eilan, R. A. McCarthy, and B. Brewer. New York: Oxford University Press.

Campbell, J. (2002). *Reference and Consciousness*. New York: Oxford University Press.

Campbell, J. (2004). Reference as attention. *Philosophical Studies, 120*, 265–276.

Canon, L. K. (1970). Intermodality inconsistency of input and directed attention as determinants of the nature of adaptation. *Journal of Experimental Psychology, 84*(1), 141–147.

Canon, L. K. (1971). Directed attention and maladaptive "adaptation" to displacement of the visual field. *Journal of Experimental Psychology, 88*(3), 403–408.

Carey, S. (forthcoming). *The Origin of Concepts*. Cambridge, Mass.: MIT Press.

Carey, S., and Xu, F. (2001). Infants' knowledge of objects: Beyond object files and object tracking. *Cognition, 80*(1/2), 179–213.

Cavanagh, P. (1992). Attention-based motion perception. *Science, 257*, 1563–1565.

Cavanagh, P. (1999). Attention: Exporting vision to the mind. In *Neuronal Basis and Psychological Aspects of Consciousness*, ed. C. Taddei-Ferretti and C. Musio, pp. 129–143. Singapore: World Scientific.

Cavanagh, P., and Alvarez, G. A. (2005). Tracking multiple targets with multifocal attention. *Trends in Cognitive Sciences, 9*(7), 349–354.

Cavanagh, P., Labianca, A. T., and Thornton, I. M. (2001). Attention-based visual routines: Sprites. *Cognition, 80*(1–2), 47–60.

Cheng, K. (1986). A purely geometric module in the rat's spatial representation. *Cognition, 23*, 149–178.

Chiang, W.-C., and Wynn, K. (2000). Infants' tracking of objects and collections. *Cognition, 75*, 1–27.

Chieffi, S., Allport, D. A., and Woodin, M. (1999). Hand-centred coding of target location in visuo-spatial working memory. *Neuropsychologia*, *37*, 495–502.

Chokron, S., Colliot, P., and Bartolomeo, P. (2004). The role of vision in spatial representations. *Cortex*, *40*, 281–290.

Chomsky, N. (1959). Review of B. F. Skinner's *"Verbal Behavior." Language*, *35*(1), 26–58.

Churchland, P. M. (1988). Perceptual plasticity and theoretical neutrality: A reply to Jerry Fodor. *Philosophy of Science*, *55*, 167–187.

Clark, A. (2000). *A Theory of Sentience*. New York: Oxford University Press.

Clark, A. (2004). Feature placing and proto-objects. *Philosophical Psychology*, *17*(4), 443–469.

Cohen, E. H., and Pylyshyn, Z. W. (2002). Searching through subsets of moving items. *Journal of Vision*, *2*(7), 541a.

Colby, C. L., and Goldberg, M. E. (1999). Space and attention in parietal cortex. *Annual Review of Neuroscience*, *22*, 319–349.

Cole, J. (1995). *Pride and a Daily Marathon*. Cambridge, Mass.: MIT Press.

Collett, M., and Collett, T. S. (2000). How do insects use path integration for their navigation? *Biological Cybernetics*, *82*, 245–259.

Collett, T. S., and Collett, M. (2002). Memory use in insect visual navigation. *Nature*, *3*, 542–552.

Crawford, J. D., Medendorp, W. P., and Marotta, J. J. (2004). Spatial transformations for eye–hand coordination. *Journal of Neurophysiology*, *92*, 10–19.

Culham, J. C., Brandt, S. A., Cavanagh, P., Kanwisher, N. G., Dale, A. M., and Tootell, R. B. H. (1998). Cortical fMRI activation produced by attentive tracking of moving targets. *Journal of Neurophysiology*, *80*(5), 2657–2670.

Currie, C. B., McConkie, G. W., and Carlson-Radvansky, L. A. (2000). The role of the saccade target object in the perception of a visually stable world. *Perception and Psychophysics*, *62*, 673–683.

Currie, C. B., and Pylyshyn, Z. W. (2003). *Maintenance of FINSTs across eye movements*. Unpublished ms. available at http://ruccs.rutgers.edu/~zenon/ccurrie/report.html/.

Dalla Barba, G., Rosenthal, V., and Visetti, Y.-V. (2002). The nature of mental imagery: How "null" is the null hypothesis? *Behavioral and Brain Sciences*, *25*(2), 187–188.

Danckert, J., and Maruff, P. (1997). Manipulating the disengage operation of covert visual spatial attention. *Perception and Psychophysics*, *59*(4), 500–508.

Dawson, M. (1991). The how and why of what went where in apparent motion: Modeling solutions to the motion correspondence problem. *Psychological Review*, *98*, 569–603.

Dawson, M., and Pylyshyn, Z. W. (1988). Natural constraints in apparent motion. In *Computational Processes in Human Vision: An Interdisciplinary Perspective*, ed. Z. W. Pylyshyn, pp. 99–120. Stamford, Conn.: Ablex Publishing.

Dehaene, S. (1997). *The Number Sense: How the Mind Creates Mathematics*. New York: Oxford University Press.

Denis, M., and Kosslyn, S. M. (1999). Scanning visual mental images: A window on the mind. *Cahiers de Psychologie Cognitive/Current Psychology of Cognition, 18*(4), 409–465.

Dennett, D. C. (1978). Toward a cognitive theory of consciousness. In *Perception and Cognition: Issues in the Foundations of Psychology* (vol. 9), ed. C. W. Savage. Minneapolis: Univ. of Minnesota Press.

Dennett, D. C. (1991). *Consciousness Explained*. Boston: Little, Brown.

Dennis, J. L. M., and Pylyshyn, Z. W. (2002). Effect of object discriminability on multiple object tracking. Paper presented at the Vision Sciences 2002, Sarasota, FL.

De Soto, C. B., London, M., and Handel, S. (1965). Social reasoning and spatial paralogic. *Journal of Personality and Social Psychology, 2*(4), 513–521.

Devitt, M. (2006). *Ignorance of Language*. Oxford: Oxford University Press.

Di Lollo, V., Enns, J. T., and Rensink, R. A. (2000). Competition for consciousness among visual events: The psychophysics of reentrant visual processes. *Journal of Experimental Psychology: General, 129*(4), 481–507.

Dretske, F. (1981). *Knowledge and the Flow of Information*. Cambridge, Mass.: MIT Press, a Bradford Book.

Dretske, F. (1991). *Explaining Behavior*. Cambridge, Mass.: MIT Press.

Dretske, F. (1993). Conscious experience. *Mind, 102*(406), 263–283.

Dretske, F. (2006). What change blindness teaches about consciousness. Invited talk to the Annual Meeting of the Society for the Scientific Study of Consiousness. Oxford, June 2006.

Driver, J., and Spence, C. (1998). Attention and the crossmodal construction of space. *Trends in Cognitive Sciences, 2*(7), 254–262.

Driver, J., and Spence, C. (2004). Crossmodal spatial attention: evidence from human performance. In *Crossmodal Space and Crossmodal Attention*, ed. C. Spence and J. Driver, pp. 179–220. New York: Oxford University Press.

Dufour, A., Despres, O., and Pebayle, T. (2002). Visual and auditory facilitation in auditory spatial localization. *Visual Cognition, 9*(6), 741–753.

Duhamel, J.-R., Colby, C. L., and Goldberg, M. E. (1992). The updating of the representation of visual space in parietal cortex by intended eye movements. *Science, 255*(5040), 90–92.

Edelman, S. (2001). Neural spaces: A general framework for the understanding of cognition. *Behavioral and Brain Sciences, 24*(4), 664–665.

Eilan, N., McCarthy, R. A., and Brewer, B. (eds.). (1993). *Spatial Representation: Problems in Philosophy and Psychology.* New York: Oxford University Press.

Enns, J. T., and Franconeri, S. L. (2006). Environmental representations in multiple object tracking. Paper presented at Visions Sciences 2006, Sarasota, Florida.

Enns, J. T., and Rensink, R. A. (1990). Sensitivity to three-dimensional orientation in visual search. *Psychological Science, 1*(5), 323–326.

Epstein, W. (1982). Percept-percept couplings. *Perception, 11,* 75–83.

Essock, E. A., Deford, J. K., Hansen, B. C., and Sinai, M. J. (2003). Oblique stimuli are seen best (not worst!) in naturalistic broad-band stimuli: A horizontal effect. *Vision Research, 43*(12), 1329–1335.

Evans, G. (1982). *Varieties of Reference.* Oxford: Oxford University Press.

Farrell, M. J., and Thomson, J. A. (1998). Automatic spatial updating during locomotion without vision. *Quarterly Journal of Experimental Psychology A, 51*(3), 637–654.

Farrell, M. J., and Thomson, J. A. (1999). On-line updating of spatial information during locomotion without vision. *Journal of Motor Behavior, 31*(1), 39–53.

Finke, R. A. (1979). The functional equivalence of mental images and errors of movement. *Cognitive Psychology, 11,* 235–264.

Finke, R. A., and Pinker, S. (1982). Spontaneous imagery scanning in mental extrapolation. *Journal of Experimental Psychology: Learning, Memory, and Cognition, 8*(2), 142–147.

Fleishman, E. A., and Rich, S. (1963). Role of kinesthetic and spatial-visual abilities in perceptual-motor learning. *Journal of Experimental Psychology, 66*(1), 6–11.

Flombaum, J. I., Scholl, B. J., and Pylyshyn, Z. W. (2006). "Attentional high-beams" in tracking through occlusion. *Journal of Vision, 6*(6), 765a.

Fodor, J. A. (1965). Explanation in psychology. In *Philosophy in America,* ed. M. Black. Ithaca: Cornell Univ. Press.

Fodor, J. A. (1968). The appeal to tacit knowledge in psychological explanation. *Journal of Philosophy, 65,* 627–640.

Fodor, J. A. (1980a). Methodological solipsism considered as a research strategy for cognitive psychology. *Behavioral and Brain Sciences, 3*(1), 63–73.

Fodor, J. A. (1980b). Reply to Putnam. In *Language and Learning: The Debate between Jean Piaget and Noam Chomsky,* ed. M. Piattelli-Palmarini. Cambridge, Mass.: Harvard Univ. Press.

Fodor, J. A. (1983). *The Modularity of Mind: An Essay on Faculty Psychology.* Cambridge, Mass.: MIT Press.

Fodor, J. A. (1990). *A Theory of Content and Other Essays*. Cambidge, Mass.: MIT Press.

Fodor, J. A. (1998). *Concepts: Where Cognitive Science Went Wrong*. Oxford: Oxford Univ. Press.

Fodor, J. A. (2003). *Hume Variations*. Oxford: Clarendon Press.

Fodor, J. A. (2007). Revenge of the given. In *Contemporary Debates in the Philosophy of Mind*, ed. B. P. McLaughlin and J. Cohen, pp. 105–116. New York: Basil Blackwell.

Fodor, J. A. (forthcoming). *The Language of Thought Revisited*. Cambridge, Mass.: MIT Press.

Fodor, J. A., and Pylyshyn, Z. W. (1981). How direct is visual perception? Some reflections on Gibson's "ecological Approach." *Cognition*, *9*, 139–196.

Fodor, J. A., and Pylyshyn, Z. W. (1988). Connectionism and cognitive architecture: A critical analysis. *Cognition*, *28*, 3–71.

Fougnie, D., and Marois, R. (2006). Distinct capacity limits for attention and working memory. Evidence from attentive tracking and visual working memory paradigms. *Psychological Science*, *17*(6), 526–534.

Franconeri, S., Hollingworth, A., and Simons, D. J. (2005). Do new objects capture attention? *Psychological Science*, *16*(4), 275–281.

Franconeri, S. L., Pylyshyn, Z. W., and Scholl, B. J. (2006). Spatiotemporal cues for tracking objects through occlusion. *Journal of Vision*, *5*(6), 1102a.

Freeman, J. T. (1955). Set versus perceptual defense: A confirmation. *Journal of Abnormal and Social Psychology*, *51*, 710–712.

Frisby, J. P., and Clatworthy, J. L. (1975). Learning to see complex random-dot stereograms. *Perception*, *4*(2), 173–178.

Gallistel, C. R. (1990). *The Organization of Learning*. Cambridge, Mass.: MIT Press.

Gallistel, C. R. (1999). Coordinate transformations in the genesis of directed action. In *Cognitive Science: Handbook of Perception and Cognition, 2nd ed.*, ed. Benjamin Martin Bly and David E. Rumelhart, pp. 1–42. New York: Academic Press.

Gallistel, C. R., and Cramer, A. E. (1996). Computations on metric maps in mammals: Getting oriented and choosing a multi-destination route. *Journal of Experimental Biology*, *199*(1), 211–217.

Gandevia, S. C., and Burke, D. (1992). Does the nervous system depend on kinesthetic information to control natural limb movements? *Behavioral and Brain Sciences*, *15*(4), 614–632.

Gazzaniga, M. S. (1995). Consciousness and the cerebral hemispheres. In *The Cognitive Neurosciences*, ed. M. S. Gazzaniga, pp. 1391–1400. Cambridge, Mass.: MIT Press.

Gazzaniga, M. S. (2000). Cerebral specialization and interhemispheric communication: Does the corpus callosum enable the human condition? *Brain*, *123*(7), 1293–1326.

Gentaz, E., and Hatwell, Y. (1998). The haptic oblique effect in the perception of rod orientation by blind adults. *Perception and Psychophysics*, *60*(1), 157–167.

Ghahramani, Z., Wolpert, D. M., and Jordan, M. I. (1996). Generalization to local remappings of the visuomotor coordinate transformation. *Journal of Neuroscience*, *16*(21), 7085–7096.

Gibson, J. J. (1979). *An Ecological Approach to Visual Perception*. Boston: Houghton Mifflin.

Gilchrist, A. (1977). Perceived lightness depends on perceived spatial arrangement. *Science*, *195*, 185–187.

Gilden, D., Blake, R., and Hurst, G. (1995). Neural adaptation of imaginary visual motion. *Cognitive Psychology*, *28*(1), 1–16.

Gnadt, J. W., and Andersen, R. A. (1988). Memory related motor planning activity in posterior parietal cortex of macaque. *Experimental Brain Research*, *70*, 216–220.

Gnadt, J. W., Bracewell, R. M., and Andersen, R. A. (1991). Sensorimotor transformation during eye movements to remembered visual targets. *Vision Research*, *31*(4), 693–715.

Gold, M. E. (1967). Language identification in the limit. *Information and Control*, *10*, 447–474.

Goldman, A. (1986). *Epistemology and Cognition*. Cambridge, Mass.: Harvard Univ. Press.

Goodale, M., and Milner, D. (2004). *Sight Unseen*. New York: Oxford Univ. Press.

Goodale, M. A., Jacobson, J. S., and Keillor, J. M. (1994). Differences in the visual control of pantomimed and natural grasping movements. *Neuropsychologia*, *32*(10), 1159–1178.

Goodale, M. A., Pelisson, D., and Prablanc, C. (1986). Large adjustments in visually guided reaching do not depend on vision of the hand or perception of target displacement. *Nature*, *320*, 748–750.

Goodman, N. (1968). *Languages of Art*. Indianapolis: Bobbs-Merrill.

Graziano, M. S. A., and Gross, C. G. (1995). The representation of extrapersonal space: A possible role for bimodal, visuo-tactile neurons. In *The Cognitive Neurosciences*, ed. M. S. Gazzaniga, pp. 1021–1034. Cambridge, Mass.: MIT Press.

Gul, E., and Atherton, D. (1989). Transputer implementation for multiple target tracking. *Microprocessors Microsystems*, *13*(3), 188–194.

Gumperz, J., and Levinson, S. (eds.). (1996). *Rethinking Linguistic Relativity: Studies in the Social and Cultural Foundations of Language*. Cambridge: Cambridge Univ. Press.

Gunther, Y. H. (ed.). (2003). *Essays on Nonceptual Content*. Cambridge, Mass.: MIT Press.

Hagenzieker, M. P., van der Heijden, A. H. C., and Hagenaar, R. (1990). Time course in visual-information processing: Some empirical evidence for inhibition. *Psychological Research*, *52*, 13–21.

Haladjian, H. H., and Pylyshyn, Z. W. (2006). Implicit multiple object tracking without an explicit tracking task. *Journal of Vision*, *6*(6), 773a.

Halsey, R., and Chapanis, A. (1951). On the number of absolutely identifiable spectral hues. *Journal of the Optical Society of America*, *41*, 1057–1058.

Hannus, A., Cornelissen, F. W., Lindemann, O., and Bekkering, H. (2005). Selection-for-action in visual search. *Acta Psychologica*, *118*(1–2), 171–191.

Hansen, B. C., and Essock, E. A. (2004). A horizontal bias in human visual processing of orientation and its correspondence to the structural components of natural scenes. *Journal of Vision*, *4*(12), 1044–1060.

Haugeland, J. (1978). The nature and plausibility of cognitivism. *Behavioral and Brain Sciences*, *2*, 215–260.

Heeley, D. W., Buchanan-Smith, H. M., Cromwell, J. A., and Wright, J. S. (1997). The oblique effect in orientation acuity. *Vision Research*, *37*(2), 235–242.

Henriques, D. Y. P., Klier, E. M., Smith, M. A., Lowy, D., and Crawford, J. D. (1998). Gaze-centered remapping of remembered visual space in an open-loop pointing task. *Journal of Neuroscience*, *18*(4), 1583–1594.

Hermer, L., and Spelke, E. (1996). Modularity and development: The case of spatial reorientation. *Cognition*, *61*(3), 195–232.

Hinton, C. H. (1906). *The Fourth Dimension*. London: George Allen and Unwin.

Hirsch, E. (1997). Basic objects: A reply to Xu. *Mind and Language*, *12*(3–4), 406–412.

Hirstein, W. (2005). *Brain Fiction: Self-Deception and the Riddle of Confabulation*. Cambridge, Mass.: MIT Press.

Hochberg, J. (1968). In the mind's eye. In *Contemporary Theory and Research in Visual Perception*, ed. R. N. Haber, pp. 309–331. New York: Holt, Rinehart, and Winston.

Hoffman, D. D. (1998). *Visual Intelligence: How We Create What We See*. New York: W. W. Norton.

Horn, B. K. P. (1986). *Robot Vision*. Cambridge, Mass.: MIT Press.

Hubel, D. H., and Wiesel, T. N. (1968). Receptive fields and functional architecture of monkey striate cortex. *Journal of Physiology*, *195*, 215–243.

Huntley-Fenner, G., Carey, S., and Salimando, A. (2002). Objects are individuals but stuff doesn't count: Perceived rigidity and cohesiveness influence infants' representation of small number of discrete entities. *Cognition*, *85*(3), 203–221.

Huttenlocher, J. (1968). Constructing spatial images: A strategy in reasoning. *Psychological Review*, *75*(6), 550–560.

Ingle, D. (2005). Central visual persistences: I. Visual and kinesthetic interactions. *Perception*, *34*(9), 1135–1151.

Intriligator, J., and Cavanagh, P. (2001). The spatial resolution of attention. *Cognitive Psychology*, *4*(3), 171–216.

Irwin, D. E. (1992). Memory for position and identity across eye movements. *Journal of Experimental Psychology: Learning, Memory, and Cognition*, *18*(2), 307–317.

Irwin, D. E., and Gordon, R. D. (1998). Eye movements, attention, and trans-saccadic memory. *Visual Cognition*, *5*(1–2), 127–155.

Ishai, A., and Sagi, D. (1995). Common mechanisms of visual imagery and perception. *Science*, *268*(5218), 1772–1774.

Jackson, F. (1997). *Perception: A Representative Theory*. Cambridge: Cambridge Univ. Press.

Johnson, S. P. (2001). Visual development in human infants: Binding features, surfaces, and objects. *Visual Cognition*, *8*(3–5), 565–578.

Johnson-Laird, P. N. (2001). Mental models and deduction. *Trends in Cognitive Sciences*, *5*(10), 434–442.

Jolicoeur, P., and Kosslyn, S. M. (1985). Is time to scan visual images due to demand characteristics? *Memory and Cognition*, *13*, 320–332.

Jovich, J., Peters, R., Koch, C., Braun, J., Chang, L., and Ernst, T. (2001). Brain areas specific for attentional load in a motion-tracking task. *Journal of Cognitive Neuroscience*, *13*, 1048–1058.

Julesz, B. (1971). *Foundations of Cyclopean Perception*. Chicago: Univ. of Chicago Press.

Kabanza, F., Barbeau, M., and St-Denis, R. (1997). Planning control rules for reactive agents. *Artificial Intelligence*, *95*, 67–113.

Kahneman, D., Treisman, A., and Gibbs, B. J. (1992). The reviewing of object files: Object-specific integration of information. *Cognitive Psychology*, *24*(2), 175–219.

Kanizsa, G., and Gerbino, W. (1982). Amodal completion: Seeing or thinking? In *Organization and Representation in Perception*, ed. B. Beck, pp. 167–190. Hillsdale, N.J.: Lawrence Erlbaum.

Kappers, A. M. L., and Koenderink, J. J. (1999). Haptic perception of spatial relations. *Perception*, *28*(6), 781–795.

Karnath, H. O. (1997). Spatial orientation and the representation of space with parietal lobe lesions. *Philosophical Transactions of the Royal Society of London Series B: Biological Sciences*, *352*(1360), 1411–1419.

Karnath, H. O., Christ, K., and Hartje, W. (1993). Decrease of contralateral neglect by neck muscle vibration and spatial orientation of trunk midline. *Brain*, *116*(2), 383–396.

Kazanovich, Y., and Borisyuk, R. (2006). An oscillatory neural model of multiple object tracking. *Neural Computation, 18*(6), 1413–1440.

Keane, B. (2004). A case for visual objects in early vision: A response to Austen Clark's theory of sentience. Ph.D. dissertation, Rutgers University, New Brunswick, N.J.

Keane, B. P., and Pylyshyn, Z. W. (2006). Is motion extrapolation employed in multiple object tracking? Tracking as a low-level, non-predictive function. *Cognitive Psychology, 52*(4), 346–368.

Klein, R. M. (1988). Inhibitory tagging system facilitates visual search. *Nature, 334*(6181), 430–431.

Klier, E. M., Wang, H., and Crawford, J. D. (2001). The superior colliculus encodes gaze commands in retinal coordinates. *Nature Neuroscience, 4*(6), 627–632.

Koch, C., and Ullman, S. (1985). Shifts in selective visual attention: Towards the underlying neural circuitry. *Human Neurobiology, 4,* 219–227.

Koenderink, J. J. (1990). *Solid Shape.* Cambridge, Mass.: MIT Press.

Kohler, W. (1947). *Gestalt Psychology: An Introduction to New Concepts in Modern Psychology.* New York: Liveright.

Kolers, P. A., and von Grunau, M. (1976). Shape and color in apparent motion. *Vision Research, 16*(4), 329–335.

Kosslyn, S. M. (1973). Scanning visual images: Some structural implications. *Perception and Psychophysics, 14,* 90–94.

Kosslyn, S. M. (1975). The information represented in visual images. *Cognitive Psychology, 7,* 341–370.

Kosslyn, S. M. (1978). Measuring the visual angle of the mind's eye. *Cognitive Psychology, 10,* 356–389.

Kosslyn, S. M. (1980). *Image and Mind.* Cambridge, Mass.: Harvard Univ. Press.

Kosslyn, S. M. (1981). The medium and the message in mental imagery: A theory. *Psychological Review, 88,* 46–66.

Kosslyn, S. M. (1994). *Image and Brain: The Resolution of the Imagery Debate.* Cambridge, Mass.: MIT Press.

Kosslyn, S. M., Ball, T. M., and Reiser, B. J. (1978). Visual images preserve metric spatial information: Evidence from studies of image scanning. *Journal of Experimental Psychology: Human Perception and Performance, 4,* 46–60.

Kosslyn, S. M., Sukel, K. E., and Bly, B. M. (1999). Squinting with the mind's eye: Effects of stimulus resolution on imaginal and perceptual comparisons. *Memory and Cognition, 27*(2), 276–287.

Kosslyn, S. M., Thompson, W. L., and Ganis, G. (2006). *The Case for Mental Imagery.* New York: Oxford Univ. Press.

Krekelberg, B. (2001). The persistence of position. *Vision Research*, *41*(4), 529–539.

Kripke, S. (1980). *Naming and Necessity*. Cambridge, Mass.: Harvard Univ. Press.

Krojgaard, P. (2004). A review of object individuation in infancy. *British Journal of Developmental Psychology*, *22*(2), 159–183.

Kuhn, T. (1957). *The Copernican Revolution: Planetary Astronomy in the Development of Western Thought*. Cambridge, Mass.: MIT Press.

Làdavas, E. (2002). Functional and dynamic properties of visual peripersonal space. *Trends in Cognitive Sciences*, *6*(1), 17–22.

Leonard, C., and Pylyshyn, Z. W. (2003). Measuring the attentional demand of multiple object tracking (MOT). *Journal of Vision*, *3*(9), 582a.

Lepore, E., and Ludwig, K. (2000). The semantics and pragmatics of complex demonstratives. *Mind*, *109*, 199–240.

Leslie, A. M. (1982). The perception of causality in infants. *Perception*, *11*, 173–186.

Leslie, A. M. (1984). Spatiotemporal continuity and the perception of causality in infants. *Perception*, *13*(3), 287–305.

Leslie, A. M. (1988). The necessity of illusion: Perception and thought in infancy. In *Thought without Language*, ed. L. Weiskrantz. Oxford: Oxford Science Publications.

Leslie, A. M., and Keeble, S. (1987). Do six-month-old infants perceive causality? *Cognition*, *25*, 265–288.

Levine, J. (forthcoming). Demonstrative thought.

Levy, J. (1972). Autokinetic illusion: A systematic review of theories, measures, and independent variables. *Psychological Bulletin*, *78*, 457–474.

Lewis, D. (1971). Analog and digital. *Noûs*, *5*(3), 321–327.

Libet, B. (2004). *Mind Time: The Temporal Factor in Consciousness*. Cambridge, Mass.: Harvard Univ. Press.

Libet, B., Gleason, C. A., Wright, E. W., and Pearl, D. K. (1983). Time of conscious intention to act in relation to onset of cerebral activity (readiness-potential): The unconscious initiation of a freely voluntary act. *Brain*, *106*(pt. 3), 623–642.

Lindberg, D. C. (1976). *Theories of Vision from al-Kindi to Kepler*. Chicago: Univ. of Chicago Press.

Liu, G., Austen, E. L., Booth, K. S., Fisher, B. D., Argue, R., Rempel, M. I., and Enns, J. T. (2005). Multiple-object tracking is based on scene, not retinal, coordinates. *Journal of Experimental Psychology: Human Perception and Performance*, *31*(2), 235–247.

Lormand, E. (1996). Nonphenomenal consciousness. *Noûs*, *30*(2), 242–261.

Luce, R. D., D'Zmura, M., Hoffman, D. D., Iverson, G. J., and Romney, A. K. (eds.). (1995). *Geometric Representations of Perceptual Phenomena: Papers in Honor of Tarow Indow on His 70th Birthday*. Mahwah, N.J.: Lawrence Erlbaum.

Mack, A., and Rock, I. (1998). *Inattentional Blindness*. Cambridge, Mass.: MIT Press.

Marr, D. (1977). Artificial intelligence—A personal view. *Artificial Intelligence, 9*, 37–48.

Marr, D. (1982). *Vision: A Computational Investigation into the Human Representation and Processing of Visual Information*. San Francisco: W.H. Freeman.

Mather, J. A., and Lackner, J. R. (1977). Adaptation to visual rearrangement: Role of sensory discordance. *Quarterly Journal of Experimental Psychology, 29*(2), 237–244.

Mather, J. A., and Lackner, J. R. (1981). Adaptation to visual displacement: Contribution of proprioceptive, visual, and attentional factors. *Perception, 10*(4), 367–374.

McCloskey, M., and Kargon, R. (1988). The meaning and use of historical models in the study of intuitive physics. In *Ontogeny, Phylogeny, and Historical Development*, ed. S. Strauss. Westport, Conn.: Ablex Publishing.

McCloskey, M., Washburn, A., and Felch, L. (1983). Intuitive physics: The straight-down belief and its origin. *Journal of Experimental Psychology: Learning, Memory, and Cognition, 9*(4), 636–649.

McDaniel, K. D., and McDaniel, L. D. (1991). Anton's syndrome in a patient with posttraumatic optic neuropathy and bifrontal contusions. *Archives of Neurology, 48*(1), 101–105.

McMahon, M. J., and MacLeod, D. I. A. (2003). The origin of the oblique effect examined with pattern adaptation and masking. *Journal of Vision, 3*(3), 230–239.

Medendorp, W. P., Goltz, H. C., Villis, T., and Crawford, J. D. (2003). Gaze-centered updating of visual space in human parietal cortex. *Journal of Neuroscience, 23*(15), 6209–6214.

Meltzoff, A. N. (1993). Molyneux's babies: Cross-modal perception, imitation, and the mind of the preverbal infant. In *Spatial Representation: Problems in Philosophy and Psychology*, ed. N. Eilan, R. McCarthy, and B. Brewer, pp. 219–235. New York: Oxford Univ. Press.

Menzel, R., Greggers, U., Smith, A., Berger, S., Brandt, R., Brunke, S., Bundrock, G., Hulse, S., Plumpe, T., Schaupp, F., Schuttler, E., Stach, S., Stindt, J., Stollhoff, N., and Watzl, S. (2005). Honey bees navigate according to a map-like spatial memory. *Proceedings of the National Academy of Sciences of the United States of America, 102*(8), 3040–3045.

Metcalfe, J., and Shimamura, A. P. (eds.). (1994). *Metacognition: Knowing about Knowing*. Cambridge, Mass.: MIT Press.

Michotte, A. (1946/1963). *The Perception of Causality*. Andover: Methuen.

Milner, A. D., and Goodale, M. A. (1995). *The Visual Brain in Action*. New York: Oxford Univ. Press.

Mitchell, J. F., Sundberg, K. A., and Reynolds, J. H. (2006). Attentive tracking of multiple objects modulates neuronal responses in area V4 of the macaque. *Journal of Vision*, *6*(6), 772–772.

Moore, C., Yantis, S., and Vaughan, B. (1998). Object-based visual selection: Evidence from perceptual completion. *Psychological Science*, *9*, 104–110.

Mounts, J. R. W. (2000). Attentional capture by abrupt onsets and feature singletons produces inhibitory surrounds. *Perception and Psychophysics*, *62*(7), 1485–1493.

Mueller, H. J., and Rabbitt, P. M. (1989). Reflexive and voluntary orienting of visual attention: Time course of activation and resistance to interruption. *Journal of Experimental Psychology: Human Perception and Performance*, *15*(2), 315–330.

Musseler, J., and Prinz, W. (1996). Action planning during the presentation of stimulus sequences: Effects of compatible and incompatible stimuli. *Psychological Research*, *59*(1), 48–63.

Newell, A., and Simon, H. A. (1972). *Human Problem Solving*. Englewood Cliffs, N.J.: Prentice-Hall.

Nicod, J. (1970). *Geometry and Induction*. Berkeley: Univ. of California Press.

Nisbett, R. E., and Valins, S. (1987). Perceiving the causes of one's own behavior. In *Attribution: Perceiving the Causes of Behavior*, ed. E. E. Jones, D. E. Kanouse, H. H. Kelley, R. E. Nisbett, and S. Valins, pp. 63–78. Hillsdale, N.J.: Lawrence Erlbaum.

Nisbett, R. E., and Wilson, T. D. (1977). Telling more than we can know: Verbal reports on mental processes. *Psychological Review*, *84*(3), 231–259.

Nissen, M. J. (1985). Accessing features and objects: Is location special? In *Attention and performance XI*, ed. M. I. Posner and O. S. Marin, pp. 205–219. Hillsdale, N.J.: Lawrence Erlbaum.

Noë, A. (2004). *Action in Perception*. Cambridge, Mass.: MIT Press.

Noles, N. S., Scholl, B. J., and Mitroff, S. R. (2005). The persistence of object file representations. *Perception and Psychophysics*, *67*(2), 324–334.

Oberle, C. D., McBeath, M. K., Madigan, S. C., and Sugar, T. G. (2005). The Galileo bias: A naive conceptual belief that influences people's perceptions and performance in a ball-dropping task. *Journal of Experimental Psychology: Learning, Memory, and Cognition*, *31*(4), 643–653.

Ogawa, H., Takeda, Y., and Yagi, A. (2002). Inhibitory tagging on randomly moving objects. *Psychological Science*, *13*(2), 125–129.

Ogawa, H., and Yagi, A. (2002). The effect of information of untracked objects on multiple object tracking. *Japanese Journal of Psychonomic Science*, *22*(1), 49–50.

O'Hearn, K., Landau, B., and Hoffman, J. E. (2005). Multiple object tracking in people with Williams Syndrome and in normally developing children. *Psychological Science*, *16*(11), 905–912.

O'Keefe, J., and Nadel, L. (1978). *The Hippocampus as a Cognitive Map*. Oxford: Oxford Univ. Press.

O'Regan, J. K. (1992). Solving the "real" mysteries of visual perception: The world as an outside memory. *Canadian Journal of Psychology, 46*, 461–488.

O'Regan, J. K., and Noë, A. (2002). A sensorimotor account of vision and visual consciousness. *Behavoral and Brain Sciences, 24*(5), 939–1031.

Paillard, J. (ed.). (1991). *Brain and Space*. New York: Oxford University Press.

Pashler, H. E. (1998). *The Psychology of Attention*. Cambridge, Mass.: MIT Press.

Peacocke, C. (1992). *A Study of Concepts*. Cambridge, Mass.: MIT Press.

Peacocke, C. (1993). Intuitive mechanics, psychological reality, and the idea of a meterial object. In *Spatial Representation: Problems in Philosophy and Psychology*, ed. N. Eilan, R. A. McCarthy, and B. Brewer. New York: Oxford Univ. Press.

Perry, J. (1979). The problem of the essential indexical. *Noûs, 13*, 3–21.

Philipona, D., O'Regan, K., and Nadal, J.-P. (2003). Is there something out there? Inferring space from sensorimotor dependencies. *Neural Computation, 15*(9), 2029–2049.

Podgorny, P., and Shepard, R. N. (1978). Functional representations common to visual perception and imagination. *Journal of Experimental Psychology: Human Perception and Performance, 4*(1), 21–35.

Poggio, T., Torre, V., and Koch, C. (1990). Computational vision and regularization theory. In *Image Understanding 1989*, vol. 3, ed. S. Ullman and W. Richards, pp. 1–18. Norwood, N.J.: Ablex Publishing.

Poincaré, H. (1913/1963). Why space has three dimensions. Trans. J. W. Bolduc. In *Mathematics and Science: Last Essays*, pp. 25–44. New York: Dover.

Posner, M. I. (1980). Orienting of attention. *Quarterly Journal of Experimental Psychology, 32*, 3–25.

Pylyshyn, Z. W. (1973a). The role of competence theories in cognitive psychology. *Journal of Psycholinguistics Research, 2*, 21–50.

Pylyshyn, Z. W. (1973b). What the mind's eye tells the mind's brain: A critique of mental imagery. *Psychological Bulletin, 80*, 1–24.

Pylyshyn, Z. W. (1979). The rate of "mental rotation" of images: A test of a holistic analog hypothesis. *Memory and Cognition, 7*, 19–28.

Pylyshyn, Z. W. (1980). Cognition and computation: Issues in the foundation of cognitive science. *Behavioral and Brain Sciences, 3*(1), 111–132.

Pylyshyn, Z. W. (1981). The imagery debate: Analog media versus tacit knowledge. *Psychological Review, 88*, 16–45.

Pylyshyn, Z. W. (1984). *Computation and Cognition: Toward a Foundation for Cognitive Science*. Cambridge, Mass.: MIT Press (also available through CogNet).

Pylyshyn, Z. W. (ed.). (1987). *The Robot's Dilemma: The Frame Problem in Artificial Intelligence.* Norwood, N.J.: Ablex Publishing.

Pylyshyn, Z. W. (1989). The role of location indexes in spatial perception: A sketch of the FINST spatial-index model. *Cognition, 32,* 65–97.

Pylyshyn, Z. W. (1991). Rules and representation: Chomsky and representational realism. In *The Chomskian Turn,* ed. A. Kashir. Oxford: Basil Blackwell.

Pylyshyn, Z. W. (1994). Some primitive mechanisms of spatial attention. *Cognition, 50,* 363–384.

Pylyshyn, Z. W. (1996). The study of cognitive architecture. In *Mind Matters: Contributions to Cognitive Science in Honor of Allen Newell,* ed. D. Steier and T. Mitchell. Hillsdale, N.J.: Lawrence Erlbaum.

Pylyshyn, Z. W. (1999). Is vision continuous with cognition? The case for cognitive impenetrability of visual perception. *Behavioral and Brain Sciences, 22*(3), 341–423.

Pylyshyn, Z. W. (2001). Visual indexes, preconceptual objects, and situated vision. *Cognition, 80*(1/2), 127–158.

Pylyshyn, Z. W. (2002a). Mental imagery: In search of a theory. *Behavioral and Brain Sciences, 25*(2), 157–237.

Pylyshyn, Z. W. (2002b). Seeing, acting, and knowing: Commentary on O'Regan and Noë. *Behavioral and Brain Sciences, 24*(5), 999.

Pylyshyn, Z. W. (2003). *Seeing and Visualizing: It's Not What You Think.* Cambridge, Mass.: MIT Press.

Pylyshyn, Z. W. (2004). Some puzzling findings in multiple object tracking (MOT): I. Tracking without keeping track of object identities. *Visual Cognition, 11*(7), 801–822.

Pylyshyn, Z. W. (2006). Some puzzling findings in multiple object tracking (MOT): II. Inhibition of moving nontargets. *Visual Cognition, 14*(2), 175–198.

Pylyshyn, Z. W., and Annan, V. J. (2006). Dynamics of target selection in multiple object tracking (MOT). *Spatial Vision, 19*(6), 485–504.

Pylyshyn, Z. W., Burkell, J., Fisher, B., Sears, C., Schmidt, W., and Trick, L. (1994). Multiple parallel access in visual attention. *Canadian Journal of Experimental Psychology, 48*(2), 260–283.

Pylyshyn, Z. W., and Cohen, J. (1999). Imagined extrapolation of uniform motion is not continuous. *Investigative Ophthalmology and Visual Science, 40*(4), S808.

Pylyshyn, Z. W., and Dennis, J. L. M. (forthcoming). Can multiple object tracking make use of individual object properties?

Pylyshyn, Z. W., Elcock, E. W., Marmor, M., and Sander, P. (1978). Explorations in visual-motor spaces. Paper presented at the Proceedings of the Second International Conference of the Canadian Society for Computational Studies of Intelligence, University of Toronto.

Pylyshyn, Z. W., and Storm, R. W. (1988). Tracking multiple independent targets: Evidence for a parallel tracking mechanism. *Spatial Vision, 3*(3), 1–19.

Quine, W. V. O. (1960). *Word and Object.* Cambridge, Mass.: MIT Press.

Quine, W. V. O. (1992). *Pursuit of Truth,* revised ed. Cambridge, Mass.: Harvard Univ. Press.

Rauschenberger, R. (2004). Attentional capture by auto- and allo-cues. *Psychonomic Bulletin and Review, 10*(4), 814–842.

Rensink, R. A., and Enns, J. T. (1995). Preemption effects in visual search: Evidence for low-level grouping. *Psychological Review, 102*(1), 101–130.

Reynolds, R. I. (1978). The microgenetic development of the Ponzo and Zollner illusions. *Perception and Psychophysics, 23,* 231–236.

Reynolds, R. I. (1981). Perception of an illusory contour as a function of processing time. *Perception, 10,* 107–115.

Robertson, I. H., Nico, D., and Hood, B. M. (1995). The intention to act improves unilateral left neglect: two demonstrations. *Neuroreport, 7*(1), 246–248.

Rock, I. (ed.). (1997). *Indirect Perception.* Cambridge, Mass.: MIT Press.

Rolls, E. T. (1999). Spatial view cells and the representation of place in the primate hippocampus. *Hippocampus, 9,* 467–480.

Rosenfeld, A., Hummel, R. A., and Zucker, S. W. (1976). Scene labeling by relaxation operators. *IEEE Transactions on Systems, Man, and Cybernetics, SMC-6,* 420–433.

Rosenthal, D. M. (2005). *Consciousness and Mind.* New York: Oxford Univ. Press.

Rossotti, H. (1983). *Colour: Why the World Isn't Grey.* Princeton: Princeton Univ. Press.

Saarinen, J. (1996). Localization and discrimination of "pop-out" targets. *Vision Research, 36*(2), 313–316.

Saiki, J. (2003). Feature binding in object-file representations of multiple moving items. *Journal of Vision, 3*(1), 6–21.

Salinas, E., and Thier, P. (2000). Gain modulation: A major computational principle of the central nervous system. *Neuron, 27,* 15–21.

Schindler, I., Kerkhoff, G., Karnath, H. O., Keller, I., and Goldenberg, G. (2002). Neck muscle vibration induces lasting recovery in spatial neglect. *Journal of Neurology, Neurosurgery, and Psychiatry, 73*(4), 412–419.

Scholl, B. J., and Pylyshyn, Z. W. (1999). Tracking multiple items through occlusion: Clues to visual objecthood. *Cognitive Psychology, 38*(2), 259–290.

Scholl, B. J., Pylyshyn, Z. W., and Feldman, J. (2001). What is a visual object: Evidence from target-merging in multiple-object tracking. *Cognition, 80,* 159–177.

Scholl, B. J., Pylyshyn, Z. W., and Franconeri, S. L. (1999). When are featural and spatiotemporal properties encoded as a result of attentional allocation? *Investigative Ophthalmology and Visual Science, 40*(4), 4195.

Scholl, B. J., and Tremoulet, P. D. (2000). Perceptual causality and animacy. *Trends in Cognitive Sciences*, *4*(8), 299–308.

Schulz, T. (1991). A microgenetic study of the Müller-Lyer illusion. *Perception*, *20*(4), 501–512.

Sears, C. R., and Pylyshyn, Z. W. (2000). Multiple object tracking and attentional processes. *Canadian Journal of Experimental Psychology*, *54*(1), 1–14.

Sekuler, A. B., and Palmer, S. E. (1992). Visual completion of partly occluded objects: A microgenetic analysis. *Journal of Experimental Psychology: General*, *121*, 95–111.

Selfridge, O. (1959). Pandemonium: A paradigm for learning. *Symposium on Mechanization of Thought Processes: National Physical Laboratory Symposium.* London: HM Stationery Office.

Sellars, W. (1956). Empiricism and the Philosophy of Mind. In *Minnesota Studies in the Philosophy of Science*, volume I: *The Foundations of Science and the Concepts of Psychology and Psychoanalysis*, ed. M. Scriven, pp. 253–329. Minneapolis: Univ. of Minnesota Press. (Reprinted in Sellars, Wilfrid. (1963). *Science, Perception, and Reality*, London: Routledge and Kegan Paul.)

Shadlen, M. N., and Newsome, W. T. (1996). Motion perception: seeing and deciding. *Proceedings of the National Academy of Science*, *93*, 628–633.

Shapiro, L. (1995). *Affine Analysis of Image Sequences.* New York: Cambridge Univ. Press.

Shepard, R. N. (2001). Perceptual-cognitive universals as reflections of the world. *Behavioral and Brain Sciences*, *24*, 581–601.

Shepard, R. N., and Metzler, J. (1971). Mental rotation of three dimensional objects. *Science*, *171*, 701–703.

Simons, D. J., and Chabris, C. F. (1999). Gorillas in our midst: Sustained inattentional blindness for dynamic events. *Perception*, *28*(9), 1059–1074.

Simons, D. J., and Levin, D. T. (1997). Change blindness. *Trends in Cognitive Sciences*, *1*, 261–267.

Simons, D. J., and Rensink, R. A. (2005). Change blindness: Past, present, and future. *Trends in Cognitive Sciences*, *9*(1), 17–20.

Slemmer, J. A., and Johnson, S. P. (2002). Object tracking in ecologially valid occlusion events. Paper presented at Vision Sciences 2002, Sarasota, Florida.

Slezak, P. (1992). When can images be reinterpreted: Non-chronometric tests of pictorialism. In *Proceedings of the Fourteenth Conference of the Cognitive Science Society*, pp. 124–129. Mahwah, N.J.: Lawrence Erlbaum.

Slezak, P. (1995). The "philosophical" case against visual imagery. In *Perspective on Cognitive Science: Theories, Experiments, and Foundations*, ed. P. Slezak, T. Caelli, and R. Clark, pp. 237–271. Stamford, Conn.: Ablex Publishing.

Smith, A. D. (2003). *The Problem of Perception*. Cambridge, Mass.: Harvard Univ. Press.

Smith, B. C. (1996). *On the Origin of Objects*. Cambridge, Mass.: MIT Press.

Snodgrass, M. (2002). Disambiguating conscious and unconscious influences: Do exclusion paradigms demonstrate unconscious perception? *American Journal of Psychology, 115*, 545–580.

Snyder, L. H. (2000). Coordinate transformations for eye and arm movements in the brain. *Current Opinion in Neurobiology, 10*(6), 747–754.

Snyder, L. H., Batista, A. P., and Andersen, R. A. (2000). Intention-related activity in the posterior parietal cortex: A review. *Vision Research, 40*(10–12), 1433–1441.

Snyder, L. H., Grieve, K. L., Brotchie, P., and Andersen, R. A. (1998). Separate body- and world-referenced representations of visual space in parietal cortex. *Nature, 394*(6696), 887–891.

Spelke, E. S. (1990). Principles of object perception. *Cognitive Science, 14*, 29–56.

Spence, C., and Driver, J. (eds.). (2004). *Crossmodal Space and Crossmodal Attention*. New York: Oxford Univ. Press.

Sperling, G. (1960). The information available in brief visual presentations. *Psychological Monographs, 74*(11), 1–29.

Sperling, G. (1967). Successive approximations to a model for short-term memory. *Acta Psychologica, 27*, 285–292.

Sperling, G., and Weichselgarter, E. (1995). Episodic theory of the dynamics of spatial attention. *Psychological Review, 102*(3), 503–532.

Stich, S. (1978). Beliefs and subdoxastic states. *Philosophy of Science, 45*, 499–518.

Strawson, P. F. (1959). *Individuals: An Essay in Descriptive Metaphysics*. London: Methuen.

Stricanne, B., Andersen, R. A., and Mazzoni, P. (1996). Eye-centered, head-centered, and intermediate coding of remembered sound locations in area LIP. *Journal of Neurophysiology, 76*(3), 2071–2076.

Suganuma, M., and Yokosawa, K. (2002). Is multiple object tracking affected by three-dimensional rigidity? Paper presented at Vision Sciences Society 2002, Sarasota, Florida.

Swets, J. A. (ed.). (1964). *Signal Detection and Recognition by Human Observers*. New York: Wiley.

Tipper, S., Driver, J., and Weaver, B. (1991). Object-centered inhibition of return of visual attention. *Quarterly Journal of Experimental Psychology A, 43A*, 289–298.

Tipper, S. P., Weaver, B., Jerreat, L. M., and Burak, A. L. (1994). Object-based and environment-based inhibition of return of selective attention. *Journal of Experimental Psychology: Human Perception and Performance, 20*, 478–499.

Titchener, E. B. (1912). The schema of introspection. *American Journal of Psychology, 23*, 485–508.

Tlauka, M., and McKenna, F. P. (1998). Mental imagery yields stimulus-response compatibility. *Acta Psychologica*, 67–79.

Tolman, E. C. (1948). Cognitive maps in rats and men. *Psychological Review, 55*(4), 189–208.

Tootell, R. B., Silverman, M. S., Switkes, E., and de Valois, R. L. (1982). Deoxyglucose analysis of retinotopic organization in primate striate cortex. *Science, 218*(4575), 902–904.

Treisman, A. (1988). Features and objects: The fourteenth Bartlett memorial lecture. *Quarterly Journal of Experimental Psychology, 40A*(2), 201–237.

Treisman, A., and Gelade, G. (1980). A feature integration theory of attention. *Cognitive Psychology, 12*, 97–136.

Tremoulet, P. D., and Feldman, J. (2000). Perception of animacy from the motion of a single object. *Perception, 29*(8), 943–951.

Tremoulet, P. D., Leslie, A. M., and Hall, D. G. (2000). Infant individuation and identification of objects. *Cognitive Development, 15*(4), 499–522.

Tresillian, J. R. (1995). Perceptual and cognitive processes in time-to-contact judgments: Analysis of prediction-motion and relative judgment tasks. *Perception and Psychophysics, 57*(2), 231–245.

Trick, L. M., Audet, D., and Dales, L. (2003). Age differences in enumerating things that move: Implications for the development of multiple-object tracking. *Memory and Cognition, 31*(8), 1229–1237.

Trick, L. M., Perl, T., and Sethi, N. (2005). Age-related differences in multiple-object tracking. *Journals of Gerontology: Series B: Psychological Sciences and Social Sciences, 2*, 102.

Trick, L. M., and Pylyshyn, Z. W. (1993). What enumeration studies tell us about spatial attention: Evidence for limited capacity preattentive processing. *Journal of Experimental Psychology: Human Perception and Performance, 19*(2), 331–351.

Trick, L. M., and Pylyshyn, Z. W. (1994a). Cueing and counting: Does the position of the attentional focus affect enumeration? *Visual Cognition, 1*(1), 67–100.

Trick, L. M., and Pylyshyn, Z. W. (1994b). Why are small and large numbers enumerated differently? A limited capacity preattentive stage in vision. *Psychological Review, 101*(1), 80–102.

Tsang, E. (1993). *Foundations of Constraint Satisfaction*. London: Academic Press.

Tye, M. (1991). *The Imagery Debate*. Cambridge, Mass.: MIT Press.

Tyrrell, R. A., Rudolph, K. K., Eggers, B. G., and Leibowitz, H. W. (1993). Evidence for the persistence of visual guidance information. *Perception and Psychophysics, 54*(4), 431–438.

Ullman, S. (1976). Relaxation and constrained optimization by local processes. *Computer Graphics and Image Processing, 10,* 115–125.

Ullman, S. (1979). *The Interpretation of Visual Motion.* Cambridge, Mass.: MIT Press.

Ullman, S. (1984). Visual routines. *Cognition, 18,* 97–159.

Van de Walle, G., Carey, S., and Prevor, M. (2000). Bases for object individuation in infancy: Evidence from manual search. *Journal of Cognition and Development, 1,* 249–280.

vanMarle, K., and Scholl, B. J. (2003). Attentive tracking of objects versus substances. *Psychological Science, 14*(4), 498–504.

Viswanathan, L., and Mingolla, E. (1998). Attention in depth: Disparity and occlusion cues facilitate multi-element visual tracking (Abstract). *Investigative Ophthalmology and Visual Science, 39*(4), 634.

Viswanathan, L., and Mingolla, E. (2002). Dynamics of attention in depth: Evidence from multi-element tracking. *Perception, 31*(12), 1415–1437.

von Holst, E., and Mittelstaedt, H. (1950/1971). The principle of reafference: Interactions between the central nervous system and the peripheral organs. In *Perceptual Processing: Stimulus Equivalence and Pattern Recognition,* ed. P. C. Dodwell, pp. 41–71. New York: Appleton.

Voss, P., Lassonde, M., Gougoux, F., Fortin, M., Guillemot, J. P., and Lepore, F. (2004). Early- and late-onset blind individuals show supra-normal auditory abilities in far-space. *Current Biology, 14*(9), 1734–1738.

Wallach, H., and O'Connell, D. N. (1953). The kinetic depth effect. *Journal of Experimental Psychology, 45,* 205–217.

Waltz, D. (1975). Understanding line drawings of scenes with shadows. In *The Psychology of Computer Vision,* ed. P. H. Winston, pp. 19–91. New York: McGraw-Hill.

Warren, D. H. (1970). Intermodality interactions in spatial localization. *Cognitive Psychology, 1*(2), 114–133.

Washburn, M. F. (1922). Introspection as an objective method. *Psychological Review, 29,* 89–112.

Watson, D. G., and Humphreys, G. W. (1997). Visual marking: Prioritizing selection for new objects by top-down attentional inhibition of old objects. *Psychological Review, 104*(1), 90–122.

Watson, D. G., and Humphreys, G. W. (2000). Visual marking: Evidence for inhibition using a probe-dot detection paradigm. *Perception and Psychophysics, 62*(3), 471–481.

Watt, D. G. D. (1997). Pointing at memorized targets during prolonged microgravity. *Aviation, Space, and Environmental Medicine, 68*(2), 99–103.

Wegner, D. M. (2002). *The Illusion of Conscious Will.* Cambridge, Mass.: MIT Press.

Wegner, D. M. (2003). The mind's best trick: How we experience conscious will. *Trends in Cognitive Sciences*, *7*(2), 65–69.

Wehner, R., Boyer, M., Loertscher, F., Sommer, S., and Menzi, U. (2006). Ant navigation: One-way routes rather than maps. *Current Biology*, *16*(1), 75–79.

Weiskrantz, L. (1995). Blindsight: Not an island unto itself. *Current Directions in Psychological Science*, *4*(5), 146–151.

Wexler, K., and Cullicover, P. (1980). *Formal Principles of Language Acquisition.* Cambridge, Mass.: MIT Press.

Wexler, M., Kosslyn, S. M., and Berthoz, A. (1998). Motor processes in mental rotation. *Cognition*, *68*(1), 77–94.

Whorf, B. L. (1958). *Language, Thought, and Reality.* Cambridge, Mass.: MIT Press.

Wiggins, D. (1997). Sortal concepts: A reply to Xu. *Mind and Language*, *12*(3–4), 413–421.

Wilson, H. R., Loffler, G., Wilkinson, F., and Thistlethwaite, W. A. (2001). An inverse oblique effect in human vision. *Vision Research*, *41*(14), 1749–1753.

Wilson, J. A., and Robinson, J. O. (1986). The impossibly-twisted Pulfrich pendulum. *Perception*, *15*(4), 503–504.

Wittreich, W. J. (1959). Visual perception and personality. *Scientific American*, *200* (April), 56–75.

Wong, E., and Mack, A. (1981). Saccadic programming and perceived location. *Acta Psychologia*, *48*, 123–131.

Wright, R. D., Dawson, M. R., and Pylyshyn, Z. W. (1987). Spatio-temporal parameters and the three-dimensionality of apparent motion: Evidence for two types of processing. *Spatial Vision*, *2*(4), 263–272.

Xu, F. (1997). From Lot's wife to a pillar of salt: Evidence that *physical object* is a sortal concept. *Mind and language*, *12*, 365–392.

Xu, F., Carey, S., and Quint, N. (2004). The emergence of kind-based object individuation in infancy. *Cognitive Psychology*, *49*, 155–190.

Yantis, S. (1992). Multielement visual tracking: Attention and perceptual organization. *Cognitive Psychology*, *24*, 295–340.

Yantis, S., and Johnson, D. N. (1990). Mechanisms of attentional priority. *Journal of Experimental Psychology: Human Perception and Performance*, *16*(4), 812–825.

Yantis, S., and Jones, E. (1991). Mechanisms of attentional selection: Temporally modulated priority tags. *Perception and Psychophysics*, *50*(2), 166–178.

Index